BOOKMARKS

A MANUAL FOR COMBATING HATE SPEECH ONLINE THROUGH HUMAN RIGHTS EDUCATION

Revised edition (2016), with the inclusion
of the Guide to Human Rights for Internet Users

WRITTEN AND EDITED BY

ELLIE KEEN, MARA GEORGESCU

WITH CONTRIBUTIONS TO THE SECOND EDITION FROM

MARA GEORGESCU, SATU VALTERE, OLENA CHERNYKH

FINAL EDITING

RUI GOMES

Joint Programme between the European Union and the Council of Europe
Strengthening Information Society in Ukraine

Funded
by the European Union
and the Council of Europe

Implemented
by the Council of Europe

This publication was printed under the support of the Joint Programme between European Union and the Council of Europe Strengthening the Information Society in Ukraine.

Bookmarks - A manual for combating hate speech online through human rights education

Revised edition, 2016

The views expressed in this manual do not necessarily reflect the opinions of the Council of Europe.

All other correspondence concerning this document should be addressed to the Youth Department of the Council of Europe:

European Youth Centre Strasbourg
30, rue Pierre de Coubertin
F- 67075 Strasbourg Cedex – France
Email: youth@coe.int

Credits for photos on the cover (from left to right):

- Council of Europe
- Földi László
- Horváth Dániel
- National Campaign Committee Slovakia

Proofreading: Rachel Appleby

Layout and design: Horváth Dániel – danielhorvath.com

Printed in Ukraine

ISBN 978-92-871-8201-2

PREFACE

The manual Bookmarks you have in your hands is a precious tool to stop hate speech and strengthen human rights. You may ask: "Why should we bother? Don't people have the right to express themselves freely in a democratic society?" It is true that freedom of expression is a fundamental human right that applies also to ideas that may offend, shock or disturb people. But exercising this right carries clear duties and responsibilities. Hate speech is not "protected" speech; words of hate can lead to real-life crimes of hate, and such crimes have already ruined and taken the lives of too many people.

Hate speech has become one of the most common forms of intolerance and xenophobia in Europe today. Of particular concern is the increasing presence of hate speech in political discourse and how it has become commonplace in the public sphere, in particular via the Internet. When the unacceptable starts to be accepted, becomes "the norm", there is a true threat to human rights. The No Hate Speech Movement of the Council of Europe was launched to reduce the acceptance of hate speech online and put an end to its "normalisation".

No one would deny that the Internet provides us with remarkable new tools for communication, solidarity, organising social change and entertainment. And yet we must not let it be misused as an instrument of online torture and propaganda for the industries and ideologies of hate. Freedom of expression online must also mean freedom from fear online.

The Council of Europe has been a pioneer in defining hate speech and in calling for the condemnation of racism and xenophobia on the Internet. Legal measures are very important, but they are not enough. Education is the only long-term solution: to prevent hate speech, to denounce hate speech and to promote solidarity with the victims.

Learning about, through and for human rights is essential in maintaining an active climate of human rights in the face of the rapid changes which our societies are facing today. This is especially relevant to children and young people, and nowadays should certainly be an integral part of education about media and Internet literacy.

The No Hate Speech Movement campaign of the Council of Europe is carried out by young people themselves: they called for its creation and are deciding how it is run. This is important because it is also young people who are among the most regular victims of human rights abuse online through various forms of hate speech and bullying.

I hope this guide finds its way into schools, youth centres and youth organisations – and onto the Internet too. I encourage students, educators and others to use it freely and to join in with the campaign. Let us use Bookmarks to make a stand against hate speech.

Thorbjørn Jagland
Secretary General of the Council of Europe

ACKNOWLEDGEMENTS

We would like to express our gratitude to all those who contributed to this manual, with their suggestions and feedback, in particular:

- The members of the Follow-up Group of the No Hate Speech Movement campaign, chiefly the representatives of the Advisory Council on Youth and of the European Steering Committee on Youth, and the observers representing the European Steering Committee on Educational Policy and Practice, the European Youth Information and Counselling Agency, the European Youth Forum, the European Youth Card Association, the EEA Norway Grants and the online activists.
- Claudia Lenz (The European Wergeland Centre), Anni Siltanen (Insafe) and Vitor Tomé (consultant).
- Anne Weber (Office of the Commissioner for Human Rights), Gordana Berjan (Children's Programme), Lee Hibbard, Elvana Thaci and James Lawson (Internet Governance Unit); Paula Eck-Walters (Secretariat of the European Commission against Racism and Intolerance); Josef Huber, Yulia Pererva (Education Department); Anca-Ruxandra Pandea, Menno Ettema, Aileen Donegan, Claire Uszynski and Maud Hoffman Boivin (Youth Department), all at the Council of Europe.

We have made all possible efforts to trace references of texts and activities to their authors and give them the necessary credits. We apologise for any omissions and will be pleased to correct them in the next edition.

TABLE OF CONTENTS

CHAPTER 1

ABOUT THE MANUAL

1.1 INTRODUCTION TO THE MANUAL

This manual has been designed to support the No Hate Speech Movement, the Council of Europe's youth Campaign against hate speech online, and will be useful for educators working to address this problem, both inside and outside the formal education system. The manual is designed for working with young people aged 13 to 18; however, activities can be adapted to other age ranges and other profiles of learners.

'Sticks and stones may break my bones but words can never hurt me'

Do you agree?

Bookmarks was first published at the beginning of 2014 and has already been translated into 10 languages. In this revised edition, the manual has been updated to include the most recent information about the No Hate Speech Movement youth campaign and about the Council of Europe *Guide to Human Rights for Internet Users*. This has also resulted in three new educational activities in this edition.

The need for educational initiatives which target cyberhate can partly be seen in the growing amount of abuse to be found on the Internet, much of which is extreme and racist in tone and can threaten the fundamental values of a democratic society. However, cyberhate is not just a problem related to racism and discrimination; it is also a problem related to the way that people use the Internet. This makes it a relatively new phenomenon, and one which is not fully recognised or understood. The 'novelty' of online hate speech means that this is a problem that the world does not yet quite know how to deal with.

Many existing attempts to combat cyberhate tend to focus on controlling mechanisms: cutting out the hate when it appears. The approach in these pages views hate speech as a *symptom* of a deeper problem. The activities have been designed to address the underlying causes of hate speech as well as learning how to deal with it when it occurs.

Hate speech online represents the leaves of a particularly malicious plant, whose roots lie deep in society. Pruning the leaves cannot address the wider causes of the problem.

A HUMAN RIGHTS APPROACH

The activities in the manual should help young people in developing the knowledge, skills and attitudes which will be needed if the Internet is to reflect the fundamental principles which have been established for the *real* world. Those principles were drawn up and agreed on over 60 years ago: they are known as human rights, and they reflect the basic dignity of every human being, their equality in rights, their freedom, and their role in deciding and establishing the rules which should govern our daily existence.

Like the youth Campaign, this manual sees hate speech as a human rights concern and the approach used in the activities is based on human rights principles and standards. This makes the manual useful not only in addressing online hate speech but also as a way of understanding human rights themselves and the way they apply both in offline as well as online settings. You can find more information on the educational approach in Chapter 3, and some basic information about human rights online and offline in Chapter 5.

DEMOCRACY AND CITIZENSHIP ... ONLINE

The manual is based on the firm belief that online space is public space, and hence, all principles of a democratic society *can* and *should* apply online. In this context, the role of young people online is extremely important in combating hate speech.

Young people are citizens online, which means they can express their aspirations and concerns online, take action, and hold accountable those who violate human rights online. What's more, they can be human rights defenders online.

The online space is also a space for participation, including the awareness about Internet governance processes. The manual explores, through activities, ways of interaction online, how young people can take action online and how they can campaign online for a better and safer Internet.

Background themes related to democracy, online campaigning and Internet literacy are included in Chapter 5.

1.2 THE PROBLEM OF HATE SPEECH ONLINE

NEW POSSIBILITIES, NEW DANGERS

The possibilities for human interaction have exploded with the coming of the Internet. The Internet has given us the possibility, in theory, to communicate with almost any other person in the world; it has even made it possible, in theory, for one thought in a back room in a small and unknown corner of the world to be picked up by *every* other person! Everyone with access to the Internet is now both publisher and public speaker. Few, it seems, can interfere with what we want to say.

Do *you* know what's out there?

See page 151 for some examples. Or do an online search yourself.

This is a novelty that few would want reversed, but it should not surprise us that the ever-expanding world of online interaction has also come to reflect and feed back into many of the difficulties that human beings have historically encountered in their 'real' existence. Intolerance and 'hate' have been a feature of human society almost since time began. A number of studies have seen an increase in these attitudes over recent years.

Who's checking!?

Is it easier to speak our darkest thoughts online?

The problem is that if there is less tolerance of difference, and if the constraints on that intolerance are not

watched, then intolerance – and hate – will find expression, both in the things that people do and in the things they say. The Internet has opened up new ways of saying things, and it has opened up new avenues to say them to more people. The constraints, however, on what we can say online are far fewer than those which exist offline: we can say things over the Internet that we would not dare to say in public in the 'real' world.

If hate speech offline is a problem that societies have recognised, and found the need to address, is online hate speech something that we can ignore?

Which is worse...?

Spoken at a public meeting	Posted on an Internet forum
"If you're gay – get a cure. Then join the human race."	*"If you're gay – get a cure. Then join the human race."*

THE EXTENT OF THE PROBLEM

"I will rape you tomorrow at 9pm. Shall we meet near your house????"[1]
"We dont want you here, stay in your own country and destroy it, not ours!!!"[2]
*"You're a silly ****. Your mother's a wog and your dad is a rapist"*[3]

Monitoring the amount of hate speech online is notoriously difficult. In fact, it is precisely this difficulty which makes it so easy for those who want to spread hate to do so online, and makes it so difficult for governments, or others, to control. A few organisations have attempted to track the extent of the problem. All of them have found that online hate appears to be increasing.

An increase in hate sites

- The 2011 edition of the Simon Wiesenthal annual Digital Terror & Hate Report[4] notes a 12% increase to 14,000 "problematic social networks websites, forums, blogs, twitter, etc. (up from 11,500 last year), comprised on the subculture of hate".
- The Internet Security system, Websense, which claims to be tracking about 15,000 'hate and militancy' sites, reported that racism, hate, and militancy sites tripled in number during 2009.[5]

Other studies have tried to investigate the extent to which young people are encountering hate in their online activities.

Young people and online hate

- Across Europe, 6% of 9 to 16-year-old Internet users reported having been bullied online, and 3% confessed to having bullied others.[6]
- 16% of young Internet users in Canada say they have posted comments on the Internet that were hateful towards a person or group of people.[7]
- 78% of the respondents of an online survey stated they had encountered hate speech online on a regular basis. The three most recurrent targets of hate speech were: LGBT people (70%), Muslims (60%) and women.[8]

ENDNOTES

1 Tweet to Stella McCreasy (UK Member of Parliament)
2 From the Facebook page 'Bugger off Asylum Seekers'
3 Tweet sent out when a footballer – Fabrice Muamba originally from the Democratic Republic of Congo – suffered a cardiac arrest during a football match.
4 Digital Terrorism and Hate Report launched at Museum of Tolerance, February 2011 www.wiesenthal.com/site/apps/nlnet/content2.aspx?c=lsKWLbPJLnF&b=4441467&ct=9141065
5 Racism, hate, militancy sites proliferating via social networking, Networkworld, May 2009 www.networkworld.com/news/2009/052909-hate-sites.html
6 From a survey by EU KidsOnline: www2.lse.ac.uk/media@lse/research/EUKidsOnline/EU%20Kids%20II%20(2009-11)/EUKidsOnlineIIReports/Final%20report.pdf
7 From 'Young Canadians in a Wired World', a national school-based survey of 5,272 children and youth in Grades 4 to 11, and qualitative research findings from focus groups with parents and young people aged 11 to 17, 2003 – 2005.
8 Council of Europe online survey in view of the No Hate Speech Movement, 2012. www.coe.int/youthcampaign

CHAPTER 2

NO HATE SPEECH MOVEMENT

THE COUNCIL OF EUROPE YOUTH CAMPAIGN FOR HUMAN RIGHTS ONLINE

"Hate speech, as defined by the Committee of Ministers of the Council of Europe, covers all forms of expression which spread, incite, promote or justify racial hatred, xenophobia, antisemitism or other forms of hatred based on intolerance, including: intolerance expressed by aggressive nationalism and ethnocentrism, discrimination and hostility against minorities, and migrants and people of immigrant origin. For the purpose of the campaign, other forms of discrimination and prejudice, such as antigypsyism, christianphobia, islamophobia, misogyny, sexism and discrimination on the grounds of sexual orientation and gender identity fall clearly within the scope of hate speech."

Presentation of the campaign – www.nohatespeechmovement.org

2.1 ABOUT THE CAMPAIGN

The Council of Europe's campaign against online hate speech was launched on 22 March 2013 and runs until the end of 2017. The first phase of the Campaign (2013-2015) was designed to raise awareness of the problem, change attitudes towards it and mobilise young people to act against it. The second phase of the Campaign (2015-2017) will focus more on educational responses and prevention strategies. The No Hate Speech Movement youth campaign is part of the Council of Europe's wider efforts to promote human rights online.

The Council of Europe views hate speech as a threat to democracy and human rights. The No Hate Speech Movement has human rights at its core but is not only about using legal mechanisms to combat cyberhate – nor is it necessarily about 'cutting out the hate' wherever it occurs. The Campaign encourages respect for freedom of expression and aims to develop alternative responses to hate speech, including prevention, education, awareness raising, the development of self-regulation by users and encouraging support for victims. In essence, the Campaign is about promoting human rights online, and making the Internet a safer space for all.

CAMPAIGN GOALS

The Campaign addresses and combats hate speech by mobilising young people as actors and multipliers for a culture of human rights and democratic citizenship, online and offline.

The Campaign has the following goals:

- To raise awareness about hate speech online and offline
- To support human rights education activities for action against hate speech and the risks it poses for democracy and to the well-being of young people
- To develop and disseminate tools and mechanisms for reporting hate speech, especially in its online dimension, including at national level
- To mobilise national and European partners to prevent and counter hate speech and intolerance online and offline
- To promote media literacy and digital citizenship and support youth participation in Internet governance
- To contribute to the implementation of the Council of Europe Action Plan on the fight against violent extremism and radicalisation leading to terrorism, notably by addressing root causes for the violent radicalisation of young people.

THE CAMPAIGN TOOLS

NATIONAL CAMPAIGN COMMITTEES

The Campaign is promoted by the Council of Europe and its European partners and implemented by national campaign committees in the member states.

CAMPAIGN COORDINATION WEBSITE

www.coe.int/youthcampaign

This is the portal for the Campaign organisers at national and European levels. It contains updated information about the work behind the campaign, including contacts for national campaigns' committees and coordinators.

NO HATE SPEECH MOVEMENT ONLINE PLATFORM

www.nohatespeechmovement.org

The online platform exists to support the movement and to serve as the public face of the Campaign. It includes personal testimonials from young people – including self-made videos and photos. Anyone can register as a user of the site, and join the movement. The platform is moderated by online volunteers and activists.

HATE SPEECH WATCH

www.nohatespeechmovement.org/hate-speech-watch

This is an area of the Campaign Internet platform consisting of examples of hate speech online submitted by users. It offers the possibility to discuss possible approaches with other young people in the movement and organise actions against hate speech.

BLOG "THE CAMPAIGN IN ACTION"

The www.nohatespeechmovement.org has a blog for campaign activists and partners to provide information about activities and initiatives carried out across Europe. It also enables discussions about current issues related to hate speech and to the Campaign.

FORUM "JOIN THE DISCUSSION"

In this forum http://forum.nohatespeechmovement.org anyone can join a discussion about hate speech online and offline and many other issues related to the Campaign. The forum is moderated by the online volunteers and activists.

EVENTS

Although the main activities take place online, the Campaign also includes offline activities, such as training courses, seminars, conferences, youth events, festivals and flashmobs. And, of course, many educational activities in formal and in non-formal learning settings.

EUROPEAN ACTION DAYS

These are organised action events which run throughout the Campaign and involve activists in the national and European campaigns alike. Each action day focuses on different aspects of hate speech and encourages action in support of particular target groups. The Action Days include a programme and various online activities co-ordinated by volunteer moderators. Dates and themes for the Action Days are updated regularly: check the campaign website!

Here are some examples of Action Days:

- The second week of February: Safer Internet Action Day
- 8 March: Action Day against Misogyny and Sexism
- 21 March: Action Day against Racism and Xenophobia
- 8 April: Action Day against Antigypsyism and in Solidarity with Roma people
- 17 May: Action Day against Homophobia and Transphobia
- 20 June: Action Day in support of Refugees and Asylum Seekers
- 22 July: Action day in solidarity with Victims of Hate Crimes
- 21 September: Action Day against Islamophobia and Religious Intolerance
- 9 November: Action Day against Fascism and Antisemitism
- 10 December: Action Day for Human Rights Online

LEARNING TOOLS

BOOKMARKS

This manual is an important tool of the Campaign. It is designed for teachers and educators and should help to increase the number of young people aware of the Campaign – and those ready to join the movement.

CAMPAIGN VIDEOS

The videos provide introductions to the problem of hate speech online and present the "No Hate Speech Movement" tools and approaches. You can find various videos on the Campaign's main page www.nohatespeechmovement.org

GUIDE TO HUMAN RIGHTS FOR INTERNET USERS

The Guide is a tool for Internet users to learn about human rights online, their possible limitations, and available remedies for such limitations. The Guide provides information about what rights and freedoms mean in practice in the context of the Internet, how they can be relied and acted upon, as well as how to access remedies.

The Guide is accessible at: www.coe.int/en/web/internet-users-rights/guide.

2.2 WHAT CAN YOUNG PEOPLE DO?

There are many more possible ways of contributing to the Campaign than are listed below. Some further suggestions are included as 'Ideas for Action' at the end of the activities in this manual. Here is a brief list to bring your groups into the Campaign.

- Join the Movement on www.nohatespeechmovement.org
- Sign up to the Campaign newsletter, post photos or videos and interact with others on the Campaign website (http://forum.nohatespeechmovement.org)
- Monitor hate speech online and report examples to Hate Speech Watch: www.nohatespeechmovement.org/hate-speech-watch
- Watch out for the European Action Days and organise your own national event
- Visit the campaign co-ordination website at www.coe.int/youthcampaign . Find out who your national co-ordinator is and see how you and your group can get involved in the campaign in your country
- Share your activities – and learn about others' – in the blog "The Campaign in Action"
- Join the discussions about hate speech online and the campaign in the forum http://forum.nohatespeechmovement.org
- Disseminate the campaign in Facebook - https://www.facebook.com/nohatespeech and Twitter - #nohatespeech @nohate_speech
- Carry out educational activities about hate speech using this manual
- Take action online and offline to promote human rights for all and fight hate speech!

The Campaign is evolving all the time, thanks to the dedication of online and offline volunteers and activists. This is why you can find many more materials on the campaign website, including ideas, resources, petitions, and details of upcoming events. Give your group time to browse the website and then discuss as a group how you can join the Campaign.

CHAPTER 3

USING THE MANUAL

This chapter contains a brief outline of the manual's overall structure, aims and methodology. It should help with understanding the educational approach and with planning and conducting activities with your group.

3.1 THE NEED FOR THE MANUAL

Hate speech is an attack on those who are often already vulnerable, and it sows the seeds for tension, further inequality and often violence. The Council of Europe views hate speech as a threat to democracy and human rights.

The No Hate Speech Movement campaign recognises that efforts to address the problem need to include work at a number of different levels. The problem and the solutions are not always straightforward. This manual has been designed to support the educational work that will enable young people to find their own ways of addressing and coping with hate speech online. It aims to develop the understanding, skills and motivation that they will need in order to play an active role in the Campaign, and an active role in shaping an Internet which pays due respect to human rights and democratic participation principles. The manual has also been designed to be used as a tool for the promotion of the rights of Internet users.

Young people are not only 'bystanders' to hate speech online: many are already victims, and some have been drawn into victimising. Educational initiatives need to take this into account and need to address young people in all three roles. With this in mind, the activities in this manual have been designed to address seven key objectives.

THE MANUAL'S OBJECTIVES

- To enable actors in formal and non-formal education contexts to address hate speech with young people and involve school communities in the No Hate Speech Movement campaign
- To develop the skills and motivation for young people to recognise online hate speech and to become 'online activists' for human rights
- To raise awareness of human rights principles and promote a vision of the Internet which reflects these principles
- To support human rights education through non-formal learning approaches and develop critical spirit among children and young people
- To empower those who are already victims of online hate speech, or who are likely to become victims
- To encourage empathy for groups or individuals who may be targets of hate speech online
- To break down myths and prejudice about some of the most common targets of hate speech.

THE MANUAL'S EDUCATIONAL APPROACH

This manual uses the educational approaches of human rights education. The Council of Europe Charter on Education for Democratic Citizenship and Human Rights Education (2010) defines human rights education as:

> "education, training, awareness raising, information, practices and activities which aim, by equipping learners with knowledge, skills and understanding and developing their attitudes and behaviours, to **empower learners to contribute to the building and defence of a universal culture of human rights in society**, with a view to the promotion and protection of human rights and fundamental freedoms."

Human rights education involves three dimensions:

- **Learning about** human rights, knowledge about human rights, what they are, how they are safeguarded and protected, and how they apply offline and online.
- **Learning through** human rights, recognising that the context and the way human rights learning is organised and imparted has to be consistent with human rights values (e.g. participation, freedom of thought and expression, etc.) and that in human rights education the process is as important as the content of the learning
- **Learning for** human rights, by developing skills, attitudes and values for the learners to apply human rights values in their lives and to take action, alone or with others, for promoting and defending human rights.

Compass, the Council of Europe manual for human rights education with young people, offers more information about human rights education that can support facilitators in understanding its approaches and practices. Learn more: www.coe.int/compass

3.2 STRUCTURE OF THE MANUAL

INTRODUCTORY CHAPTERS

This chapter, and the two preceding chapters, are important in setting the context for the activities. It is recommended that you familiarise yourself with the contents in order to understand the context for the manual and the Campaign.

Much of the material in Chapter 1 is also explored more fully in Section 5.1, Hate Speech Online. The information presented in this section will give you a good idea of the range of issues relating to hate speech online, and an understanding of the urgency of working to address it.

Chapter 2 offers a brief overview of the Council of Europe's Campaign against hate speech online. Since this manual is strongly action-orientated, becoming involved in the Campaign will strengthen the activities, and add force to the Campaign. It is recommended that you also look at the Campaign Internet platform (www.nohatespeechmovement.org) which provides more detailed information, and numerous opportunities for young people to become involved.

UNDERLYING THEMES

The manual has been built around eight themes of direct relevance to hate speech online. The themes themselves, and some of the underlying issues they address, are laid out in the diagram on page 20. The questions are not exhaustive: they only pick out some of the more important issues falling under each theme.

Most of the activities address issues relating to a number of different themes, each of which is an important area in itself. For this reason, many of the activities will also be useful in supporting more general work on anti-racism, Internet literacy, citizenship education, human rights education, and other areas.

THE ACTIVITIES

The main body of the manual consists of 24 activities, each of which has been designed to address one or more of the themes. Activities have also been classified according to 'level of complexity': a level 4 activity assumes some pre-existing experience or knowledge of the area; a level 1 activity can be run with groups who are new to the topic.

You can use the table of activities on page 22 to identify appropriate activities according to theme, time required, and level of complexity. Although it is not expected that many educators will have the opportunity, or need, to run all the activities, the importance of the interrelated themes means that all the activities can be used not only to address hate speech but also to support work across a number of other concerns.

Each activity also contains a section consisting of 'Ideas for Action'. These are an important way of consolidating the knowledge and skills acquired in the activities, and they will help young people to become engaged in the Campaign and to feel their own power to make it a success.

THE BACKGROUND TEXTS

The background texts in Chapter 5 have been designed to support the activities. Sections 5.1 and 5.2, dealing with hate speech online and human rights online and offline, are of central importance to all the activities. Other texts can be referred to as needed, and as indicated by specific activities.

3.3 RUNNING THE ACTIVITIES

The instructions for the activities are relatively detailed and contain additional advice in the 'tips for facilitators'. These tips also warn of potential difficulties, so it is important to look at them beforehand.

Further support and recommendations on running human rights activities can be found in Chapter 1 of Compass. www.coe.int/compass

The following section contains general recommendations for getting the best out of the activities, and a brief outline of the educational approach used in the manual. Refer to the list of 'Dos and Don'ts' at the end for a quick checklist of things to bear in mind.

THE ROLE OF FACILITATOR

The activities use the term 'facilitator' to refer to the person running the activities. A facilitator is someone who 'makes something happen', who supports and encourages others to learn and develop their own potential. Effective facilitation is the key to human rights education, and the key to giving life to these activities.

Do not feel you need to be an 'expert' in order to work on the issues: good facilitation does not require any particular knowledge or expertise, except perhaps an 'expertise' in understanding and relating to young people. The activities in this manual will be most successful in an environment where your group is encouraged to explore and find their own approach to issues which are complicated, and often controversial. There is no harm in letting them know that you are exploring together with them! The direct participation of learners in the education processes increases the impact and quality of learning and is inherent to learning *through* human rights. The facilitator, therefore, does not have to be the expert in all matters but should be able to help learners find information and form their own answers and opinions.

CREATING A SAFE ENVIRONMENT

Many of the activities and the issues raised in the manual may touch some of your participants directly. Some participants may have been the victims of bullying or cyberbullying, perhaps even by others in the group; some may have been targeted by racist abuse or discriminatory behaviour. It is very important that you are sensitive to these possibilities and that you let participants know that there is support available if needed. Make sure that you are able to offer that support, or able to point them in the direction of someone else who can help. The InSafe (www.saferinternet.org) and the InHope (www.inhope.org) networks provide useful contacts and helplines to report abuse online in many countries. Many member states have their own specific services to support and receive complaints. Facilitators are advised to inform themselves and, where relevant, to invite these services to support their educational activities.

As far as possible, participants need to feel 'safe' discussing the issues. You could set some base rules with the group, for example, agreeing to respect the opinions of others and to avoid any form of abuse, mockery or personal criticism.

3.4 TEN DO'S AND DON'TS

1	Do encourage participants to voice their opinions and ideas, and speak from their own experiences.	Don't condemn any suggestions as 'useless', 'irrelevant' or 'stupid'!
2	Do try to develop a culture of mutual respect, a safe environment where everyone feels comfortable about expressing their opinion.	Don't allow the group to exclude, ignore, pre-judge, or disrespect anyone else: try to establish some basic principles from the outset.
3	Do encourage discussion and questioning: they will learn by expressing their doubts or uncertainty.	Don't try to give lengthy presentations: that will only turn participants off!
4	Do make links with the reality of the participants and with real issues in their environment.	Don't hand out generalisations which they can't relate to.
5	Do abandon dogma! Allow them to question 'established truths', and do so yourself.	Don't 'preach', or use your position to close an argument.
6	Do be honest with participants. They will respect you more and will be more likely to open up themselves.	Don't pretend to know if you aren't sure! Tell them you will find out, or encourage them to do so.
7	Do trust participants. They need to find the answers for themselves.	Don't talk down to them, and don't try to lead them where they won't be led.
8	Do take their suggestions seriously: they will be more likely to become involved if they feel ownership.	Don't feel you need to stick rigidly to what was planned: follow their interests if they prefer to move in another direction.
9	Do appeal to their natural human sympathies. Ask them how they feel, or how they *would* feel if …	Don't give up if their opinions seem unkind or thoughtless. Show them another perspective.
10	Do treat participants as equals – equal to each other, and 'equal' to you. You are all only human!	Don't exclude participants or make assumptions about what they can or can't do. Humans can be unpredictable!

3.5 THEMES AND QUESTIONS

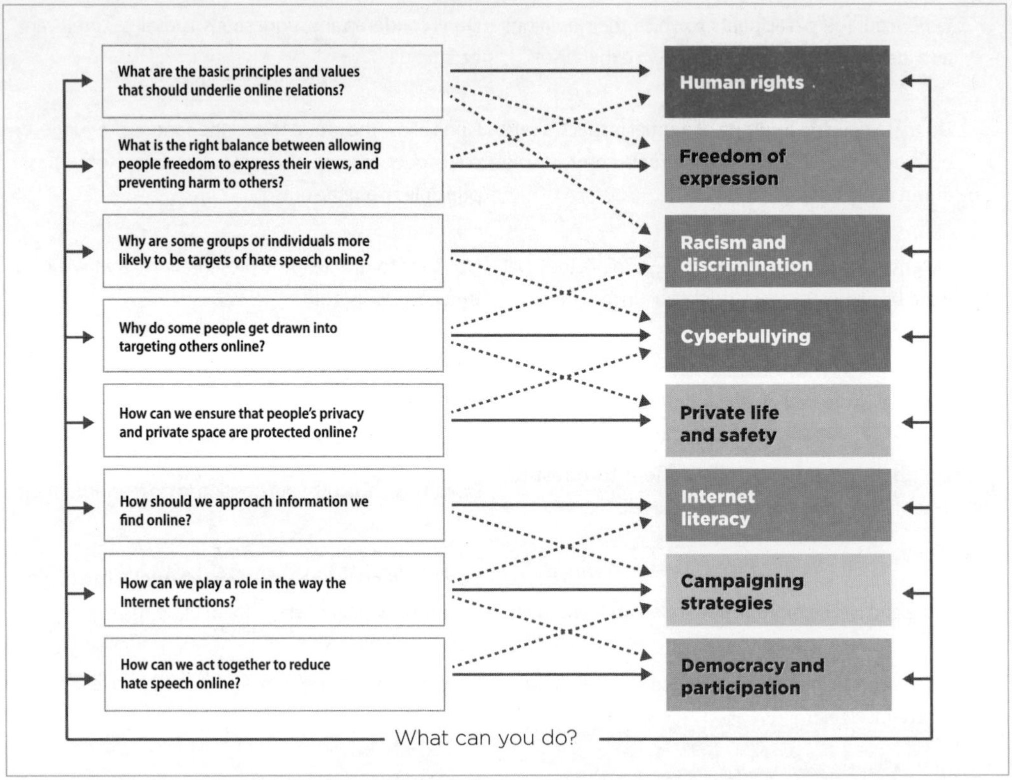

Questions	Themes
What are the basic principles and values that should underlie online relations?	Human rights
What is the right balance between allowing people freedom to express their views, and preventing harm to others?	Freedom of expression
Why are some groups or individuals more likely to be targets of hate speech online?	Racism and discrimination
Why do some people get drawn into targeting others online?	Cyberbullying
How can we ensure that people's privacy and private space are protected online?	Private life and safety
How should we approach information we find online?	Internet literacy
How can we play a role in the way the Internet functions?	Campaigning strategies
How can we act together to reduce hate speech online?	Democracy and participation

What can you do?

CHAPTER 4

24 ACTIVITIES

FOR COMBATING HATE SPEECH ONLINE THROUGH HUMAN RIGHTS EDUCATION

SYNOPTIC TABLE OF ACTIVITIES

Title	Themes	Overview	Level	Time (in min)
A day in court	Freedom of Expression Human Rights Racism and Discrimination	Participants play out a mini-trial, looking at a real case that came before the European Court of Human Rights	4	120
A new mosque in Sleepyville	Democracy and Participation Racism and Discrimination Internet Literacy	This is a simulation of an online consultation/debate. The issue under discussion is the building of a new mosque in a traditionally Christian area.	4	Up to 3 hours, or 3 sessions of 50 minutes each
Action and campaigning step by step	Racism and Discrimination Campaigning Strategies Human Rights	This is a series of 4 activities leading to an action against hate speech and hate crime. The different parts can be run separately and can also be used in combination with other activities in the manual.	4	3 sessions of 90 minutes, 60 minutes and 45 minutes for Parts 1, 2 and 3. Time is also needed for the campaigning action.
Changing the game	Racism and Discrimination Internet Literacy Campaigning Strategies Democracy and Participation	Participants are introduced to the campaign and devise a 'mini-campaign' against sexism in online gaming.	3	60
Checking the facts	Internet Literacy Racism and Discrimination Campaigning Strategies	Participants are asked to act as 'researchers' for politicians on the issue of homophobic abuse. They consider the reliability of information posted online and develop strategies for their own practice.	4	60
Clash of freedoms	Democracy and Participation Freedom of Expression Racism and Discrimination	The activity is a simulation involving two communities with opposing views on freedom of expression, but forced to live together on the same island.	4	120
Confronting cyberbullying	Cyberbullying Democracy and Participation Internet Literacy	This is an activity in which participants identify their likely response to various bullying scenarios – and discuss alternative courses of action.	1	45
Freedom unlimited?	Freedom of Expression Democracy and Participation Human Rights	Participants explore the idea of freedom of expression using a number of case studies. They need to decide what to do with comments or communications which are controversial, abusive or potentially dangerous.	2	45

Title	Themes	Overview	Level	Time (in min)
Group X	Racism and Discrimination Human Rights Private Life and Safety	Participants map rights from the European Convention on Human Rights against a series of abuses commonly experienced by young Roma.	4	60
Human rights online quiz	Human Rights	This activity is a quiz about human rights online. It helps participants to get to know their rights online by using the *Guide to Human Rights for Internet Users*.	3	60
Online participation	Internet Literacy Private Life and Safety Human Rights	Participants think about how they use the Internet and how they participate online. They identify and rate their level of online participation and plan what kind of role they would like to have online in the future.	3	45
Our rights online	Human Rights Democracy and Participation	Participants learn more about the *Guide to Human Rights for Internet Users*. They analyse key messages and statements of the Guide and reflect on its application in daily life.	2	60
Play it again	Cyberbullying Democracy and Participation Racism and Discrimination	This activity is based on a role play: someone is drawn into an act of bullying because of peer pressure. Participants are asked to replay the scenario in order to achieve a different outcome.	2	60
Race for rights!	Human Rights Racism and Discrimination Private Life and Safety	The activity provides a basic introduction to human rights through a team game. Participants have to depict different rights to members of their team using anything they like – except for words!	1	60
Reading the rules	Campaigning Strategies Internet Literacy Democracy and Participation	Participants discover the terms of use or community guidelines of a website and take steps to report inappropriate content to the website. Participants also discuss what the pluses and minuses of reporting there are, particularly in relation to the possibilities of Web 2.0.	3	60

Title	Themes	Overview	Level	Time (in min)
Roots and branches	Racism and Discrimination Human Rights Campaigning Strategies	Participants explore the causes and effects of hate speech online using a 'problem tree' approach. This activity can be used as a follow-up activity to the activity Group X, or as a standalone activity.	2	45
Saying it worse	Racism and Discrimination Democracy and Participation	This is an introductory activity to hate speech online. Participants rank different examples of anti-gay hate speech according to which they think are 'worse'.	1	45
Talking it out	Campaigning Strategies Racism and Discrimination Internet Literacy	The activity uses a 'fishbowl' discussion to explore common prejudices about particular groups in society and engages participants to think critically about commonly held beliefs and develop arguments against hate speech.	1	45
The stories they tell	Racism and Discrimination Human Rights Freedom of Expression	Participants work in small groups to analyse a news publication, focussing on the portrayal of immigrants and immigration. Results are presented as a collage.	2	60
Understanding hate speech	Human Rights Racism and Discrimination	Participants look at examples of hate speech and discuss its possible consequences for individuals and society.	2	60
Virtual action	Campaigning Strategies Racism and Discrimination Human Rights	This is an activity during which participants will be inspired by some anti-racism actions and reflect together on how they could develop similar actions online.	3	60
Wear and share	Private Life and Safety Internet Literacy Cyberbullying	Participants fill out a diagram to show their preferences in sharing particular information online and discuss ways of being more cautious when sharing personal information online.	1	40
Web attack	Internet Literacy Campaigning Strategies Racism and Discrimination	Participants redesign a (fictional) campaign website to cope with a flood of racist comments from the local community.	3	90
Web profiles	Racism and Discrimination Internet Literacy Democracy and Participation	The activity takes place in an imaginary Internet forum. Participants are asked to greet each other according to common stereotypes about particular groups. They use the activity to draw up a set of guidelines for interacting online.	1	Part I: 35 minutes Part II: 25 minutes

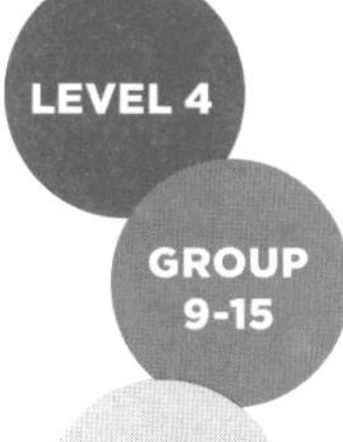

TIME
120'

A DAY IN COURT

Participants play out a mini-trial, looking at a real case that came before the European Court of Human Rights.

THEMES	Freedom of Expression, Human Rights, Racism and Discrimination
COMPLEXITY	Level 4
GROUP SIZE	9-15
TIME	120 minutes
OBJECTIVES	• To consider how freedom of expression rights should be balanced against the need to protect victims of racist abuse or hate speech • To explore the protections – and limitations – of the right to freedom of expression (Article 10) in the European Convention on Human Rights (ECHR) • To understand the role of the European Court
MATERIALS	• Copies of the cards on pages 29-31 • Pens and paper for note-taking • Space for small groups to meet – ideally in separate rooms
PREPARATION	• Photocopy and cut out the cards on page 30. Everyone will need their own card and a copy of the case. You should have the same number of judges, representatives of the Danish Government and representatives of Mr Jersild (or as close as possible). • Number the cards in each group so that you have one judge, one Mr Jersild and one Danish Government representative corresponding to each number. • You will need sufficient space so that each of the 'courts' (3 people) is able to sit apart from the others.

INSTRUCTIONS

1. Tell the group that the session will be devoted to a case against the Danish government which came before the European Court of Human Rights. Participants will play the role of the different actors in the case – the judges, the Danish government and a journalist who was punished for producing a programme containing racist views, Mr. Jersild. Refresh participants' memory, if necessary, on the Court and the ECHR, and tell them that the case concerns freedom of expression.

2. Ask participants what they understand by freedom of expression, and supplement briefly, using the information below (or in Chapter 5).

Free speech, or the right to free expression, is a fundamental human right. People should be allowed to 'express' their opinions or thoughts because thoughts, opinions, and beliefs are an important part of our identity.
Freedom of expression should also be protected because it plays a key role in a democratic society. However, sometimes the right to freedom of expression can be limited if it may harm individuals or be dangerous for society.

3. Read out the information on 'The Case' (page 29), making sure that the details are clear to everyone.
4. Divide participants into 3 roughly equal groups.
   - Group A represents Mr Jersild
   - Group B represents the Danish Government
   - Group C represents the judges in the European Court
5. Hand each group copies of the relevant role card and a copy of the information about the case. Explain that the groups will have 30 minutes to discuss and clarify their own position before moving on to meet with representatives from different groups and start the trial. They should use the time before the trial to prepare their arguments or, in the case of the judges, to prepare questions to both sides.
6. After the 30 minutes' preparation time has passed, ask participants to find the member of each of the other groups with the same number as them and form a new group with these two people. Thus, the person with number 1 in Group A will need to find the person with number 1 in Group B, and the person with number 1 in Group C.
7. Explain that each of these new small groups represents a mini-court. The courts have a further 20 minutes to listen to the arguments of both sides and for the judges to put questions.
8. After this time, each judge should come to an individual judgement on whether Article 10 has been violated. Bring the whole group back together and ask the judges to pronounce their decisions, giving their reasons.
9. Offer the representatives of the other two groups the opportunity to respond to the judgements made; then tell them how the European Court in fact ruled in this case (page 28). Ask for people's reactions to the decision.
10. Proceed to the debriefing and evaluation. Make sure that people have come out of role before discussing the questions below.

DEBRIEFING

- What were the most difficult aspects of the case you considered?
- Did you find it hard to play your role?
- Do you think the 'judge' made the right decision in your case? What were the most important factors in the final decision?

Give participants the following information:

> *Although it was not the task of the European Court to decide whether the Greenjackets' comments should have been punished, they did make a comment about this in their final judgement. The judges believed that the Greenjackets' comments were not covered by freedom of expression – in other words, they should not have been 'free' to express such opinions.*

- Do you agree with this? What are the arguments for and against restricting their rights?
- Have you ever seen similar examples of racism online? How would you react if you did?
- Do you think people should be allowed to post racist comments or hate speech online?
- Can you think of things you can do to make such abuse less common?

TIPS FOR FACILITATORS

- Some of the points made by the Greenjackets have been included as a separate handout. Use your own discretion to decide whether these can be shared with participants.
- At point 5, where people are meeting with others sharing their role, you will need to warn them that they will be split up for the actual court cases – so everyone will need to take their own notes. They will not be able to rely on others in their group!
- Encourage people to use part of the time for discussing details of the case with others, and part of it to prepare their opening statements. The judges should clarify the details of the case and think about the type of additional information they will need from both sides in order to make a judgement.
- Explain to both sides in the trial that even if they do not agree with the position they are supposed to be representing, they need to make sure that the best possible defence is presented to the judges.
- It will be best if you can either allow the different 'courts' to meet in different rooms (point 7), or at least for them to be far enough from each other so as not to be overheard or overhear the others.
- Ask the judges to manage the time during the 'trials'. They may want to plan beforehand how much time they allow for questions and how they divide the time between each side. Emphasise that they need to give each side approximately the same amount of time, but that they will also need to be sure that there is time available for clarification of any points which may be disputed.
- It may be worth mentioning to participants that the European Court was not really taking a decision about Mr Jersild's behaviour, it was considering the 'behaviour' of the Danish State towards Mr Jersild. Council of Europe member states need to make sure that national laws protect the human rights of individuals. When the European Court is asked to make a judgement, it looks at whether the law, or its interpretation, is really offering protection for those rights.
- You may familiarise yourself with the section 'Freedom of expression and information' from the *Guide to Human Rights for Internet Users* in order to be ready to make parallels to cases concerning freedom of expression on the Internet.

VARIATIONS

You could run the trial as a piece of role-play to be run by one group and observed by everyone else. The role-players could be given their role cards before the session and asked to prepare their arguments. Observers would be asked for their views on the process at the end of the role play.

IDEAS FOR ACTION

Participants could find out whether the sites they visit most often have policies on racist abuse or other forms of hate speech.

- They could gather a few examples and the whole group could compare the policies of different sites. Discuss whether they feel any are inadequate to protect users – and how they would like to adapt them. They could post their suggestions onto the No Hate Speech Movement site and encourage other online activists to lobby the sites they have targeted.
- They could also select one or two sites which do claim to have a policy on hate speech, and monitor how well the policy is implemented. Any examples they find of hate speech online could be reported to Hate Speech Watch and also to the sites hosting the content, with a complaint and reference to the policy.

Develop with participants counter-arguments to the racist opinions from this case, which participants can use if they come across these types of racist beliefs.
Create a video with participants about the value of diversity and acceptance in a democratic society.

OTHER RESOURCES

JUDGMENT OF THE EUROPEAN COURT

The case was heard by the European Court in 1994. The Court disagreed with the judgement of the Danish court and decided that Mr Jersild should not have been punished for making and showing the film. They felt that the film made it sufficiently clear that the racist comments were not acceptable or approved by the filmmaker and that there was no danger of the message being misunderstood by the public.
They commented:

> *" [the film] clearly sought - by means of an interview - to expose, analyse and explain this particular group of youths, limited and frustrated by their social situation, with criminal records and violent attitudes, thus dealing with specific aspects of a matter that already then was of great public concern."*

The Court also made the point that news reporting is essential in a democratic society and allows the press to play the role of 'public watchdog'. They said there would need to be very strong reasons for punishing a journalist who publicised statements made by someone else. It is one of the important functions of a free press that it allows and encourages public discussion of issues which are of general importance to society.

HANDOUTS

THE CASE

The applicant in the case is Mr Jens Olaf Jersild, a Danish national who works for Danmarks Radio (which also broadcasts television programmes). The news channel is regarded as a serious one and has an audience of well-informed people.

Mr Jersild wanted to broadcast a documentary on an extreme racist group called the Greenjackets. He contacted members of the group and conducted a long interview with them; then he cut the film down to a few minutes and added some commentary of his own. The final result was shown as part of a news programme and was broadcast on national television.

In the broadcast, members of the Greenjackets were shown making abusive and derogatory remarks about immigrants and ethnic groups in Denmark, comparing black men to gorillas and saying they are "not human". A Danish court found the Greenjackets members guilty of making racist comments and also found Mr Jersild guilty because he had 'encouraged' them, and had broadcast the remarks to a wider audience.

Mr Jersild appealed his conviction at the European Court of Human Rights because he thought his conviction by a Danish court was a violation of his right to freedom of expression (Article 10 of the ECHR).

The European Court needed to decide whether restricting his right to broadcast the remarks was 'legitimate'. This meant looking at whether the right balance was struck between protecting the rights of the people who were the targets of the racist comments, and the need for the public to know about the existence of such groups.

This handout is optional:

Some of the comments made in the broadcast included:

"... the Northern States [in America] wanted that the niggers should be free human beings, man, they are not human beings, they are animals."

"Just take a picture of a gorilla, man, and then look at a nigger, it's the same body structure and everything, man, flat forehead and all kinds of things."

"A nigger is not a human being, it's an animal, that goes for all the other foreign workers as well, Turks, Yugoslavs and whatever they are called."

"...we don't like their mentality ... what we don't like is when they walk around in those Zimbabwe-clothes and then speak this hula-hula language in the street ..."

"It's drugs they are selling, man, half of the prison population in 'Vestre' are in there because of drugs ... they are the people who are serving time for dealing drugs ..."

HANDOUTS

ROLE CARD FOR MR JERSILD

You are a serious journalist and you wanted to make a film about racism and xenophobia which did 2 things:

1. Illustrated the extent of the problem – including the extreme nature of views held by the Greenjackets
2. Showed that the Greenjackets are a criminalised group with many emotionally immature and socially disadvantaged members.

You believe that both these points are important ones for society to understand and you think that your programme managed to address both, partly by directly broadcasting some of the worst opinions, and partly by describing the poor level of education, the background and social difficulties experienced by the young people you interviewed. You do not think that any of your viewers would have understood your programme to be supporting the racist opinions expressed.

As a journalist, you value freedom of expression very highly: too much restriction would make it impossible for journalists to inform the public about real – and unpleasant – issues. You believe that journalists have a responsibility to bring such issues to the public's attention so that they can be recognised and addressed.

Article 10 from the European Convention (simplified)

1. Everyone has the right to freedom of expression. This right includes the freedom to hold opinions and to receive and communicate information and ideas without interference.
2. Freedom of expression can be restricted if the restriction is 'necessary in a democratic society' – in particular, in order to protect the rights of others.

ROLE CARD FOR THE DANISH GOVERNMENT

You believe it was right that Mr Jersild was convicted by the Danish court. His programme contained very extreme and racist views which should not be heard by a wide audience. The programme was sensationalist and did not contain enough commentary to say that the views expressed were unacceptable and dangerous. You believe that journalists have a responsibility to ensure that viewers are not upset or misled. You think that people watching his programme would not have understood that the journalist was shocked by the racist statements and that he did not approve of them. They would not have understood that such statements are ignorant, harmful and illegal.

Mr Jersild edited the film to show the worst comments expressed by the Greenjackets. You think he should not have interviewed the members and encouraged them to express such views, and certainly should not have given the views wide publicity by including them in his programme. You do not think the programme should have been made and Mr Jersild should be held responsible for having given wide publicity to such dangerous opinions.

Article 10 from the European Convention (simplified)

1. Everyone has the right to freedom of expression. This right includes the freedom to hold opinions and to receive and communicate information and ideas without interference.
2. Freedom of expression can be restricted if the restriction is 'necessary in a democratic society' – in particular, in order to protect the rights of others.

HANDOUTS

ROLE CARD FOR THE JUDGES

It is your task to manage the trial and then to decide whether you think the Danish courts acted rightly and Mr Jersild was indeed guilty or whether his rights were violated.

The trial process:

Begin by reminding Mr Jersild and the representative of the Danish Government that each side will be given a few minutes to present their side of the case; then you will put questions and they can respond to each other. Tell them that they must behave in an orderly manner and follow any instructions from you!

The decision you need to make:

You need to consider whether Mr Jersild should have allowed his film to be broadcast to the public. His right to freedom of expression would seem to allow him to do that, but freedom of expression is not an *absolute* right – it needs to be balanced against other social concerns and other human rights. It is your task to decide if the balance has been correctly struck in this case.

These are the key questions you will need to decide and weigh up when you hear the evidence of both sides:

- Do you think that the film might have been understood by the public to be supporting the racist opinions?
- Was it important that the public knew about the racist beliefs and the background of the Greenjackets, or was it more important that such opinions do not reach a wide audience?

Article 10 from the European Convention (simplified)

1. Everyone has the right to freedom of expression. This right includes the freedom to hold opinions and to receive and communicate information and ideas without interference.
2. Freedom of expression can be restricted if the restriction is 'necessary in a democratic society' – in particular, in order to protect the rights of others.

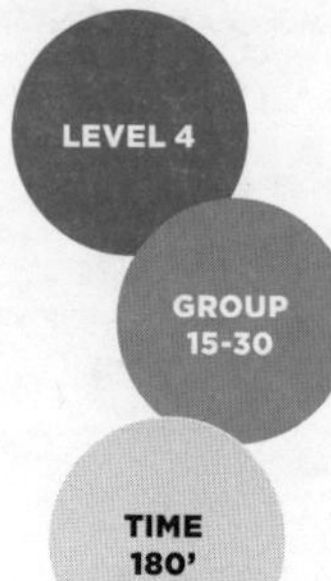

A NEW MOSQUE IN SLEEPYVILLE

This is a simulation of an online consultation / debate. The issue under discussion is the building of a new mosque in a traditionally Christian area.

THEMES	Democracy and Participation, Racism and Discrimination, Internet Literacy
COMPLEXITY	Level 4
GROUP SIZE	15-30
TIME	Either a continuous 2½-3 hour session, or three sessions of approximately 50 minutes each
OBJECTIVES	• To explore the rights of religious minorities and how they relate to hate speech online • To develop skills of online debate and analysis • To consider the use of democratic discussion / participation in increasing tolerance towards other people or other beliefs
MATERIALS	• Access to the Internet – a minimum of 5 computers • Space for groups to meet • 2 facilitators • Ballot papers for Council members (optional)
PREPARATION	• Make a copy of the handouts for all participants • Create a closed space on the Internet. See facilitators' tips for suggestions. • Create a login for each participant – or check beforehand that everyone is able to login using an existing account (see facilitators' tips).

INSTRUCTIONS

1. Read out the description of the problem on page 35. Explain that all participants are members of Sleepyville and all are troubled by the problem of whether a new mosque should be built on a piece of derelict Council land.
2. Give each participant a copy of the handouts and invite them to select roles. Talk through the Consultation Procedure and make sure everyone understands.

3. Indicate the spaces where people and groups can meet up beforehand and the computers available for the activity. Check that everyone has a login and password.
4. Remind those who are able to submit an initial statement that this should be done before the Consultation opens to the public. Encourage everyone to make use of the 30-minute Pre-Consultation phase to:
   - agree positions within the groups and allocate roles or arguments (if necessary)
   - meet with representatives of other groups
   - check they are able to login to the site.

   If computer access or time is limited, remind participants that they will need to be succinct in their arguments as they may only get one chance to make their points!
5. Announce the beginning of the Pre-Consultation phase, and explain that the Consultation will open to the public in 30 minutes.
6. After 30 minutes, announce the start of the public Consultation and invite members of the public to read the initial statements from groups – and submit their comments.
7. At the end of the Consultation, the Mayor declares the Consultation closed. Members of the Town Council then meet and take a vote. If there is no majority opinion, the Mayor has a casting vote.
8. The Mayor announces the decision. Invite participants to bring their chairs into a circle for the debriefing.

DEBRIEFING

Start the feedback round by greeting everybody by their real names. This is important to allow the participants to give up the roles they had assumed during the simulation.
Ask the participants what they feel about the process they have just been through:

- Were you surprised by the result of the vote? Would it have suited the person whose role you were playing?
- Do you think an online consultation is a good way of deciding issues like this? What are the advantages and disadvantages?

QUESTIONS ABOUT THE IDEAS REFLECTED IN THE DEBATE:

- Did interaction with other people or groups make you alter your approach or change your attitude towards any of the issues raised?
- How easy was it to identify with your role?
- Do you think that this situation could arise in real life? Can you think of any similar cases?
- How would you react if this case arose in your town / place of residence? Did the activity alter your attitude at all?

MAKING THE LINK WITH HATE SPEECH ONLINE:

- What did you think about the rule to delete comments which were racist or abusive?
- Did the presence of this rule make you think differently about the comments you posted?
- How easy was it to decide whether or not to delete a comment? (question for the Site Administrators)
- Did you agree with decisions made by the moderators? (question for all participants)

TIPS FOR FACILITATORS

- You will need to set up a secure site before the activity starts. This could be a Facebook page, or an account on another social network. You could also refer to http://cooltoolsforschools.wikispaces.com/Collaborative+Tools for other suggestions. You will need to make sure that everyone has an account which is able to access this site.
- You will need a second facilitator to help run the activity. Although the groups should be allowed to work independently, they may need support or guidance while preparing – or during the consultation. For example, during the preparation phase, it may be useful to check that people are using the time to meet others or to plan what they are going to say during the meeting.
- If computers are limited, you may need to impose a time limit (or word limit) so that everyone gets a chance to post a contribution.
- During the debriefing, it is very important to try to avoid repeating the simulation. People need to try to detach themselves from the role they played in the activity in order to be able to reflect properly on what they have been through. You should help them to look back on the simulation with their normal 'hats' rather than in their assumed roles.

VARIATIONS

You could reduce or limit the number of words that people can post – either as initial submissions or as comments. Try limiting the comments to 'tweets' – i.e. 140 characters!

The activity could also be run over a number of days, reducing the time needed as an organised session and giving participants the chance to submit comments from home.

In case you do not have access to online tools, the activity can be fully developed offline. In its current form, the activity is an adaptation of a *Compass* activity. More information: www.coe.int/compass

IDEAS FOR ACTION

What are some of the religious or ethnic minorities in your country and how does the media write about them? Look for stories on national or local news sites about any groups which are traditionally presented in a bad light. Then write to the journalists responsible – or add a comment, if the website allows it.

Are there any online consultations organised by your local authorities? Can young people use any online tools to communicate with locally elected representatives? Do an online search with participants and start using the existing tools, if any, to raise issues of concern for young people.

Contact some local minority organisations and meet them in order to discover more about how your own community tackles diversity.

HANDOUTS

For all participants; these can also be posted on the consultation site.

A MOSQUE IN SLEEPYVILLE

You live in the picturesque town of Sleepyville, a town of about 80,000 people. In the last 60 years the population has changed radically, partly because young people mostly try to move to larger cities to look for work, but also because the region has seen the arrival of a large number of immigrant families, many from Muslim countries. Some of these families have been here for several generations, but they are still treated with suspicion as 'newcomers' by many people in the town. They now make up almost 15% of the total population.

The issue that is now dividing the town is the desire of Muslims in Sleepyville to have a mosque built on a piece of derelict land belonging to the Council. This land has been undeveloped and has been a source of complaints to the Council for years: it is near the main shopping street and is an area where vandalism and drug-taking have been a regular problem.

So when a rich businessman offered to take the problem off the Council's hands, the Mayor thought his lucky day had come! The Council readily agreed to give up the land and to fund 20% of the construction costs for a new mosque on the site. The remaining 10% of the building costs, which the businessman could not cover, were to be found from among the Muslim community.

Building was meant to start this week… but the quiet town of Sleepyville has been anything but quiet ever since the decision was taken. A week ago, the Council's Twitter account was hacked by an anti-Muslim group and several abusive and racist tweets were sent out – some encouraging people to take to the streets and "hunt out the foreigners". An increase in racist attacks against Muslims followed, some resulting in violence. On one occasion, someone was critically injured. A few Muslim groups have responded, and violence between different gangs appears to be on the increase.

The Mayor of Sleepyville has called for calm and has announced that the decision to build the mosque will be reviewed after a public consultation has taken place. They have decided to hold an online consultation forum to allow as many people as possible to participate.

HANDOUTS

For all participants

CONSULTATION PROCEDURE

The Consultation is open to residents of Sleepyville over the age of 18.

The following registered groups / individuals are invited to submit an initial statement outlining their position on the proposed mosque. Initial statements must be received before the Consultation opens to the public.

- **The Mayor and Deputy Mayor of Sleepyville** (joint statement)
- **Town Council Members** representing the Traditionalist Party, Populist Party and Diversity Party (1 statement from each party)
- **Non-governmental organisations:** Youth Action Group "Young Sleepies for Human Rights!", "Past and Present Association", "Muslim Association of Sleepyville" (one submission from each organisation)

Initial statements will be posted on the Council's website and will then be open to comments from all **other residents over the age of 18. Any comment judged to be threatening, racist or abusive will be deleted from the Council website.**

The Consultation will close after 30 minutes. Council members will then vote on the proposal with the Mayor having a deciding vote if there is no majority opinion.

The decision of the Council will be final.

Role-cards

THE MAYOR OF SLEEPYVILLE

You are the town's figurehead and are very conscious of the need to re-establish calm and good relations in the town. You think it is important that you are seen to be impartial throughout the proceedings and you value your reputation as a fair mediator between different sectors of society. You would like to find a solution which is acceptable to the largest number of people possible.

Before the consultation opens to the public, you need to draft an initial statement setting out your position. You should discuss this with the Deputy Mayor. If you have time, you should also try to meet with groups or residents to gauge opinion and see if you can reduce the risk of violence.

You will not vote unless the vote results in a tie. If that is the case, your vote will decide the outcome.

HANDOUTS

DEPUTY MAYOR

You work beside the Mayor and should help him / her to draft an initial statement. You may also be asked to meet with some of the more extreme groups before the Consultation opens to see if you can convince them of the importance of finding a mutually acceptable solution.

Once the Consultation opens, it will be your task to assist the Mayor with meeting groups or residents in order to gauge opinion and see if you can reduce the risk of violence.

You do not vote in the debate.

SITE ADMINISTRATORS (2 PEOPLE)

Your role is to try to follow the discussion and make sure that comments are not racist or likely to be hurtful. Any such comments should immediately be deleted from the Council website. Spend the time before the Consultation opens thinking about how you will decide whether comments are unacceptable. You may want to draw up a brief set of guidelines.

You can also post comments warning people that their language is unacceptable, or encouraging participants to be polite and considerate to others involved in the debate.

You do not vote in the debate.

TOWN COUNCIL MEMBERS: TRADITIONALIST PARTY (2 OR 3 PEOPLE)

You represent the Traditionalist Party on the Town Council, and you are very strongly opposed to the mosque. You do not think it is right that Council land and Council resources should be spent on a place of worship that does not respect the traditions of this country and this town. You feel that immigrant families are privileged to be allowed to live here and that they should not try to impose different lifestyles on a country where they are guests.

Some of your members are strongly anti-Muslim, believing that the current violence was only to be expected from a community which believes in such a violent religion. You would really like to reduce the number of Muslims in the town because you think they have corrupted the traditional values of Sleepyville. You are also certain that the mosque will become a meeting area for recruiting terrorists.

You need to prepare an initial statement of your position which should be posted to the website before the Consultation opens to the public. Keep it brief!

Each of your members has a vote in the final decision.

HANDOUTS

TOWN COUNCIL MEMBER: POPULIST PARTY (1 OR 2 PEOPLE)

You represent the Populist Party on the Town Council. You supported the original decision to have the mosque built on the land, partly because you realise that the Muslim community has been very good for the economy of the town and you do not want to alienate them. However, you have been very worried by complaints from residents and the recent violence. You are also concerned about your seat in the next Council elections, so you will probably support whichever option appears to be least controversial.

You need to prepare an initial statement on your position which should be posted to the website before the Consultation opens to the public. Keep it brief!

Each of your members has a vote in the final decision.

TOWN COUNCIL MEMBER: DIVERSITY PARTY (1 OR 2 PEOPLE)

You represent the Diversity Party on the Town Council. You believe that the relatively large proportion of people from different parts of the world has added to the culture and interest of Sleepyville and you have felt it unfair that the town has deprived many of these people of the opportunity to practise their religion for so long. You would like to see more dialogue between the different communities in Sleepyville and you have been engaged in trying to calm the violence and bringing the opposing sides together to talk. You can see that the derelict land is causing social problems in the town and that the Council does not at the moment have the money to develop it themselves.

You need to prepare an initial statement of your position which should be posted to the website before the Consultation opens to the public. Keep it brief!

Each of your members has a vote in the final decision.

MEMBERS OF THE "PAST AND PRESENT" ASSOCIATION OF SLEEPYVILLE (2-4 PEOPLE)

You are one of the main groups opposed to this mosque. Your members are from traditional (non-Muslim) communities in Sleepyville, and you think it is very important to keep the ancient character of the town, where most of you have lived all your lives. The site that is proposed for the mosque is very central and it would be visible from most places in the town centre. In particular, the mosque could block out the view of the main church from the town square. You feel that the character of your hometown is being completely changed by a community that arrived here only recently. You do not see why people who arrived in this country from somewhere else should not live by the same rules as you have here.

Your members have become increasingly radical over the past few years and your organisation has been accused of being openly racist and responsible for some of the violence on the streets. You have close connections with the Traditionalist Party which is represented on the Council.

You need to prepare an initial statement of your position which should be posted to the website before the Consultation opens to the public. Keep it brief!

HANDOUTS

MEMBERS OF THE YOUTH ACTION GROUP "YOUNG SLEEPIES FOR HUMAN RIGHTS!" (2-4 PEOPLE)

Your group was set up to address some of the worst problems for young people today in Sleepyville. You see the building of the mosque as a solution both to the Muslim community's need for a place of worship, and as a solution to the numerous social problems which have been a result of the land being left derelict for so long. You support the building of this mosque but you are concerned that other social problems may be neglected by the Council if they have to contribute to the building. In particular, the youth budget over the past 5 years has been cut to a level where it cannot begin to meet the needs in the town.
You need to prepare an initial statement of your position (not exceeding 250 words) which should be posted to the website before the Consultation opens to the public.

MEMBERS OF THE "MUSLIM ASSOCIATION OF SLEEPYVILLE" (2-4 PEOPLE)

You have been asking the Council for years to provide a place of worship for the Muslim community, but it has always been refused on financial grounds. You feel that it is unfair that the Muslim community is being asked to find 10% of the building costs, when economic conditions are so harsh for most people, and when the Christian community has 11 different places of worship and these are used by far fewer people than the mosque would be. You feel that the contribution that your community has made to the town is not appreciated, that people in your community are unfairly discriminated against in various aspects of their life, and that in refusing to allow this mosque, the council is denying members of your community their fundamental right to religious worship. You are aware that some of your members hold more extreme views than the official views of the Association and you are concerned that some Muslims have responded violently to attacks on their community. You worry that a reversal of the decision will further alienate Muslim residents and may lead to a further increase in inter-community violence.
You need to prepare an initial statement of your position which should be posted to the website before the Consultation opens to the public. Keep it brief!

CITIZENS OF SLEEPYVILLE

You are worried about the conflict that seems to have taken over the town of Sleepyville. You do not know which position you support yet: you want to gain a better understanding of the positions of the non-governmental organisations and the Parties represented on the Council; then you plan to make up your mind.
You may not post comments until the Consultation opens to the public (30 minutes after the start) but you can read initial statements as they are posted and should try to meet with other residents and representatives of Associations or Town Council members to hear their arguments.
Think about what you would like to say when the Consultation goes public – and be aware that each comment must not exceed 150 words. After everyone has had a chance to comment, you may make a second comment if time allows.

This activity has been developed from 'A Mosque in Sleepyville' in Compass, the Manual for Human Rights Education with Young People - www.coe.int/compass

ACTION AND CAMPAIGNING STEP BY STEP

This is a series of 4 activities leading to an action against hate speech and hate crime. The different parts can be run separately and can also be used in combination with other activities in the manual.

THEMES	Racism and Discrimination, Campaigning Strategies, Human Rights
COMPLEXITY	Level 4
GROUP SIZE	Any
TIME	3 sessions of 90 minutes, 60 minutes and 45 minutes for Parts 1, 2 and 3. Time is also needed for the campaigning action.

PART 1 (60 minutes) looks at the historical suffering of the Roma people, including during the time of the Nazi holocaust. The activity can be run without the other parts. The aim is to give the group an understanding of the hate-fuelled crimes against Roma people which have gone unacknowledged and continue to have consequences today.

PART 2 (60 minutes) involves planning an action to raise public awareness of this suffering and to express solidarity with Roma people. This part can be used to plan any activity under the Campaign and as a follow-up activity to other activities in the manual.

PART 3 is the action itself. The instructions are drawn up by your group!

PART 4 (45 minutes) is a debriefing of the action. The questions can be used in general form to debrief any action your group undertakes as part of the Campaign.

PART 1: LESSONS OF HISTORY

TIME 60 minutes

OBJECTIVES
- To raise awareness of Roma victims of the Nazi Holocaust and build solidarity towards Roma people
- To highlight an extreme example of deeply ingrained prejudice and hate speech and examine the consequences today
- To develop solidarity for Roma people and motivate the group to act against racism and discrimination

MATERIALS
- Flipchart paper and markers
- Copies of the handout, "A brief history of the persecution of the X" (optional)

PREPARATION
- Tell the group before the session that you are planning to discuss the Holocaust, and speak separately with anyone who may be likely to find it difficult.
- Make copies of the handouts, one copy per small group.

INSTRUCTIONS

1. Ask participants to form small groups of 2 to 3 people who share the same sense of identity. This may relate to their ethnicity or nationality, but it may also be connected with different social or religious groupings (even football teams!). Give them about 10 minutes to share their feelings about this identity within their small groups.
2. Give participants the handout, "A brief history of the persecution of the X", or present some of the information to give them a feeling for the successively brutal treatment that had to be endured by the Roma population. Do not tell them yet the name of the population that was targeted.
3. Briefly discuss their reactions, if possible without moving people from their groups. Then ask each group to pair up with another and give them 15 minutes to address the following questions:
   - What would they feel if 'their' people had been the target of this kind of treatment at some point in recent history? (Ask them to concentrate on the group they selected under point 1.)
   - What do they feel would be the most difficult aspects for a community that had lived through this?
   - What if there were people today denying there was a Holocaust? What would determine them to deny these facts?
4. Bring the group together and ask them to feed back on their discussions. Then ask whether participants know or can guess which people the handout was about. If they don't guess, tell them it was the Roma, and ask what they know about the situation of Roma people today. How are they treated and how much is known about their historical suffering? How does hate speech affect them today?
5. Tell participants that there have been cases at the European Court of Human Rights which have found numerous violations of human rights against this group in almost every country of Europe. Remind participants that the media and the population as a whole have very intolerant attitudes towards

Roma people and they are frequent targets of abuse and hate crime. Ask if participants have come across any examples, in their 'real' lives or on the Internet.

6. If you are running the activity as an introduction to a Campaign action, give participants some information about the Dosta! Campaign and tell them that the next session will look at ways they can take action to address discrimination against Roma people.

TIPS FOR FACILITATORS

- The extreme content presented in the activity may make it upsetting for certain members of the group. Obviously, if there are Roma people in your group, you should alert them beforehand and be prepared to offer support if this is needed. However, there were many other groups targeted by the Nazi holocaust and representatives of these groups may also be affected. This applies perhaps particularly to Jews, since the extent of their suffering is very widely known. Make sure you are aware beforehand of the composition of the group and their likely reaction to the activity.
- You could provide participants with information about other groups which were targeted by the Nazi regime – or ask if they can name them. Some of these groups include:
  - Poles (about 2.5 million gentile Poles were killed)
  - Other Slavic peoples
  - Soviets (particularly prisoners of war)
  - 'Non-Europeans' – particularly people of African or Asian origin
  - The mentally ill and those with learning disabilities
  - The deaf and physically disabled
  - Homosexuals and transgender people
  - Political opponents – in particular, communists and leftists
  - Religious 'dissidents', in particular members of Jehovah's Witnesses

  See https://en.wikipedia.org/wiki/Holocaust_victims for more information.
- You will need to approach the discussion with maximum sensitivity and flexibility, and should not rush the group if you feel that people need more time to express their feelings.
- For the work in small groups, you would be advised to think beforehand about whether there are likely to be any difficulties for certain individuals. If this is the case, it may be easier to 'assign' a group identity for everyone, for example, you could ask people to pair up as 'males' and 'females', people who study different subjects, people who prefer football / tennis / athletics, and so on.
- In the Brief Romani Holocaust Chronology (below) any reference to Roma or "gypsy" has been replaced everywhere by X. When you use this information, you could refer to 'the group' or even ask participants to imagine it is their group.
- The purpose of asking participants to select an identity which is important for them is in order that they try to perceive what it would be like to be targeted as a group. However, if the group has strong prejudices about Roma, they may even so find it difficult to identify with the Roma's problems. You should certainly address this, if this is the case: leave plenty of time at point 4 of Part 1 for them to discuss their concerns. Tell them that it is estimated that between 75% and 80% of the Roma popula-

tion in Europe was killed during the Holocaust, and in some countries this figure was as high as 90%. You could ask them to imagine what it would be like for them to lose 90% of their people, or 90% of the people in this group: in a group of 20 only 2 people would remain.

- You may want to give participants some information about 'hate crimes' and explore the link with hate speech, and hate speech online. 'Hate crimes' are crimes committed against individuals or groups which are motivated by an attitude of hate towards the group as a whole. You could explore the ways that 'mild' expressions of hate or racial slurs can easily escalate into more extreme forms, and can then make crimes against individuals appear to be justified.
- The word 'dosta' means 'enough' in Romani. The Dosta! campaign is an awareness-raising campaign which aims at bringing non-Roma closer to Roma citizens. You can find information about the campaign at http://dosta.org. It may be helpful if you have access to the Internet, so that participants can spend some time looking at the site. There are other sites which address the Roma holocaust which they could also use for research:
  www.romagenocide.org
  www.sintiundroma.de/en/sinti-roma/the-national-socialist-genocide-of-the-sinti-and-roma.html
  http://romafacts.uni-graz.at/index.php/history
  www.romasinti.eu/
  www.romasintigenocide.eu/en/home

DEBRIEFING

Give participants some time at the end of the activity to speak about their feelings as a result of the information and the activity. You could begin by doing a round and asking everyone to use one word to describe their feelings.

- Did you gain any new information or understanding as a result of the activity?
- Did the activity alter your attitudes towards Roma people?
- Why do you think the suffering of the Roma people under the Nazi regime is so little known about today?
- Do you think if this was more widely known it would make a difference to the way Roma people are treated today?
- What can you do to make the information more widely known?
- What, if anything, have we 'learned' from the Nazi holocaust? Can you explain how hate speech became so widespread that terrible crimes could be committed against large numbers of people? Do you see any parallels with hate speech online and offline today?

VARIATIONS

You could use the form of this activity to look at any of the other groups targeted by the holocaust, and whose suffering is not widely known. Some of these groups are listed in the tips for facilitators.

PART 2: PLANNING AN ACTION

This part of the activity is based on Chapter 3 of Compass – Taking Action – and you can use the guidelines under the section, "Getting Results" for more detailed ideas. This is available at www.coe.int/compass.

TIME	60 minutes
OBJECTIVES	• To develop an understanding of how to plan an effective action • To consider ways that the Internet can be used as a campaigning tool • To develop a plan of action – to be implemented by the group
MATERIALS	• Copies of the flowchart (optional) • Flipchart paper and markers
PREPARATION	• Make copies of the flowchart – or draw an empty version on a piece of flipchart paper

INSTRUCTIONS

1. Explain that the group will be designing an action to address the problem of online hate speech against the Roma people (or another group). Remind them about the extent and impact of online hate. Ask participants to give some examples from their own experience.
2. Ask the group to brainstorm some of the problems associated with online hate speech, thinking particularly about those aspects they could address. Prompt them to consider different degrees of hate, from mild abuse to incitement which may lead to hate crime; prompt them to consider the different forums and actors who contribute to the volume of hate speech online. Write the suggestions up on a flipchart.
3. Explain that the group will need to select one of their 'solutions' to work on. Remind them that it is not particularly important which one they choose, but it will need to be achievable and should not be too ambitious!
4. Discuss the most popular solutions briefly and try to reach a consensus on one that all members will be happy to work on.
5. Hand out copies of the flowchart on page 48 – or use an empty version on a piece of flipchart paper. Use the headings in the flowchart on page 48 and work through each box with participants. Check that:
   - The action they have identified will contribute to resolving the problem
   - The action is realistic, given the resources of the group and given the obstacles they may come up against
   - The 'solution' is concrete enough so that they will know whether they have achieved it or not.
6. Draw up a Decision Sheet, so that everyone knows what they are supposed to be doing, and when. See the end of the Taking Action section of *Compass* for a model – www.coe.int/compass .
7. Use the debriefing to check everyone is happy with the process and the result – and ready to implement the plan.

DEBRIEFING

- How do you feel about the plan for the action you have come up with?
- Does everyone feel they have a role to play – and are you happy with your role?
- Is there anything else we need to consider or be aware of before running the action?
- How will we know whether our action has been 'successful'?

TIPS FOR FACILITATORS

- You could run the activity 'Roots and Branches' focussing to select a problem for the group to work on. This will give them a broader picture of the ways that some of their problems are interrelated, and will result in a more cohesive plan of action.
- Try to give the group as much autonomy as possible in selecting the problem and working through the flowchart. The action will be more effective if they feel ownership of the plan. However, you should make sure you consider any potential difficulties in running the action and think about how these could be minimised.
- It is strongly advised that, if at all possible, at the stage of planning and before the actual action, you try to involve members of the Roma community, or your target group, if this is different. If you are able to invite someone to speak to the group this will make the whole activity more realistic, and will certainly be a useful source of ideas. At the very least, you should check with members of the community that the action your group is planning will be received well. Alternatively, contact a group locally that works with, or supports, your target group.
- When working through the flowchart, if you do not want to provide participants with the suggestions in the boxes you can use the more generic version in Taking Action from Compass, or draw your own version on a piece of flipchart paper. If participants find it difficult to think of ways to address hate speech online, use some of the suggestions in Campaigning Strategies to give them a few ideas.

VARIATIONS

The activity can obviously be run with a different group commonly targeted by hate speech online. It is recommended that you run an introductory activity before planning any action as this will deepen participants' understanding and motivate them to work on the problems they have identified. You can use many of the other activities as an introduction, for example:

- 'Changing the Game' can be used to look at gender-based hate speech
- 'Saying it Worse' can be used to look at homophobia
- 'Web attack' can be used to look at hate speech against asylum seekers and immigrant communities.

Online hate speech can of course be addressed both through online and offline actions. When considering actions that can be taken, you could suggest that the group confine itself to online actions.

PART 3: THE ACTION ITSELF

PART 4: REFLECTING AND LEARNING FROM THE PROCESS

- It is important to debrief the action once it has been carried out, as well as the process leading up to it. If it is an ongoing campaign, you should take some time to reflect on the process shortly after it has begun. This is very important as many one-off actions can appear to have little effect and the group may become discouraged. Use the session to address any concerns they have that the action "was not worth doing" or that it "went badly". Remind them that campaigns typically consist of numerous actions and activities, all of which, when taken together, can help to change behaviours and attitudes.
- Use their reflections as a learning point in planning any future actions.
- Begin the session by asking participants to describe their feelings after the day of action. This can be done as a brief run round the group.
- Divide participants into groups of 4-5 people and give them the following questions to discuss as a small group.
  - What did you feel went well?
  - Was there anything which was more difficult than you had imagined it to be, or anything unexpected?
  - What do you think were the main achievements of the action? Do these fit with the objectives you set out initially?
  - Do you think there are any lessons we could learn for next time?
- Bring the small groups back together and discuss the different responses to the questions. Finish the session with a few general impressions about the whole process:
  - Do you feel satisfied with your work in planning and carrying out this action?
  - What would you list as the main 'learning points' if you were to organise another action (on any theme)?
  - What have been the most important results for you personally? Do you feel that your views or attitudes have changed in any way?
  - How do you think it would be possible to build on what you have done? Would you like to try to do this?

IDEAS FOR (FURTHER) ACTION

Encourage the group to keep working on the problems they have identified! They could use other problems in the list drawn up at the beginning of Part 2 or could try other approaches to the problem they selected. The groundwork undertaken in the process of planning this activity will be useful in preparing for other actions, and may have motivated them to do more as part of the campaign.

Make sure that participants send an account of their action to the No Hate Speech Movement. They could also link up with other groups – including groups in different countries – and plan a continuation of the work they have already carried out.

HANDOUTS

A BRIEF HISTORY OF THE PERSECUTION OF THE X

1890	Conference organised in Germany on the " X scum". Military empowered to regulate movements of X.
1909	A policy conference on 'The X Question' is held. It is recommended that all Xs be branded with easy identification.
1920	2 academics introduce the notion of 'lives unworthy of life', suggesting that Xs should be sterilised and eliminated as a people.
1922	(And throughout the 1920s): All Xs in German territories are photographed and fingerprinted.
1926	A law is passed to control the 'X plague.' (This treatment is in direct violation of the terms of the Constitution.)
1927	In Bavaria, special camps are built to imprison Xs. Eight thousand Xs are put into these camps.
1928	All Xs placed under permanent police surveillance. A professor publishes a document suggesting that "it was the Xs who introduced foreign blood into Europe". More camps are built to contain Xs.
1934	Xs taken for sterilisation by injection and castration, and sent to camps at Dachau, Dieselstrasse, Sachsenhausen and elsewhere. Two laws issued in this year forbid Germans from marrying "Jews, Xs and Negroes".
1938	Between 12-18 June, hundreds of Xs throughout Germany and Austria are arrested, beaten, and imprisoned. Xs are the first targeted population to be forbidden to attend school.
1939	The Office of Racial Hygiene issues a statement saying "All Xs should be treated as hereditarily sick; the only solution is elimination. (The aim should therefore be the elimination without hesitation of this defective element in the population)".
1940	The first mass genocidal action of the Holocaust: 250 X children are used as guinea pigs to test the cyanide gas crystal, at the concentration camp at Buchenwald. Employment of any kind is forbidden to Xs in this same year.
1941	In July the Nazi Final Solution to "kill all Jews, Xs and mental patients" is put into operation. The Holocaust begins. Eight hundred Xs are murdered in one action on the night of 24 December in the Crimea.
1944	1 August: 4,000 Xs are gassed and incinerated at Auschwitz-Birkenau in one mass action.
1945	By the end of the war, 70-80% of the X population had been annihilated by Nazis. No Xs were called to testify at the Nuremberg Trials, no one testified on their behalf. No war crime reparations have been paid to the X as a people.
1950	First of many statements over the years to follow, by the German government, that they owe nothing to the X people by way of war crime reparations.
1992	Germany "sells" X asylum seekers back to Romania for USD 21 million, and begins shipping them in handcuffs on 1 November. Some X commit suicide rather than go. The German press agency asks western journalists not to use the word 'deportation' because that word has 'uncomfortable historical associations'.

Edited version of a Brief Romani Holocaust Chronology, by Ian Hancock

Activity developed from Dosta!, in Compass – Manual for Human Rights Education with Young People, Council of Europe, 2012

HANDOUT - FLOWCHART

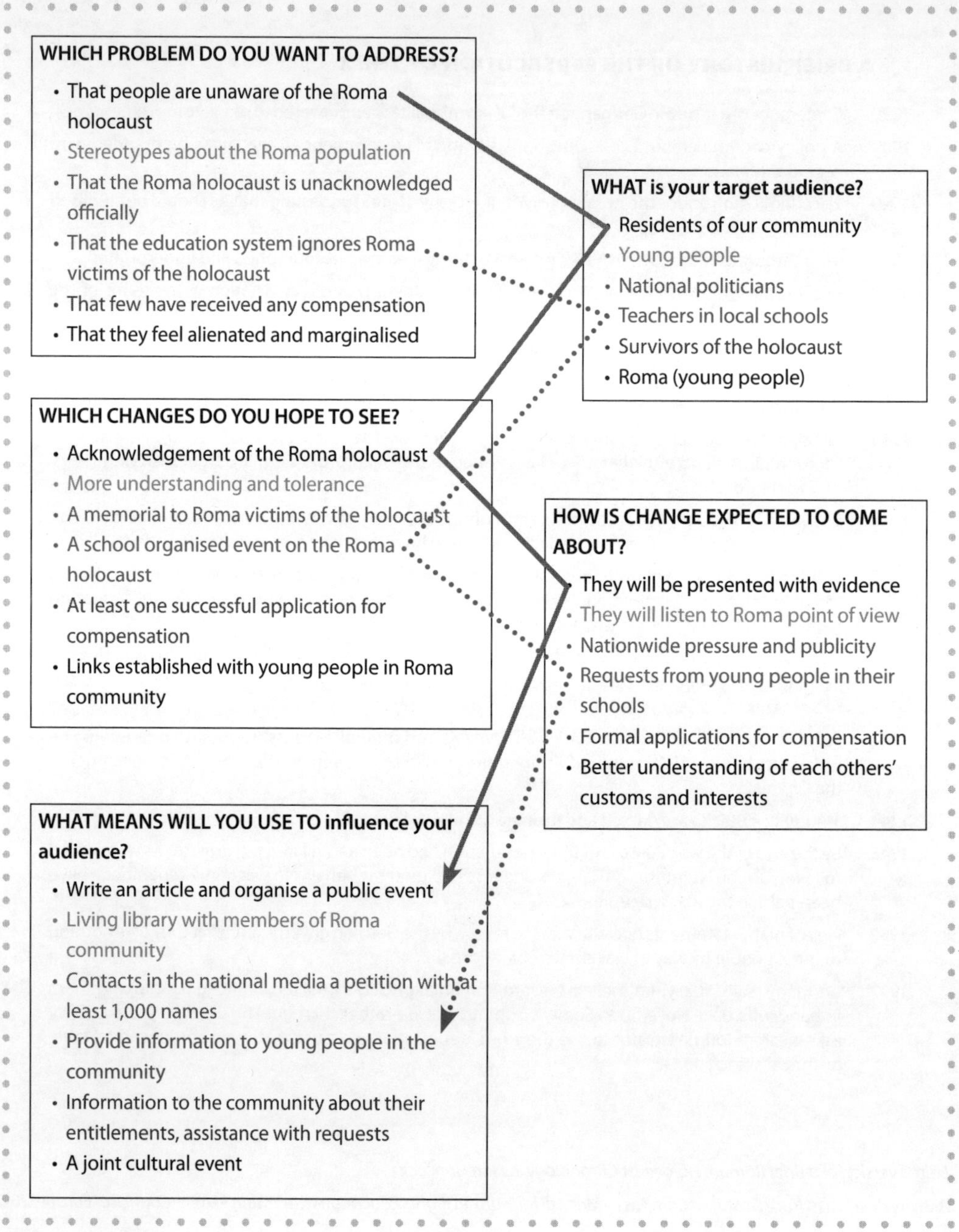

WHICH PROBLEM DO YOU WANT TO ADDRESS?

- That people are unaware of the Roma holocaust
- Stereotypes about the Roma population
- That the Roma holocaust is unacknowledged officially
- That the education system ignores Roma victims of the holocaust
- That few have received any compensation
- That they feel alienated and marginalised

WHAT is your target audience?

- Residents of our community
- Young people
- National politicians
- Teachers in local schools
- Survivors of the holocaust
- Roma (young people)

WHICH CHANGES DO YOU HOPE TO SEE?

- Acknowledgement of the Roma holocaust
- More understanding and tolerance
- A memorial to Roma victims of the holocaust
- A school organised event on the Roma holocaust
- At least one successful application for compensation
- Links established with young people in Roma community

HOW IS CHANGE EXPECTED TO COME ABOUT?

- They will be presented with evidence
- They will listen to Roma point of view
- Nationwide pressure and publicity
- Requests from young people in their schools
- Formal applications for compensation
- Better understanding of each others' customs and interests

WHAT MEANS WILL YOU USE TO influence your audience?

- Write an article and organise a public event
- Living library with members of Roma community
- Contacts in the national media a petition with at least 1,000 names
- Provide information to young people in the community
- Information to the community about their entitlements, assistance with requests
- A joint cultural event

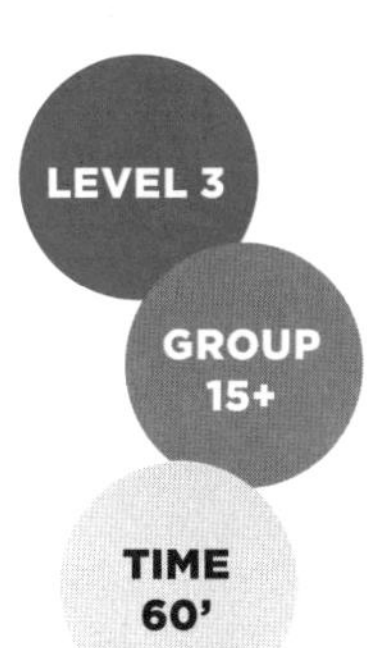

CHANGING THE GAME

Participants are introduced to the Campaign and devise a 'mini-campaign' against sexism in online gaming.

THEMES	Racism and Discrimination, Internet Literacy, Campaigning Strategies, Democracy and Participation
COMPLEXITY	Level 3
GROUP SIZE	15 upwards
TIME	60 minutes
OBJECTIVES	• To explore the problem of sexist abuse online, particularly in the gaming community • To develop online campaigning skills • To involve participants in the No Hate Speech Movement
MATERIALS	• Flipchart paper and markers
PREPARATION	• Photocopy the 'instruction cards' (pages 52-53) and the examples of hate speech on page 54 (or use an overhead slide) • Familiarise yourself with the No Hate Speech Movement (Chapter 2 of this manual or visit the Campaign platform www.nohatespeechmovement.org)

INSTRUCTIONS

1. Show participants the handout on page 54 – and ask for their views. Prompt with a few questions, if necessary, for example:
   - How do you think a woman might feel if she received something like this?
   - Do you think this kind of abuse is common?
   - What do you think a woman might feel if she wanted to join a game and saw lots of comments like this directed at other women gamers?
2. Tell participants that abuse against women is extremely common, not only in the online gaming community, but also in other online interaction. You could ask whether anyone has seen examples in their own activity online and whether any female participants have received such abuse.
3. Explain that these are all examples of hate speech online and that hate speech is a violation of human rights. If statements like these were to be directed at women or girls *offline*, they would often be illegal.

4. Tell participants that a Europe-wide campaign has been set up by the Council of Europe to mobilise young people to act against hate speech online. Give them some information about the Campaign using the information below or from Chapter 2 of this manual. You can also use the campaign website at www.nohatespeechmovement.org

> The Council of Europe's Campaign against hate speech online has been set up to address the problem of hate speech online. This is becoming increasingly common on the Internet and it can cause serious harm to those who are targeted, as well as to society as a whole. The Campaign aims to work in a number of different ways, for example, by raising awareness of the problem, working to address the attitudes and prejudices which drive online hate, mobilising young people to act against it, supporting and building solidarity for victims of online hate, and so on. All young people are encouraged to join the movement.

5. Explain that the activity will explore some ways in which the group can become involved in the Campaign by looking at the specific issue of sexist abuse against women gamers. Participants will design their own 'mini-campaign' around this issue. They will work in small groups to explore ways of addressing different target audiences who have some relation to the problem.
6. Show participants the list of 'target audiences' and invite them to select one to work on for the activity. Try to make sure there are roughly equal numbers in each group.
   - **Group 1:** women gamers
   - **Group 2:** those who abuse women gamers, or are likely to abuse them
   - **Group 3:** other gamers (those who don't necessarily engage in abuse, but allow it to happen)
   - **Group 4:** policy makers, local or national parliamentary representatives, Ministries, and so on
   - **Group 5:** online service and content providers, as website owners and hosts, online community managers
   - **Group 6:** the general public, so that they can understand the seriousness of the problem and help to support the Campaign
7. Give each group a piece of flipchart paper and their instruction card. Tell them they have about 20 minutes to think about the specific methods they will use to engage their audience. Remind them that others are working on different audiences: they should try to concentrate on the methods and messages that will be most likely to engage their audience's attention and make a positive contribute to the campaign. A good campaign brings as many people on board as possible!
8. After about 20 minutes, invite the groups to present their suggestions. Allow some time for questions of clarification and comments.
9. Explain to participants that a real campaign strategy needs more than 15 minutes! Very often, initial suggestions are modified or even rejected in favour of different ideas. A good strategy will be worked on by a number of people often over many months, and may be tested out before it is actually implemented. The debriefing will look at participants' views on their 'first draft' of a strategy!

DEBRIEFING

QUESTIONS ON THE STRATEGY AND ONLINE CAMPAIGNING:

- How easy did you find it to think of online actions? What are the advantages and disadvantages of acting online?
- Did you feel happy with your proposed strategy? Do you foresee any problems in implementing it?
- Do you think your campaign could have been strengthened by adding some offline actions? Can you suggest any?
- Do you think you managed to 'target' your audience successfully? How did you go about this?

QUESTIONS ON SEXISM AND ONLINE ABUSE:

- Is it important to address the problem of sexism in online gaming? Why or why not?
- Is it important to address hate speech online generally? Why or why not?
- Do you think you can make a difference to these problems? Do you feel motivated to do so?
- Do you feel you 'learned' anything from this activity? Have your opinions altered in any way, or did you come to understand anything more fully?

TIPS FOR FACILITATORS

- You may feel that the examples of abuse are not suitable for your group. You could modify them or remove those which are most offensive, or make up some of your own. It is also likely that some female participants have experienced sexist abuse online: you could ask them for examples.
- The activity would benefit from more time: if this is a possibility, you could give groups 30 minutes to discuss their strategies and allow them to look online at the Campaign website, or at other online campaigns.
- If the group is small, you do not need to use all target audiences: select those that seem most important for your participants.
- Many methods or messages will be similar for the different target audiences: the purpose of concentrating on one is to focus participants' attention on the particular messages that will be most likely to resonate with their audience.
- Be aware of the gender mix in the small group work. Ideally, there should be a roughly equal balance.
- When participants present their strategies, encourage other groups to offer 'constructive criticism'. You could suggest they always find something positive to say about the strategy, and then offer any suggestions for how it could be improved.

VARIATIONS

The group work could be given to participants as a project they work on over the course of a week. They could be encouraged to research other websites, explore the extent of the problem and look at the laws or regulations relating to sexist abuse online.

Participants could take another issue to concentrate on in their planning, for example, racism online, cyberbullying, or sexism across all areas of the Internet. The groups could also select their own issue to concentrate on, but in this case it would still be useful for them to identify a specific target audience.

IDEAS FOR ACTION

Participants could follow up the issue of sexism in gaming, for example, by conducting their own research into the extent of the problem. Small groups of participants could take particular games and monitor any instances of hate speech. These could be reported to Hate Speech Watch, and also to the websites themselves, if appropriate.

Participants could develop further the most promising strategies, and then implement them! They could make use of their social media profiles, online forums or other commenting spaces to spread information and raise awareness about the problem.

If participants are online gamers, they can also discuss this problem with other online gamers. Participants can also develop key messages they can use when involved in games and when such abuse occurs.

Invite participants to present some of the games they know of and discuss hate speech in games.

HANDOUTS

GROUP 1: SUPPORTING WOMEN GAMERS

Your group will concentrate on women gamers, both those who have received abuse and those who may be worried about receiving it.

- What are your key messages?
- How can you make women gamers feel supported?
- What can you suggest they do?

Think about the online tools you can use to build solidarity among women gamers.

GROUP 2: REACHING THE 'ABUSERS'

Your group will attempt to address those who commonly abuse women gamers, or those who may be tempted to do so.

- What are your key messages?
- How can you persuade them to change their behaviour?
- What information do you need?

Think about the online tools you can use to reach as many members of your target audience as possible.

HANDOUTS

GROUP 3: ENCOURAGING ACTION BY ONLINE GAMERS

Your group will target those members of the online gaming community who witness hate speech against gamers, but don't engage in it themselves.

- What do they need to know?
- What do you want them to do?
- How can you persuade them to do it?

Think about the online tools you can use to encourage action by as many gamers as possible.

GROUP 4: REACHING POLICY MAKERS

Your group will focus on those who may be able to address the problem because they are policy makers or members of your country's government.

- What are your key messages?
- How can you persuade your target audience to engage with the problem?
- What are you recommending as action they should take?

Think about the tools you can use to reach as many members of your target audience as possible.

GROUP 5: REACHING ONLINE SERVICE AND CONTENT PROVIDERS

Your group will focus on those who may be able to address the problem directly, for example website owners, Internet providers, and online community managers.

- What are your key messages?
- How can you persuade your target audience to engage with the problem?
- What are you recommending as action they should take?

Think about the tools you can use to reach as many members of your target audience as possible.

GROUP 6: RAISING PUBLIC AWARENESS

Your group will concentrate on engaging members of the public to address the problem.

- What are your key messages?
- What do you want people to do?
- What information do you need?

Think about the online tools you can use to mobilise people to join your campaign.

HANDOUTS

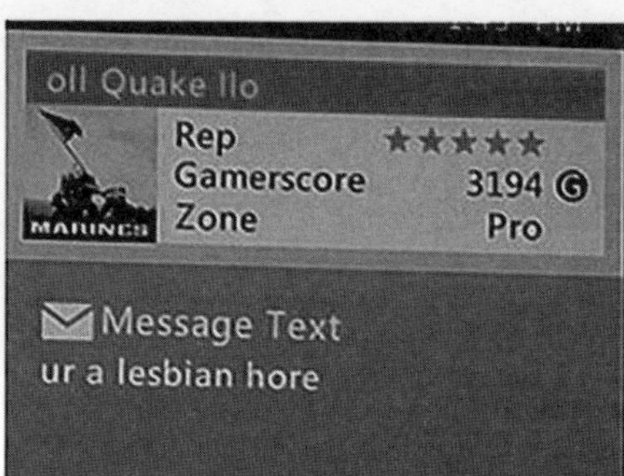

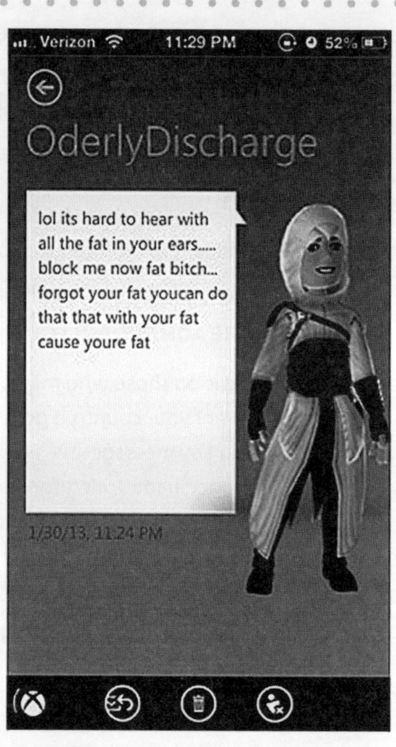

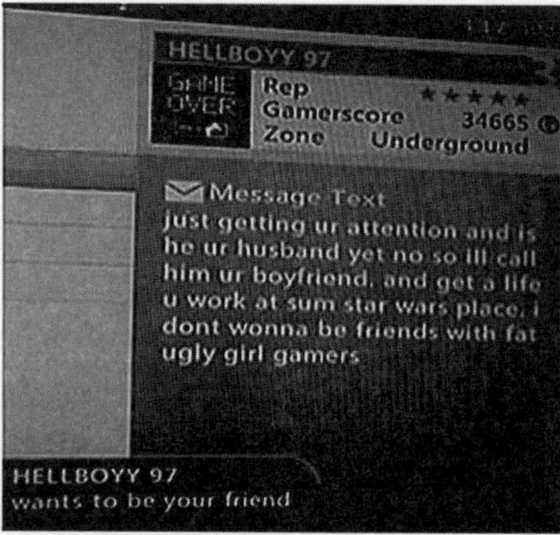

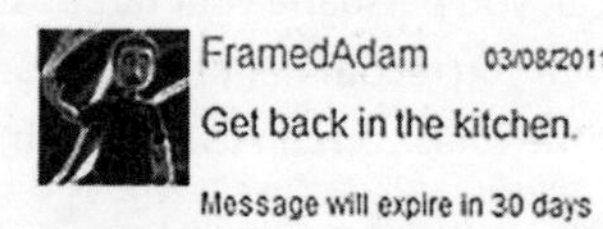

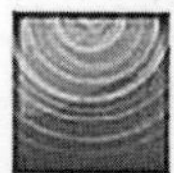

ON 4/29/2012 AT 1:43 PM
Garry Garry69 wrote:

am gonna slit your throat you fucking slut for having a full friends list you fucking cunt i hate you go an fucking die you slag!

Message will expire in 30 days | Block user

Say something here...

Source of the captions: http://fatuglyorslutty.com/ *(retrieved on 9 October 2013)*

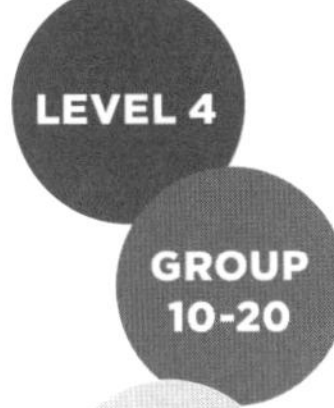

CHECKING THE FACTS

Participants are asked to act as 'researchers' for politicians on the issue of homophobic abuse. They consider the reliability of information posted online and develop strategies for their own practice.

THEMES	Internet Literacy, Racism and Discrimination, Campaigning Strategies
COMPLEXITY	Level 4
GROUP SIZE	10-20
TIME	60 minutes
OBJECTIVES	• To assess the reliability of information found online • To explore some of the difficulties faced by young gay people with hate speech online • To consider their own behaviour in relation to online content
MATERIALS	• Access to the Internet • Papers and pens • Flipchart and markers
PREPARATION	• Ensure that there is Internet access for participants • Make copies of the Researchers' tasks and the monitors' sheet (page 59). • *Optional:* Ask beforehand for volunteers to carry out the 'monitoring' task. About half the group will be needed as monitors. Show them the monitoring sheet and check they understand the information they will be looking for, and how to fill in the grid.

INSTRUCTIONS

1. Explain that the activity will explore the use of the Internet as an information resource. Ask how much participants use the Internet for this purpose and whether they have 'favourite' sites they use.
2. Give them the following scenario and check that everyone understands the task.

> Following a number of homophobic attacks against young gays – particularly in online sites and videos – and strong lobbying by NGOs, there is to be a debate in parliament about the issue. The government has proposed draft legislation to allocate money from the budget towards educational efforts to counter homophobic attitudes and provide support for young gays. The main opposition parties are all opposed to the new law.

You are to imagine you are working as researcher for a politician who wants to speak in the debate. She has asked you to prepare a briefing for her speech with some key points to be made in the debate. You have 20 minutes to do some preliminary research.

3. Explain that people will work in groups of 4, with 2 people acting as 'researchers' and 2 people observing the 'methodology' of the researchers. Tell them that research demands a proper methodology! Ask if they can suggest some important considerations in carrying out research and make a list of these on a flipchart.
4. Ask for volunteers to act as monitors, if this has not been done beforehand. Give them copies of the monitors' sheet and make sure they understand the task. Divide the rest of the group so that you have roughly equal numbers working for the government, and for the different opposition parties. Give each group a card with their task.
5. Tell participants they have 30 minutes to carry out their research. Suggest that they use the first 20 minutes to find relevant information, and leave 10 minutes at the end to agree on the main points they will present to their parliamentary representative.
6. When groups have finished the task, invite them to move away from the computers. Give them another 5-10 minutes so that the monitors in their group can feed back on some of their key observations.
7. Invite the researchers to present the main points they selected for their member of parliament's speech. These can be presented as 'bullet points': participants are to imagine they are briefing the member of parliament, not making the speech themselves!
8. Allow some time after each presentation for the monitors to present their results, and for any questions from other groups on the information presented or the strategy used. Then invite participants to debrief the activity.

DEBRIEFING

QUESTIONS ABOUT THE RESEARCH AND BRIEFING FOR PARLIAMENTARY REPRESENTATIVES

- How easy did you find the task? What did you find most difficult?
- How did you decide which websites to use for information? How much were you concerned by the 'trustworthiness' of the sites or the 'truth' of the information you selected?
- Did you give more importance to finding information which would support your representative's position, or to providing an 'objective' account of the issue? Which do you think a real researcher should do?
- Did you search for examples of hate speech against gays? If some groups did not, do they think this would have been relevant?
- Do you think your representative would be happy with your research? Do you think those she represents would be happy?

QUESTIONS ABOUT USING THE INTERNET FOR RESEARCH PURPOSES

- Did you find out anything important about using the Internet for research? Would you like to add

anything to the list of considerations compiled at the beginning of the activity?
- Were you surprised by the different information that people managed to find? How do you explain this?
- What are some of the ways we can check whether a website is reliable, or whether information can be trusted? Do you normally do this?

QUESTIONS ABOUT HOMOPHOBIA / HATE SPEECH ONLINE

- Did you find any examples of discrimination or abuse?
- Do you think you found any information which was 'false' or unfair?
- What are the risks of allowing anyone to post their opinions online? Can you think of things you can do to reduce the risk of other people taking these opinions as 'fact'?

TIPS FOR FACILITATORS

- The activity will be more effective if the 'monitors' are briefed beforehand. If this is possible, you could have only one monitor for each small group, and increase the number of 'researchers'.
- The researchers should not feel they are being 'tested' by the monitors. You could tell them that the monitors' task is to look at different research methods and that there are a number of ways of approaching this task!
- You may decide not to show the researchers the monitors' sheet: in this case they would not be alerted to some of the key considerations and the results might be more interesting. However, this may also put more pressure on the researchers. Showing them the sheet would give the researchers and monitor a better collaborative working relationship.
- During the debriefing you could explore whether research is likely to be biased by the result we 'want' to find. You could use this to ask how participants generally relate to information they see but do not want to believe!
- One of the dangers of misinformation or strong bias being so prevalent on the Internet is that it can easily be spread as 'fact'. You could explore whether participants think they may have passed on 'facts' they have seen on the Internet, and whether any of this information may have helped to spread prejudices about particular groups or individuals.
- You could use the checklist in the background information on Internet literacy to supplement participants' suggestions for how they can check the reliability of information posted on the Internet. Emphasise that most of what we see contains an element of 'opinion'. There are many ways of presenting information so that a particular point of view is strengthened. For example, omitting examples of homophobic hate speech gives the impression that this is not a problem!
- You can do a search about the tracking of Internet hoaxes and discuss with participants how false news contributes to fueling hate speech.

VARIATIONS

You could select a different 'target group' for participants to research, for example, women, Roma or another ethnic minority, asylum seekers, and so on.

You could also run the activity without monitors, but with everyone acting as their own 'monitor'. In this case, you should go through the monitors' sheet with the group beforehand and ask them to check their own methods as they research.

IDEAS FOR ACTION

Participants could refine the list of considerations for carrying out research online and create their own set of guidelines. They could also compile a checklist for sharing information with others, and share this with activists on the No Hate Speech Movement website. A great deal of hate speech is disseminated by people who unthinkingly share opinions which express a bias and are hurtful to others.

They could try out the checklist on page 59 – or their own – on some popular news sites. A great deal of journalism is responsible for spreading prejudices about groups in society. This can encourage readers to think it is 'acceptable' to abuse these groups.

You can find other educational activities to run with your group about strategies of misinformation here: http://mediasmarts.ca/sites/default/files/tutorials/facing-online-hate/index.html

Invite participants to present the websites they use most often to find information online and check together how reliable and impartial these websites are.

HANDOUTS

POLITICIAN 1:

Your politician is a member of the government. She needs to speak strongly in favour of the new legislation. Do an Internet search to find any information that would be useful to her in making her speech. Then make a list of about 5 key points you think she should address.

POLITICIAN 2:

Your politician is a member of the opposition. He is opposed to allocating money from the budget to address this problem. Do an Internet search to find any information that would be useful to him in making his speech. Then make a list of about 5 key points you think he should address.

POLITICIAN 3:

Your politician is a member of a minority party. Your party has not yet decided whether to support or oppose the legislation. Do an Internet search to find any information that would be useful to your politician in making up her mind. Then make a list of about 5 key points you think she should address.

HANDOUTS

MONITORS

Your task is to try to analyse the approach used by the researchers. Try to gather as much information on the questions in the monitors' sheet as possible. You can ask the researchers to explain what they are doing, or why they are taking a particular approach, as long as you don't distract them too much!

MONITORS' SHEET

Search terms used to find information	
FOR EACH SITE VISITED:	
Name of site	
Approx. no of minutes spent on the site	
'Political orientation' (pro-gay, anti-gay, neutral)	
Why was the site chosen?	
'Authority' of the site: – Why should the site be trusted? – Did the group check this?	
For any information extracted, was a source or reference given and did the group check this?	
Anything else relating to how the researchers approached their task:	

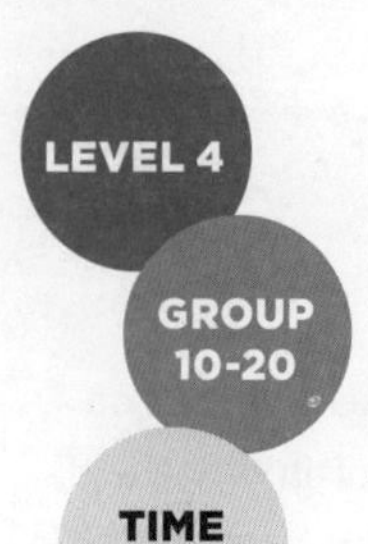

CLASH OF FREEDOMS

The activity is a simulation involving two communities with opposing views on freedom of expression, but forced to live together on the same island.

THEMES	Democracy and Participation, Freedom of Expression, Racism and Discrimination
COMPLEXITY	Level 4
GROUP SIZE	10-20
TIME	120 minutes
OBJECTIVES	• To explore issues relating to diversity, pluralism and hate speech • To consider how freedom of expression contributes to the functioning of a democratic society • To discuss the advantages and disadvantages of having no limits on freedom of expression • To practise skills of negotiation
MATERIALS	• Paper and pens • Space for the two communities to meet (separately) • 2 facilitators (ideally)
PREPARATION	• Make copies of the information about the two islands (pages 63 and 64) • Make copies of the Problems to be addressed (page 65)

INSTRUCTIONS

1. Explain that the activity will involve a simulation and divide the group into two different communities. The Ixprat community should be larger: about two thirds of participants. The remaining third of the group will represent the Pastiks. Explain that the first part of the simulation will involve work in the separate communities. After 20 minutes, the groups will be brought together.
2. One of the groups should be shown to a different room. The facilitator for each group should read out the information about the relevant community, and may then hand out copies for people to refer to.
3. Begin the discussion in each group by asking for participants' thoughts about life on the island. Ask whether they would like to live there. After some reflection, the following questions should be put to the groups:

Pastik group

What are your concerns about moving to the new island?

Ixprat group

What are your concerns about receiving a large number of immigrants with no knowledge of your culture or traditions?

4. After 20 minutes, the two groups should be brought together. Invite the islanders to introduce themselves, encouraging them to make brief statements if they would like to do so. Do not allow this to occupy more than 10 minutes.
5. After about 10 minutes, give participants the following information:

A year has passed, and a number of problems have arisen. Tensions between the communities have become increasingly acute and many people are worried about severe social unrest. The President has invited you to form a working group to try to find solutions to these problems.

6. Divide the whole community into smaller working groups, so that each working group has (roughly) 2 Pastik members and 4 Ixprat members. Give each group one of the problems on page 65.
7. Tell the groups that they have 20 minutes to reach a decision about how to resolve the problem. Explain that any proposal must be put to the vote and needs to be approved by a majority of participants (in the working group) in order to be accepted. Remind them that if they cannot approve a new decision, the status quo will continue!
8. After 20 minutes, bring everyone together to present their decisions. Give each working group 2-3 minutes to feed back and outline their solution, and ask for any brief responses. Then, move to debriefing.

DEBRIEFING

Begin by taking participants out of role and reminding them that they are now going to discuss the activity as a whole. They should try not to return to previous debates.

- How did you feel about the activity? What did you like or not like?
- How easy was it to play your role – and stay in it – when the islanders came together?
- What did you think about the negotiation process, and the process of decision making at the end? What were the most important things for you when trying to find a solution?
- Was it fair that the Ixprat community effectively had a veto on any proposal, because they were the majority? How can we make sure that the opinions and rights of minorities are fairly represented in 'real' life?
- Did the activity change any of your views? If so, which in particular, and why?
- Do you think the activity was close to reality: did it recall any problems in society today?
- How do you think we should deal with the problem of people saying things which are hurtful, intolerant and sometimes dangerous?

TIPS FOR FACILITATORS

- The descriptions of life on the two islands are relatively long, in order to get participants into the spirit of their community. They should be read out not as 'information', but more like a story!
- The working group which takes the problem about the Internet campaign could be asked to focus on the online aspect of the problem. At least, they should be directed to consider this aspect alongside any offline proposals.
- Allow the simulation to run with as little guidance from you as possible. Make sure that people understand the time limits and the nature of the task but allow them to approach the tasks in the way they think best. Interrupt only if they seem to have misunderstood, or if tensions or conflict are interfering with the process.
- Participants would benefit from some information on freedom of expression. If there is time available, use some of the information.

VARIATIONS

If time is short, the descriptions could be shortened and in the final negotiations the working groups could all be given the first problem to discuss. This will speed up the negotiations.

If time allows in the first (separate) meetings of groups, you may want to ask participants if there is any message they would like to communicate when they are brought together. These messages could then form the brief 'introductions' which take place in the first 10 minutes of the meeting.

If the group is large, it may be necessary to subdivide the 'new' community into smaller groups so that everyone has a chance to contribute. Each of the new groups should consist of roughly one third Pastiks, two thirds Ixprats. Groups may also want to nominate 1 or 2 spokespeople for their community.

IDEAS FOR ACTION

Participants could draw up a proposal for their own group, similar to the ones they produced as a result of the negotiations. This could be voted on and used as a set of guiding principles for either online or offline behaviour.

Participants could research the main immigrant groups in their country. They could find out some of the reasons why people have moved there, and look at whether they feel their rights and opinions are respected by the rest of society and how they are portrayed in the media, both online and offline. You could also invite some representatives from different communities to speak to the group.

If your country is not considered a country of immigration, you can check how the people who emigrated from your country are viewed in the hosting countries.

HANDOUTS

THE PASTIK ISLAND

You live on a small island whose borders are closed and which has seen no immigration and very few tourists for as long as anyone can remember. Your society is calm and peaceful: peace and the absence of conflict have a strong tradition and are regarded as a 'national priority'. There is even an article in the Constitution which states that:

No-one should say or do anything which might be painful or upsetting to others

This article is carefully monitored and infringements are severely punished. It is very rarely broken; it is much easier to agree with other people. Disagreement has become painful for the Pastiks as it troubles the mind.

Your country calls itself a democracy. Elections are held every year and nearly everyone votes. However, the same people tend to be elected, as there is little discussion of alternative policies.

In general, conversations, public pronouncements and even the media don't stray beyond the opinions that are generally accepted by society, and people mostly don't mind this as they have forgotten or are unable to imagine a different way of doing things. There is little news about other places on the globe, no literature from other cultures, and very little change, because change has been found to be upsetting.

People have noticed over the years that the coastline has altered: sea levels have risen and many parts of the country which used to be habitable are now under water. This did not matter to begin with: there was enough land for everyone and communities living near the coastline were simply moved further inland. However, in recent years the problem became more acute. A few people began discussing it among themselves but this was found to be upsetting, so the government introduced a ban.

Life continued, mostly calm, predictable and free from conflict and disagreement, until one terrible windy day a severe hurricane hit the island. Buildings were destroyed, many people died, and most of the land was flooded. When the waves subsided, few crops had survived and those that had survived were now dying from the salt water. Nearly all the infrastructure had been destroyed. Food became scarce, infection and disease began to spread and medical supplies were inadequate. The island fell into chaos. People even started disagreeing about what the best thing to do was!

Just when it seemed that all hope was lost, a message was received from a neighbouring island, the Island of Ixprat. The message expressed sincere concern for all Pastiks and contained an offer to accommodate anyone who wished to move to Ixprat. You are among those who have decided to move.

HANDOUTS

THE ISLAND OF IXPRAT

You live on the Island of Ixprat, located in the Pacific Ocean and in the path of one of the ancient shipping routes across the ocean. Your island has traditionally relied on trade and communication with other countries and you have had an open borders policy for hundreds of years. That has meant that travellers and immigrants from many different cultures have been a strong feature of life on the island. The result is a very diverse population, with a wide range of opinions, beliefs and cultural practices.

Your national culture embraces such diversity: people have a keen interest in other ways of doing things, different beliefs and ideologies. Of course, with such diversity, not every idea or ideology can be embraced by everyone. Disagreement and conflict are a way of life on Ixprat. Almost every meeting of two human minds contains a thrashing out of thoughts, beliefs and ideas. Furthermore, almost every meeting passes through or ends in disagreement. Disagreement is almost a national hobby.

For that reason, there are no laws which limit what one person or one group can say to another, or which limit what one person or one group can say *about* another. Some people do say terrible things. Sometimes this leads to people *doing* terrible things. The 'doing' is punishable by law; the saying is not.

Life on Ixprat is interesting, challenging, and constantly changing. You value the richness of the culture and the fact that you can say anything you like. You know that endless argument and disagreement does not always lead to happiness. In fact, you often find disagreement very tiring, and very painful: it is not always easy to hear people saying things you think are *wrong*, let alone things you think are cruel. You have also seen how some groups in society tend to be more frequent victims of cruel and intolerant language than others.

Even so, it seems to you important that no-one should ever be stopped from expressing their beliefs.

One windy day, your island received news that a very strong hurricane had hit one of the other islands in the Pacific. You know very little about that island: they have always kept themselves to themselves. You have heard tales that the people living on the island are very stupid and very backward, but you have never met anyone from there. You know it is almost impossible to visit.

The government has announced that the Island of Pastik suffered so badly as a result of the hurricane that most of the residents who have survived will be relocating to Ixprat. They can probably be squeezed in but it will mean that current residents will have to do a lot of re-adjusting. Jobs will have to be shared out and there may not be enough housing for everyone.

HANDOUTS

PROBLEMS FOR WORKING GROUPS

PROBLEM 1:

A campaign has been set up to 'Find a Pastik tongue' and it has taken the Internet by storm. The campaign site includes such slogans as

- *Poke a Pastik dummy: see if he squeaks!*
- *No tongue, no brain!*
- *Find a tongue, win a smartphone!*

People are invited to submit photos of Pastik tongues. There is a 'Tongue Gallery' with photos and videos of people forcing open the mouths of Pastiks, shining a torch into their mouths, posing with telescopes or pointing to the tongue. The campaign is gathering momentum and there have been a large number of incidents where Pastiks have been attacked in the streets. Pastiks have responded by saying they refuse to be drawn into an insulting conversation with people they don't respect.

PROBLEM 2:

A young girl from the Pastik community was shouted at in the street by a group of boys from the Ixprats. They called her a "fat slob", a "filthy slag" and told her she had no tongue in her head and no mind of her own. The girl has been miserable and has not left the house or talked to anyone for two weeks. For three days she has eaten nothing. Her parents are desperately worried.

PROBLEM 3:

A report has been released which shows that the rate of unemployment among Pastiks is far higher than in the population as a whole, there are no Pastik representatives in Parliament and few in positions of power in any organisation. The report has also monitored other social factors, for example, levels of stress and mental illness, educational qualifications, and levels of crime. On all indicators, the Pastiks appear to do worse than any other sector of society. Attitudes towards Pastiks among the rest of society are also overwhelmingly negative.

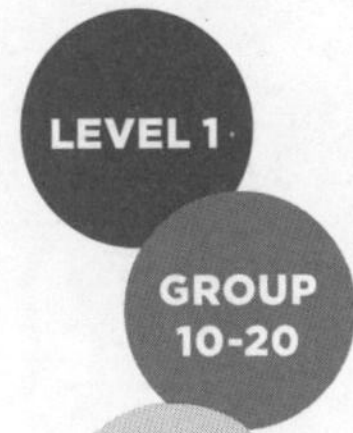

TIME 45'

CONFRONTING CYBERBULLYING

This is an activity in which participants identify their likely response to various bullying scenarios, and discuss alternative courses of action.

THEMES	Cyberbullying, Democracy and Participation, Internet Literacy
COMPLEXITY	Level 1
GROUP SIZE	10-20
TIME	45 minutes
OBJECTIVES	• To understand the different forms that bullying can take, and the connections between offline and online bullying • To identify different ways of responding to bullying, cyberbullying and hate speech online • To raise awareness of the importance of responding
PREPARATION	• Make 4 signs on pieces of A4 paper and stick each one in a different corner of the room. The signs should read: – Nothing – Respond to the bully – Report the behaviour – Something else • Make sure there is enough space for participants to move around the room.

INSTRUCTIONS

1. Start by asking participants what they understand by bullying. Prompt them to think about different ways people might bully others.
2. Point out the signs in the corners of the room and explain that you will read out a number of different scenarios. Everyone should choose which of the following options best fits what they would do:
   - Do nothing
   - Respond to the bully / bullies (for example, engage in discussion, hit back at them, or something else. If the bully is unknown, this option may not be relevant.)
   - Report the behaviour (for example to a teacher, parent, site administrator, or other authority)
   - Something else (for example, bring others into the discussion, set up a 'solidarity group', etc. You could ask them for further ideas).

3. Explain that after each scenario has been read out, participants should go to the corner which is closest to the way they would probably respond. Tell them to be honest about what they think they would do!
4. Read out the first scenario and give participants time to select their corner. Once they have taken a position, ask a few in each group to explain why they chose that response. Then read out the next scenario, and continue until you feel enough cases have been discussed.

DEBRIEFING

Use some of the following questions to debrief the activity:

- How did you find the activity? Which scenarios did you find most difficult to respond to and why?
- Do you think all were examples of bullying?
- Have you ever come across cyberbullying – either as a victim or a bystander? What can you say about the relation between offline and online bullying? Are there any important differences?
- Has the activity made you look at bullying / cyberbullying in a different way? Has it made you think you might respond differently in future?
- What can you do against cyberbullying?
- Who should take action to prevent hate speech online? What should the role of the media networks, service providers, the police, parents, the school authorities, and so on, be?

TIPS FOR FACILITATORS

- If the group is large, or unaccustomed to general discussion, it may be helpful to introduce a magic stick or imaginary microphone so that people wanting to speak must wait their turn.
- Participants may want to choose more than one option, for example, responding to the bully and reporting the abuse. If this happens, tell them to take the corner which seems most important, then give them the chance to explain their position.
- Be aware that some participants may be experiencing bullying, perhaps from others in the group. You will need to be sensitive to the different personal needs or conflicts and should not press anyone to respond if they do not seem willing to.
- If there are participants who are experiencing bullying, the activity may bring their concerns to the surface, leading them to recognise their need for further support. You should either make it clear that you can offer such support – in confidence – or should have alternative support systems you can point them to. Before the activity, you may wish to explore existing local or national services, for example, helplines or organisations offering support to the victims.
- If participants are unfamiliar with cyberbullying, or do not seem to recognise its damaging nature, you could use some of the background information to raise their awareness both about the issue and about approaches other people have used. Where relevant, the links between hate speech and bullying should be made (especially when bullying is combined with hate speech).

VARIATIONS

The activity could be simplified, with just two options for participants to select: 'Do nothing', or 'Do something'. The two signs could be put at either end of the room and participants place themselves along a line between the two signs, depending on how likely they are to select either option.

IDEAS FOR ACTION

Any further action will be more effective if the participants have decided on a group action together. You could discuss various ways for following up on the activity, for example, raising awareness of the problem (online or offline), setting up a support or solidarity group, implementing an anti-bullying policy for the group / class / school, or creating a 'No to online bullying' campaign, and so on.
You can also join the No Hate Speech Movement and use the campaign website to share video messages of solidarity with the victims of cyberbullying. You can also use the website to share advice for any Internet user on what to do in situations of cyberbullying.

HANDOUTS

SCENARIOS

You have received a number of abusive emails and text messages from addresses or numbers you don't recognise. Some have been threatening: it seems that the bullies know you. What do you do?

Some people from your school have edited some photos of yours and posted them online with nasty comments. You think you know who it is. What do you do?

A boy from a different country has just joined your class. Your friends make fun of him and have started posting racist jokes about him on their social networks. They keep telling you to re-tweet or re-post the jokes. What do you do?

A group of kids in your class have been spreading a hurtful rumour about you on social networking sites. Many kids now won't play with you or even speak to you. Even your friends are starting to think the rumours may be true. What do you do?

The teacher tells the class that some people are being badly bullied and one young person was attacked on the way home from school. She asks for anyone who knows anything about this to talk to her privately after the lesson. You think you know who did it but you're scared because you have received a lot of text messages, warning you not to say anything. What do you do?

You see a child in the playground standing alone and crying. You know other children tease her because she's learning-disabled, and they call her "thicko" and "pig ugly". Your friends are some of the worst and often laugh about her when you're all together. What do you do?

This activity is an adaptation of the activity "Bullying Scenes" from Compasito, Manual on Human Rights Education for Children – www.coe.int/compass

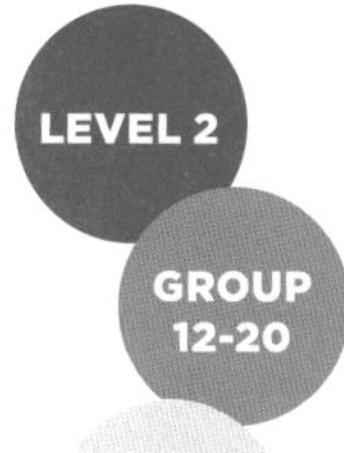

LEVEL 2

GROUP 12-20

TIME 45'

FREEDOM UNLIMITED?

Participants explore the idea of freedom of expression using a number of case studies. They need to decide what to do with comments or communications which are controversial, abusive or potentially dangerous.

THEMES	Freedom of Expression, Democracy and Participation, Human Rights
COMPLEXITY	Level 2
GROUP SIZE	12-20
TIME	45 minutes
OBJECTIVES	• To explore the concept of freedom of expression • To understand why freedom of expression is important – for individuals and for society • To look at the reasons why limiting freedom of expression may be needed to protect human rights, particularly where hate speech is involved
MATERIALS	• Flipchart and marker pens • Copies of the cards on page 72
PREPARATION	• Make copies of the cards on page 72 (enough for each small working group)

INSTRUCTIONS:

1. Ask participants what 'freedom of expression' means to them. Collect ideas on a flipchart, inviting discussion of some of the following points if they are not raised by participants:
   - Does freedom of expression mean we can say whatever we want?
   - If you think certain 'expressions' should not be permitted, how could we decide what needs banning? Who should decide?
   - Apart from through speaking or writing, what are the other ways we 'express' ourselves (music, drama, images, body language, etc.)?
2. Do not attempt to 'resolve' the issues at this moment: gather some opinions and explain that these are often controversial questions which will be explored in more detail through the activity.
3. Ask whether anyone has ever been *prevented* from saying something they wanted to – at home, school, or in public. How did it make you feel? Why was it important to you to be able to express your point of view?

4. Provide some brief information about freedom of expression. Use the information below, or add to it from the background materials (page 160):

FREEDOM OF EXPRESSION

The right to be free to express our thoughts or opinions is an important human right, and is part of international human rights law. The right is valued both because our thoughts, opinions and ability to communicate are a central part of what it means to be human, and because communication and discussion are essential in building an effective democratic society. Understanding and living side by side with others depends on open and free communication – even if we sometimes have to hear opinions we don't agree with. Nevertheless, freedom of expression is not an 'absolute' right which always applies, without limits. It is a right which has to be balanced against the rights of others, or against the good of society as a whole. When expression is either extremely damaging to certain individuals or is likely to be damaging for society, it *can* be limited.

5. Tell participants that they will work in small groups (4 - 5 people) and will discuss a number of cases in which people post things online which are harmful to others and their human rights. The groups need to decide whether this is a case where any of the material should be taken offline – in other words, whether freedom of expression should be restricted.
   - If they decide it should: what should be taken offline, and why?
   - If not, why not? What else can be done and by whom?
6. Divide participants into groups of 4 or 5 people and give each group a copy of the cases on page 72. Give them about 20 minutes to discuss each of the cases. They should try to provide reasons for the decisions.

DEBRIEFING

Go through each of the case studies asking for groups' responses. Discuss briefly the reasons behind the decisions they took. Use some of the following questions to draw out other key points:

- Were there any cases where you could not reach agreement in the group? What were the key differences in opinion?
- Did it make a difference who was responsible for the posts? Did it make a difference how many people responded, or how they responded?
- Did you arrive at any general principles to decide when freedom of expression can (or should) be restricted? What are the dangers in being over-restrictive? What are the dangers in being over-permissive?
- Do you think that closing down websites or removing harmful posts is an effective way of combatting hate speech online?
- In your country, are there restrictions on what people are allowed to say – online or offline? Do the rules differ for online expression?

TIPS FOR FACILITATORS

- When participants discuss the cases, remind them to consider how much material they would take

offline, if they decide to do so. For example, they could decide to remove the whole site (or profile) or they could remove a single post / video, ban the user who posted, and so on.

- It may be worth reminding participants that the European Court of Human Rights considers any restriction of freedom of expression as a very serious step! It should only be done when there is strong justification.
- You may want to explore with participants the extent to which the discussions themselves were useful in helping them to form their opinion, and what this may tell us about freedom of expression.
- If necessary, or if time allows, you may want to explain that human rights law, and freedom of expression, is really about how governments should behave. Limiting expression on the Internet is often more complicated because much of the Internet is 'owned' by private companies (e.g. private hosting providers, news sites 'owned' by companies, etc.). There are questions about whether or how much governments should and can regulate speech on the Internet. Have a look at Chapter 5, Background Information, on freedom of expression.
- You may want to explain that human rights law, and freedom of expression, is really about how *governments* should behave. Limiting freedom of expression on the Internet is often more complicated because much of the Internet is 'owned' by private companies (e.g. private hosting providers, news sites "owned" by companies, etc.). Familiarise yourself with the key points reflected in Chapter 5, Background Information, on freedom of expression or the section 'Freedom of expression and information' in the *Guide to Human Rights for Internet Users*.
- Try to find out before you start the activity whether any of the cases would be illegal under your national laws.
- It may be useful to end the activity by considering other ways of responding to the cases. Refer to the material on the campaign No Hate Speech Movement in Chapter 2 for some suggestions. Remind participants that removing offending material, or the site, is not the only response! It can also be very difficult to implement practically, given the amount of material posted online.

VARIATIONS

The case studies could be performed as a role play: each small group could prepare one of the scenarios and perform it to the others. Discussion about the most appropriate response would then take place in the group as a whole.

IDEAS FOR ACTION

How much do participants know about their parliamentary representatives? They could do some research into public statements they have made about minorities or other vulnerable groups, and then write to express their support or their disagreement. An individual letter from everyone in the group might even prompt a response!
Discuss with the group possible actions to take if any of the participants encounters racist posts online. Develop together some arguments and short messages that participants can use whenever they find hate speech examples online.

HANDOUTS

CASES FOR DISCUSSION

1. A group called 'Reclaim our nation' sets up a website proclaiming 'traditional values'. Many of the posts are racist. The site attracts a large number of comments and a heated discussion. Some of the discussion contains very abusive language, but there is a large community of commenters who object to the racist ideology of the site.
   - Should anything be taken offline? If so, how much and why?
   - If not, what else could be done?

2. Nikolay, a politician uses his personal website to call for the eviction of a Roma community in his constituency, and blaming them for high crime levels. Following his calls, there are a number of attacks on Roma around the country. Much of the media begins printing stories which feature crimes committed by Roma – but not the crimes committed against them.
   - Should anything be taken offline? If so, how much and why?
   - If not, why not? What else could be done?

3. On a personal blog, Rory posts a cartoon showing a well-known politician with blood dripping from his fingers, and dead bodies all around. Many people comment, mostly supporting the cartoon.
   - Should anything be taken offline? If so, how much and why?
   - If not, why not? What else could be done?

4. Ella posts a video on her public profile which makes fun of disabled people, portraying them as incompetent 'alien' beings. Site statistics show that almost no-one has viewed the video, and there are no comments from visitors.
   - Should anything be taken offline? If so, how much and why?
   - If not, why not? What else could be done?

5. A journalist sees the video (in example 4) and starts a campaign to have Ella's profile removed from the social media site As a result the video gets thousands of hits. People start commenting that this is "the best video ever", "we should start being realistic about disabled people", and so on.
   - Should anything be taken offline? If so, how much and why?
   - If not, why not? What else could be done?

6. Ditta, a well-known celebrity, posts an article on an online news site claiming that transgender women are "an abuse against humanity". A website is set up to 'bring down Ditta' with details about her personal life. She starts receiving hundreds of personally abusive emails and tweets. Some include threats.
   - Should anything be taken offline? If so, how much and why?
   - If not, why not? What else could be done?

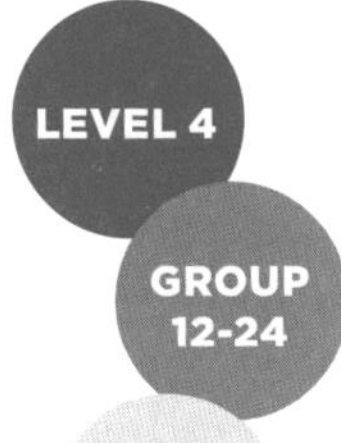

GROUP X

Participants map rights from the European Convention on Human Rights against a series of abuses commonly experienced by young Roma.

THEMES	RACISM AND DISCRIMINATION, HUMAN RIGHTS, PRIVATE LIFE AND SAFETY
COMPLEXITY	Level 4
GROUP SIZE	12-24
TIME	60 minutes
OBJECTIVES	• To consider how victims of hate speech are often deprived of numerous other human rights • To raise awareness of Roma rights and the human rights abuses they commonly experience • To relate the rights contained in the European Convention on Human Rights (ECHR) to real examples of abuse
MATERIALS	• Copies of the information about Group X (one copy for each small group) • Several copies of the ECHR (abbreviated version). You will need at least 2 copies for each small group • Flipchart paper and marker pens • Scissors and glue (optional)
PREPARATION	• Prepare a piece of flipchart paper for each small group. Stick the information about Group X in the middle of the flipchart paper.

INSTRUCTIONS

1. Read out the story about Group X (page 76). Explain that all the examples in the narrative are typical experiences for people from a particular minority, a minority which does not have its own country, but which exists in many countries of the world. Give participants the chance to guess the minority, and then confirm that the examples are all typical of Roma experiences in countries throughout Europe.
2. Ask for brief reactions to the text. Explain that most of the examples are illegal under human rights law and illegal in every country in Europe. Refresh participants' memory, if necessary, on human rights

generally and on the European Convention on Human Rights (ECHR), in particular. Use the background information on page 201.

3. Explain that participants will work in small groups (4 - 5 people) and will use an abbreviated version of the ECHR to map the examples in the text to rights contained in the Convention.
4. Hand out copies of the ECHR to everyone, and read through it together if participants need reminding. Address any questions relating to the content of the rights.
5. Ask participants to create small working groups – about 5 people in each group – and give each group one of the pieces of flipchart paper with the text about Group X. Ask them to mark on the flipchart paper, near the text, any connections between parts of the child's story and specific human rights.
6. Give groups about 20 minutes to complete the mapping. Stick up the finished flipchart papers on the wall and give participants the opportunity to look at those done by other groups – and note any similarities or differences.
7. Proceed to the debriefing.

DEBRIEFING

Bring participants back to the group and use some of the following questions to debrief the activity.

- Were you surprised by the number of different abuses which members of the Roma community commonly experience? Do you think any / all of these examples happen in this country?
- Have you ever heard or witnessed any examples of abusive speech against Roma communities? Have you seen anything online?
- Imagine you came across a nasty comment about Roma people on someone's online profile on a social network: what would you do? Do you think it would make a difference if people started objecting to such comments, or posting positive stories instead?

Use some of the following questions to explore any prejudices participants may have about Roma people:

- Those who drew up the Universal Declaration on Human Rights (and the ECHR) thought that we should never make judgements about someone based on which 'group' they belong to. Do you agree?
- What do you think about the child's comment that there are criminals in every community, but yet we don't use that to say that everyone in that community must be a criminal? Why do we say that about 'all Roma' if we don't know 'all Roma'?
- Those who drew up the UDHR also thought that there were certain things we shouldn't do to anyone, however they may have behaved. Do you agree?
- How do you think you would feel if you were constantly abused by others in the community? How might you behave?
- What do you know about the life of Roma communities? What about the problems they face?

TIPS FOR FACILITATORS

- You may find that many participants have strong prejudices about Roma. Try to avoid discussing this before the groups have worked on the flipcharts. Use some of the questions in the debriefing to explore this after the activity.

- When groups work on the flipcharts, tell them they can use any method to illustrate the links with human rights: they can cut up the information sheet or cut out the cards and stick them on the flip-chart paper. Or they can use marker pens to write up articles, draw arrows, and so on. If they run out of cards representing particular rights, tell them to use their imagination to illustrate further links!
- The narrative is not really a report from a Roma child, but each of the examples spoken about is very real in nearly every European country. You could use some of the links at the end to talk more about the abuses described.
- You may want to explain to participants that not all the human rights we possess have been included on the cards. The ECHR covers only some of our human rights, and only some of the rights in the ECHR have been included.
- Use the resource sheet 'Rights Engaged' on page 77 to feed back on the prepared flipcharts. Note that many of the abuses in the story engage more than one right, and that nearly all of them engage the right to be free from discrimination.
- Remind participants that human rights abuses are slightly different from 'normal' crimes: they apply to the behaviour of governments, or those in official positions such as teachers, police officers or prison officials. Public officials have responsibilities not to abuse people, but they also have responsibilities to make sure that people are not abused by others. If the police do not take a complaint about abuse seriously, they may be failing in their human rights responsibilities.

VARIATIONS

The activity could use the Universal Declaration on Human Rights instead of the European Convention.

IDEAS FOR ACTION

Ask participants to research the situation of Roma people in their country. Different groups could work on different topics.
Alternatively, participants could monitor sites they visit frequently, looking for negative comments about Roma. Examples could be submitted to Hate Speech Watch on the Campaign website (www.nohatespeechmovement.org/hate-speech-watch)
You can use the Factsheets about Roma history developed by the Council of Europe to familiarise participants with the past and present situation of Roma people across Europe. More information: www.coe.int/t/dg4/education/roma/histoCulture_en.asp

HANDOUTS

GROUP X

I'm a child from Group X. At school, I've been put in a special class for children with learning disabilities. We're not allowed to be in 'normal' classes. I'm often bullied by other children because I'm Group X – so are my friends. The teachers don't do anything about it. Some teachers even pick on us. *They* never get punished. In one country, I know that all the children from Group X were sent to schools for children with learning disabilities.

People don't want us around. They don't even know us, they just shout at us or beat us up because of who we are – or who they think we are. Well, we're children, just like them. And how are we meant to behave if someone shouts at us or beats us up? Should we like them for it?

If we go to the police, they often don't listen. They tell us it must have been our fault because we're all trouble-makers. How do they know? I thought the courts were meant to decide that. The police stop us in the streets all the time for no reason. They tell us they think we've stolen something and they need to search us. Sometimes I get stopped 6 times a week but I've never stolen anything.

I've heard of people from my community who've been in prison and have been beaten up by prison officers. Why should someone who beats up someone else not be punished? Even prison officers are meant to obey the law.

Last summer, groups of people dressed in the same way and singing songs against us marched in our village. We were all scared and locked ourselves in our homes. They threw stones at our homes and beat some of the young people who tried to send them away. The police did not do anything …

Members of the government often insult us, as if everyone from Group X is the same, and everyone in Group X is a criminal. Well, we're not. *Every* community has some people who commit crimes. The government doesn't insult everyone in another community, just because a few of them commit crimes. Why can't they tell some good stories about Group X people who are just like everyone else?

On the television and on the Internet, people just say whatever they want about us. I'm sick of seeing online groups telling us we're dirty or stupid or much worse things. They tell us we should get out of the country, go home, and get a job like everyone else. My Dad would love to have a job. No-one will employ him because he's Group X.

How are we supposed to live? How are we meant to feel when everyone says nasty things about us, even when they don't know us? It's hard: sometimes I don't want to go out into the street because I'm afraid I might get shouted at or beaten up.

HANDOUTS

RIGHTS ENGAGED

All examples are likely to engage the right to be free from discrimination (Article 14 or Protocol 12 of the ECHR). Other rights which may be engaged:

Special classes or schools for Roma children	Protocol 1, Article 2
Teachers picking on children	Maybe Article 8 (Private life). If the abuse is very bad, maybe Article 3. If it is affecting their education, may also engage Protocol 1, Article 2
Teachers not being 'punished'	If no-one is taking complaints seriously, maybe Article 8 (or Article 3, if the abuse is very bad). Possibly Protocol 1, Article 2
People 'shouting at' Roma, people marching in the villages where Roma live	Maybe Article 8 if the abuse is bad, is happening regularly, and if the police are doing nothing about it
People beating them up	Maybe Article 8 if the police are not responding to complaints. If the beating up is very bad or happening regularly, maybe Article 3
The police not listening to complaints	Article 8 or 3, depending on how bad the complaint is. If there are any threats to people's life, maybe Article 2
The police stopping and searching Roma	Maybe Article 5 (Liberty) if people are being stopped very regularly for no good reason. Also Article 8 (Private life)
Prison officers beating up Roma	Maybe Article 3 if the beating up is very bad. Also Article 8
Prison officers not being 'punished'	Maybe Article 3 if the beating up is very bad. Also Article 8
Members of the government abusing Roma	Maybe Article 8 if the abuse is very bad and is affecting how others treat Roma people
Abuse on the Internet / in the media	This may not be a strict violation of human rights because it's not a public official who is responsible. The abuse would have to be very bad, and there would need to be formal complaints which have been ignored by public officials.
Not being able to get a job 'because you're Roma'	Maybe Article 8 – particularly if any governmental organisations are refusing to employ someone because they are Roma
Being afraid to go out into the streets	If there is a real threat for Roma children on the streets and the police are doing nothing about it, this may engage Article 8 or 3 (or 2)

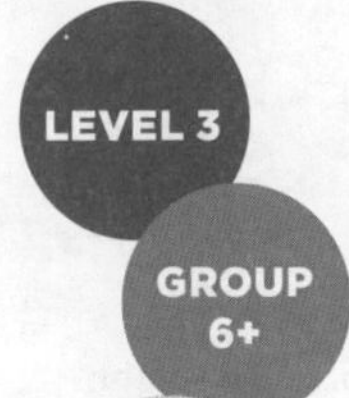

TIME 60'

HUMAN RIGHTS ONLINE QUIZ

The activity is a quiz about human rights online. It helps participants to get to know their rights online by using the Guide to Human Rights for Internet Users.

THEMES	Human Rights
COMPLEXITY	Level 3
GROUP SIZE	6 upwards
TIME	60 minutes
OBJECTIVES	• To understand how human rights apply online • To expand understanding about the universality of human rights • To think about human rights protections in the online world
PREPARATION	• Handout • The *Guide to Human Rights for Internet Users* • Pens or pencils, one per group

INSTRUCTIONS

OPTIONAL STARTER (FOR GROUPS UNFAMILIAR WITH HUMAN RIGHTS)

1. Ask participants what they understand by human rights. Write suggestions on a flipchart and prompt with further questions, if necessary. For example:
- Who has human rights?
- Can you name any human rights?
- Where do human rights come from?
- Do human rights apply online?
2. Provide a brief summary of human rights, for example:

> Human rights belong to everyone, and they are "laws for governments". Human rights mean that governments have to make sure that individuals are protected from unfair treatment, extreme abuse and violence, amongst other things. Human rights are important because they protect us, and because they mean we shouldn't behave towards others in a way that does not respect their rights.

MAIN ACTIVITY

1. Explain that the activity is a quiz about human rights online and that it involves a team game to learn about the rights that apply online.
2. Hand out the simplified version of the *Guide to Human Rights for Internet Users* or give the link to it. Give participants time to read it though and ask questions if they do not understand some of the rights.
3. When everyone is ready, divide the group into teams of 2 to 6. Give the handout to each team.
4. Tell participants that they will play the quiz as a team and they should pick one person who writes the answers on a handout. Tell then that they will have about 30 minutes to finish the quiz by using the Guide as a source for the questions.
5. After they have finished the quiz, go through the correct answers together with participants and decide who was the best team. Correct answers are: 1B, 2A and B, 3B, 4C, 5A, 6B, 7B, 8C, 9C, 10B, 11C, 12C, 13A, 14B.

DEBRIEFING

REFLECTIONS ON THE QUIZ:

- Which of the questions were the most difficult? Why?

REFLECTIONS ON HUMAN RIGHTS:

- Were any of the rights particularly difficult to understand?
- Do you think you could "do without" any of these rights? If so, which ones?
- Do you think these rights apply to the online world as well as the "real" world? Can you think of examples where some of these rights are relevant to online activity?
- Do you think that human rights are respected on the Internet?

REFLECTIONS ON HATE SPEECH:

- Explain briefly that hate speech is any 'expression' of hatred towards a group or member of a group which is nasty, hurtful and likely to lead to violent reactions towards members of the group. Ask for a few examples to clarify.
- Which of the rights in the quiz might be relevant to hate speech? Why?
- If you were a target of hate speech online, which rights would you be most likely to need?
- What can be done about the spread of hate speech online?

TIPS FOR FACILITATORS

- Participants could work in pairs to convey the rights. This may be helpful to allow them to discuss what the rights mean, but it may also add time to the activity.
- You may wish to concentrate on one or two of the areas of 'reflection' in order to explore issues more fully.
- You can learn more about human rights and human rights online from the background information on page 155.
- You can learn more about the topics related to the Guide by looking in more detail at the background section.

IDEAS FOR ACTION

Ask participants to write a status update or a blog post that relates to the Guide to raise awareness about how human rights apply online.

HANDOUTS

PART I: INTRODUCTORY

1. When was the Guide published?
   A. 1990
   B. 2014
   C. 2010.
2. Why was the Guide made?
   A. To have a tool for Internet users
   B. To raise awareness about human rights online
   C. To get people to read more.
3. The Guide is based on
   A. The Lisbon Treaty of the European Union
   B. The European Convention on Human Rights
   C. A collection of good ideas.
4. Who has to follow the instructions of the Guide?
   A. Only EU member states
   B. All countries in the world
   C. All Council of Europe member states
5. What does the European Convention on Human Rights do?
   A. It secures human rights
   B. It convinces people
   C. It secures only adults rights.
6. Who do human rights belong to?
   A. People who have behaved well
   B. Everyone
   C. Only people who pay their taxes.

HANDOUTS

PART II: ACCESS AND NON-DISCRIMINATION / FREEDOM OF EXPRESSION AND INFORMATION / ASSEMBLY, ASSOCIATION AND PARTICIPATION

7. When surfing online or using different social network channels, you must not be discriminated against because of
   A. Eye colour
   B. Gender and language, for example
   C. Using a smartphone or a computer.
8. What does freedom of expression mean online?
   A. To have the freedom to express yourself but only in writing
   B. To have the freedom to express yourself in certain channels
   C. To have the freedom to express yourself online and to access information.
9. Which of the following is not included in freedom of expression?
   A. Political speech
   B. Views on religion
   C. Expressions which incite to discrimination, hatred or violence.
10. What does it mean to have a right to participate online?
   A. To have the freedom to choose any website or application but only to participate in four different ones at the same time
   B. To have the freedom to choose any website, application or other service in order to form, join, mobilise and participate in social groups and assemblies
   C. To have the freedom to choose any website or application but not be allowed to protest online.

HANDOUTS

PART III: PRIVACY AND DATA PROTECTION / EDUCATION AND LITERACY / CHILDREN AND YOUNG PEOPLE / EFFECTIVE REMEDIES

11. According to the Guide, everyone has the right to education. What does it mean online?
    - A. For example, every child should do their homework on a computer
    - B. For example, everyone should have access to newspapers online
    - C. For example, everyone should have access to online courses and digital education.
12. Who is entitled to special protection and guidance when using the Internet?
    - A. Everyone
    - B. Only children and young people from 14 to 16 years old
    - C. Children and young people.
13. Internet service providers should
    - A. Give information to people on how to report and complain about interferences with their rights
    - B. Give information to people on how many discrimination cases there are
    - C. Give information to people on how many people work work in each company.
14. Who is the authority to which you need to turn to first of all for protection from criminal offences committed on or using the Internet?
    - A. International authorities
    - B. National authorities
    - C. European authorities.

ONLINE PARTICIPATION

This activity helps participants to think about the way they use the Internet and how they participate online. Participants will identify and scale their level of online participation and also plan what kind of role they would like to have online in the future. Participants also learn how to address hate speech and how to protect human rights online in a more effective way.

THEMES	Internet Literacy, Private Life and Safety, Human Rights
COMPLEXITY	Level 3
GROUP SIZE	Any
TIME	45 minutes
OBJECTIVES	• To identify one's participation level and roles online • To learn how to address hate speech and how to protect human rights online in a more effective way • To understand the risk that may occur when acting against hate speech online
MATERIALS	• Big cardboards • Flipchart paper • Coloured pens / markers • Post-its • Copies of the handout Ladder of participation on page 86
PREPARATION	• Prepare large cards with online roles and place them on the floor. You can write on them roles such as creator, conversationalist / discusser, critic, collector, "joiner", spectator, inactive, viewer and member. • Make copies of the handout on page 86.

INSTRUCTIONS

1. Explain to participants that you have placed cards on the floor of the room and that all the cards represent different online roles: creator, conversationalist / discusser, critic, collector, "joiner", spectator, inactive, viewer and member. Provide examples of what each role means.

2. Ask participants to place themselves on one of the cards according to what they do on the Internet "in general". How do they see their role online? How do they participate online?
3. After they have chosen their place, ask them to look around and pay attention to where others have placed themselves. You can also ask for examples of actions participants do online.
4. Ask participants to place themselves on the cards again depending on what they do on the Internet regarding combating hate speech online. After they have chosen their place ask them to look around and pay attention where others have placed themselves. You can also ask for examples of their actions to combat hate speech online.
5. Ask participants to place themselves on the cards again, according to where they would like to see their online participation one year from now when it comes to combating hate speech online. After they have chosen their place you can ask for clarification of why they have chosen that specific role.
6. Ask participants to form small groups of 2 to 4 people. Ask groups to come up with actions they would like to take to reach the level of participation they have chosen when combating hate speech online.
7. Ask groups to share their actions with others.

DEBRIEFING

- What did you think about the activity?
- How was it to identify your role online? What did you discover about your online behaviour?
- How was it to identify your role online regarding actions against hate speech online?
- How was it to identify what kind of role online you would like to have when combating hate speech? How was it to think of things you could do more of online?
- What do you think about these examples of online participation? What is their link to "offline" participation? Can people participate online as they do offline?
- Is it important to address hate speech online in general? Why or why not?
- How easy did you find it to think of online actions against hate speech?
- Do you feel that you can freely participate online?

TIPS FOR FACILITATORS

- You can learn more about online participation in Chapter 5.6, 'Democracy and participation' on page 174.
- You can also learn more about human rights online reading the *Guide to Human Rights for Internet Users*, and specifically the section 'Assembly, association and participation'. It may also be worth mentioning the Guide to participants as well. Internet users need their human rights to be protected online. Knowing their rights and challenging any abuses is important in making sure that this happens. The Guide is accessible at: www.coe.int/en/web/internet-users-rights/guide.

IDEAS FOR ACTION

Participants could make their own "map of online participation" to plan how to be more active online and how to combat hate speech online.

Invite participants to imagine an activity or action to share with the activists of the No Hate Speech Movement youth campaign.

This activity has been developed during the first regional training course based on Bookmarks, held in Belgium, October 2014.

HANDOUT

LADDER OF ONLINE PARTICIPATION*

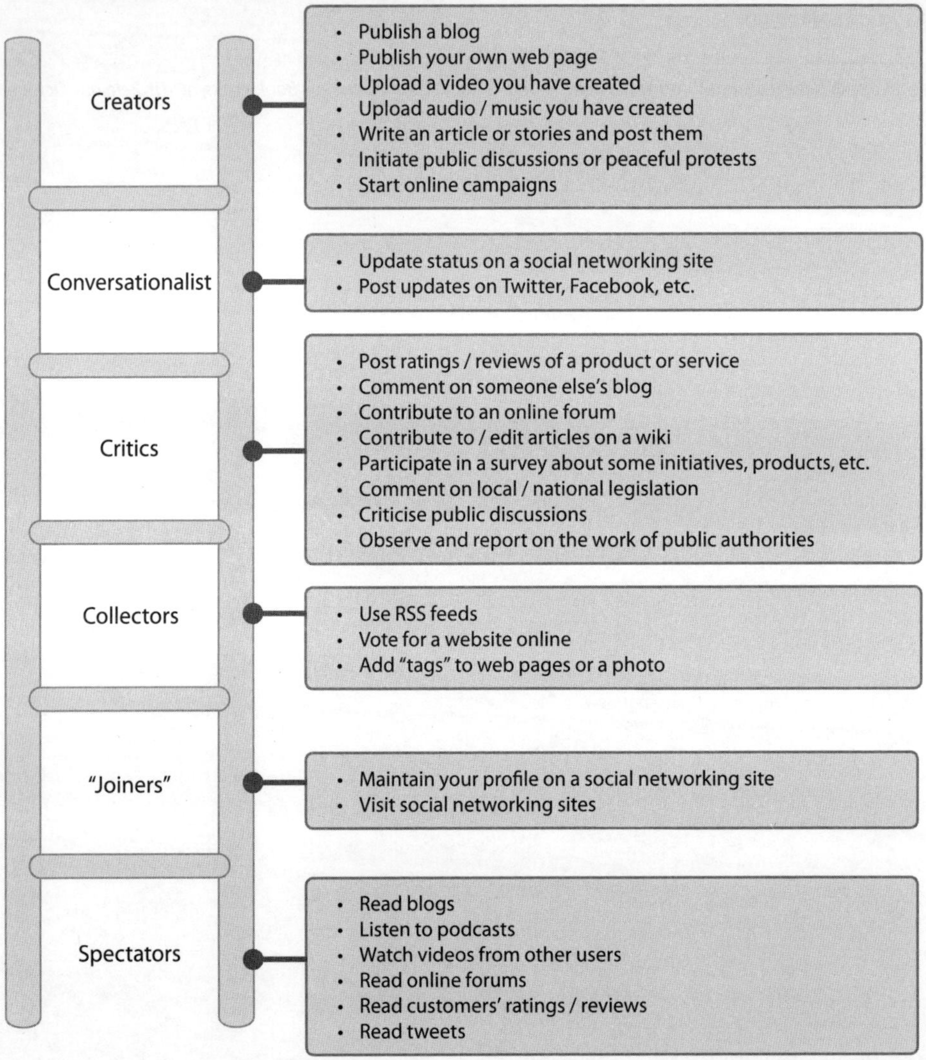

Creators
- Publish a blog
- Publish your own web page
- Upload a video you have created
- Upload audio / music you have created
- Write an article or stories and post them
- Initiate public discussions or peaceful protests
- Start online campaigns

Conversationalist
- Update status on a social networking site
- Post updates on Twitter, Facebook, etc.

Critics
- Post ratings / reviews of a product or service
- Comment on someone else's blog
- Contribute to an online forum
- Contribute to / edit articles on a wiki
- Participate in a survey about some initiatives, products, etc.
- Comment on local / national legislation
- Criticise public discussions
- Observe and report on the work of public authorities

Collectors
- Use RSS feeds
- Vote for a website online
- Add "tags" to web pages or a photo

"Joiners"
- Maintain your profile on a social networking site
- Visit social networking sites

Spectators
- Read blogs
- Listen to podcasts
- Watch videos from other users
- Read online forums
- Read customers' ratings / reviews
- Read tweets

* Based on the 2010 model by Bernoff, J. and Li, C. (2010), 'Social technographics revisited – mapping online participation'. In Participation Models: Citizens, Youth, Online, available at: www.nonformality.org/wp-content/uploads/2012/11/Participation_Models_20121118.pdf

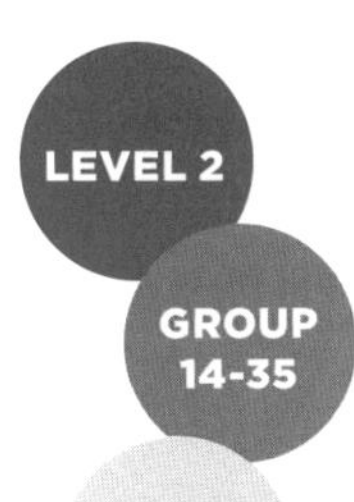

TIME
60'

OUR RIGHTS ONLINE

Participants are introduced to the Guide to Human Rights for Internet Users. They have to analyse key messages and statements of the Guide and to reflect on its application in daily life.

THEMES	Human Rights, Democracy and Participation
COMPLEXITY	Level 2
GROUP SIZE	14-35
TIME	60 minutes
OBJECTIVES	• To explore with participants the human rights online of Internet users • To introduce the simplified version of the *Guide to Human Rights for Internet Users* • To discuss ways of applying the Guide in daily life • To reflect on participants' role in promoting the Guide
MATERIALS	• Copy of the simplified version of the Guide on page 90. • Pens and paper for note-taking • Flipchart paper and markers • Space for small groups to work
PREPARATION	• Copy the simplified version of the Guide and cut into 7 parts for small group work.

INSTRUCTIONS

1. Make a small introduction of the *Guide to Human Rights for Internet Users* using the description below, or the short version on page 206.
2. Explain to participants that they will read and work on 7 different areas of the Guide.
3. Divide participants into 7 small groups. Give each group one area of the simplified version of the Guide on page 90, and ask them to read it.

The *Guide to Human Rights for Internet Users* is part of a recommendation that the Council of Europe adopted for its 47 member states.

The Guide is the set of statements and principles regarding the exercising of human rights on the Internet.

The Guide is particularly helpful to the general public, educators and young people to learn about human rights and freedoms online, their possible limitations and available means of protection.

The Guide does not establish new human rights. It is based on the European Convention on Human Rights, other Council of Europe conventions and other instruments of human rights protection.

The Guide describes how human rights can be fulfilled and protected in the following areas: "Access and non-discrimination", "Freedom of expression and information", "Assembly, association and participation", "Privacy and data protection", "Education and literacy", "Children and young people" and "Effective remedies".

The Guide stresses what kind of responsibilities users, public authorities, Internet providers and online content providers have when it comes to exercising human rights online.

4. Ask each group to prepare a short performance reflecting the human rights from the area they read about. Ask the groups not to tell each other what their performance is going to be about.
5. After 15 minutes of preparation, have every group present their performance.
6. Allow a few minutes after each performance for feedback. Ask the other groups to guess what human rights the performance illustrated.
7. Then give the group itself one minute for a short explanation of what they tried to reflect from the content they read. Write their ideas or messages on flipchart paper.
8. Repeat this for each of the performances.
9. Follow to debriefing.

DEBRIEFING

- How was this exercise?
- What new information about your rights have you learnt from this activity?
- Is there any difference between human rights offline and human rights online?
- Who has the responsibility to apply these rights online?
- How can we make sure these rights apply online? What can we do? What should our government do? What should the website owners do?
- After becoming acquainted with the content of the Guide, what would you tell other Internet users when they come across hate speech online?
- What kind of support one can get from the Guide in combating hate speech online?

TIPS FOR FACILITATORS

- Familiarise yourself with the full version of the Guide to be ready for the introduction and participants' questions.
- Ask participants to concentrate on key ideas they would want to bring to others while creating a performance.
- While debriefing, pay attention to the flipchart paper with key ideas prepared as a result of groups performing.
- When participants discuss their role in promoting human rights online, ask for specific examples of what young people can do in their daily online activity.

VARIATIONS

If the group feel uncomfortable doing performances, you could ask them to draw the content they read, or to express their ideas in some other relevant and creative way.

IDEAS FOR ACTION

You may establish with your group a list of key points regarding what Internet users should know about their rights online.

You may check with your group who the institutions and organisations protection human rights online in your country are.

Invite participants to join the No Hate Speech Movement youth campaign at the European level or in their own country. They can also prepare a photo, meme or video about human rights and hate speech online, based on the ideas they expressed in their performances.

As the result of the activity, participants can elaborate action plans promoting human rights online among their friends, schoolmates, and so on.

HANDOUTS

GUIDE TO HUMAN RIGHTS FOR INTERNET USERS

SIMPLIFIED VERSION

GROUP 1

Access to the Internet and non-discrimination

Anyone should have access to the Internet without discrimination by gender, age, race, colour, language, religion or belief, political or other opinion, ethnicity or sexual orientation.

If you live in rural and geographically remote areas, are on a low income and/or have special needs or disabilities, authorities should facilitate your access to the Internet.

GROUP 2

Freedom of expression and information

Anyone has the freedom to express themselves online and to access information online. There can be limits to this in case of expressions which incite to discrimination, hatred or violence. You may be able to mask your identity online, for instance by using a pseudonym; however, in some cases your identity can be revealed by authorities.

GROUP 3

Assembly, association and participation

Anyone has the right to associate with others using the Internet and to protest peacefully online. You may choose any online tools in order to join any social groups or participate in public policy debates.

GROUP 4

Privacy and data protection

Anyone has the right to private and family life on the Internet. This includes the confidentiality of your private online correspondence and communications. Personal information should only be used online if people previously agreed to this.

Public authorities and private companies have an obligation to respect specific rules and procedures when they process your personal data.

GROUP 5

Education and literacy

Anyone has the right to education, culture and knowledge online.

You should be supported in developing skills to understand and use different Internet tools, and to check the accuracy and trustworthiness of content and services that you access.

HANDOUTS

GROUP 6

Children and young people

Children and young people are entitled to special protection and guidance when using the Internet.
You can expect training from your teachers, educators and parents about safe use of the Internet.
You are entitled to receive, from authorities, Internet service and content providers, clear information about illegal online content or behaviour which can harm you.

GROUP 7

Support and help

Anyone has the right to receive help and support when their rights are not respected online, including the possibility for having access to a court.
An Internet service provider (providers of access to online content) should inform you about your rights and how to complain about violations.
Your digital identity, computer and the data it contains are protected by authorities from illegal access, forgery and other fraudulent manipulation.

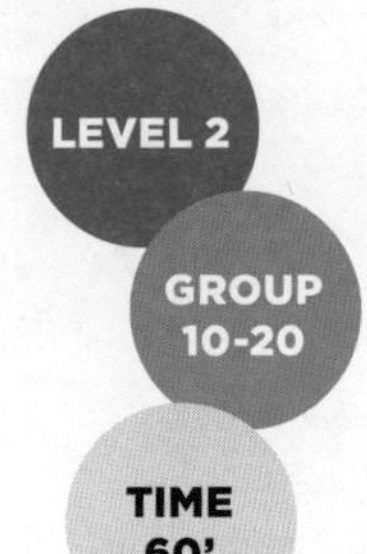

PLAY IT AGAIN

This activity is based on a role play: someone is drawn into an act of bullying because of peer pressure. Participants are asked to replay the scenario in order to achieve a different outcome.

THEMES	Cyberbullying, Democracy and Participation, Racism and Discrimination
COMPLEXITY	Level 2
GROUP SIZE	10-20
TIME	60 minutes
OBJECTIVES	• To understand how bullying works • To develop solidarity and empathy for victims of bullying • To encourage participants to take action against bullying and hate speech online
PREPARATION	• Identify 4 volunteers before the activity begins. They will be asked to perform a short role play for the rest of the group (not more than 5 minutes). Give them copies of the scenario on page 95 so that they can prepare beforehand. Help them to get started if necessary. • Make sure you have enough space for the role play.

INSTRUCTIONS

1. Tell the group that the activity will begin with a brief role play. Read out the following background to the scenario then introduce the volunteers and invite them to begin the role play.

Scenario:

Albert is quiet and is seen as a bit 'different'. He doesn't have many friends and often worries that others in the class don't like him. Sometimes he plays the fool to make the other children laugh, and he is very good at that (even if the teacher doesn't always approve!).

After one lesson when he had made all the class laugh a lot, he was approached as he was leaving school by Derek and Jared, two of the most popular boys in the class. The three of them laughed together about his behaviour, and then walked home together. Albert felt very proud, as if he'd at last been accepted.

2. Now run the role play.
3. After the role play, ask participants for their reactions. Prompt with a few questions if necessary, for example:
   - Do you think the scenario is realistic?
   - What do you think about Albert's behaviour?
   - How do you think Ahmed must have felt?
4. Invite participants to think about how they might have behaved if they had been in Albert's position. Then tell them that the role play will be run again, but this time you would like to invite others to step in and see if they can produce a better outcome for Ahmed (and Albert).
5. Start the role play again (with the same volunteers) but stop it at certain points and ask for new volunteers to change places with one of the characters. You may want to do this a couple of times to allow more people to take part in the activity.
6. After the role play, invite everyone to come up with something else that Albert could have posted online at the end of the original scenario – something which might have helped to repair the damage. This could be a tweet, a personal message, a comment, or anything else. Then move on to the debriefing.

DEBRIEFING

Make sure participants have come out of their roles, if they took part in the role play. Emphasise that the following questions should be answered from their own point of view, not from the point of view of characters that featured in the role play.

- What did you think about this activity?
- What were the things that made Albert join in with the bullying?
- How easy do you find it to resist these pressures in your own life?
- What if this happened online? What would be similar? What would be different?
- Have you ever seen posts on someone's personal profile, or elsewhere on the Internet, which target people in the way Albert did in this scenario?
- Is there anything you can do to stop things like this being posted, or lessen their impact?
- Did you learn anything from the activity, or did it make you think about bullying in a different way?

TIPS FOR FACILITATORS

- Make sure you are aware of any potential tensions in the group before running the activity. You may need to alter the scenario so that it does not reflect any strong negative attitudes towards people in the group. In particular, you may want to change the nationality of Ahmed or change the comments made by Albert, or you may want to substitute female characters into the scenario.
- Be careful when selecting volunteers: try to choose volunteers who are unlikely to have any relation to issues raised in the scenario. Brief the first volunteers that the role play does not need to be long.
- You may want to allow some time after the role play for people who did not have an opportunity to participate to make their own suggestions. Running the role play more than 3 times will become repetitive, but people could be asked to describe other possible ways of altering the outcome.

- If the role play arouses strong emotions among participants, it may be useful to run a further brief activity before the debriefing to allow them to distance themselves from their roles. It is normally sufficient to ask them to say their names out loud or do a quick physical energiser.
- Try not to offer your own judgement on any of the behaviour in the role play: use questions instead to make participants see a different point of view. It is important that participants feel free to speak honestly about their own attitudes or behaviour, including any difficulties they may feel in not succumbing to peer pressure.

VARIATIONS

Instead of using role play, the example could be used as a case study, with alternative scenarios discussed in small groups, or in the whole group.

IDEAS FOR ACTION

Invite participants to develop solidarity messages with victims of cyberbullying or to draw up a list of suggestions for people who feel 'pressured' to join in with bullying. These messages could be shared on the No Hate Speech Movement website www.nohatespeechmovement.org
Draw up an action plan for instances when participants come across cyberbullying online, either as a victim, or as an observer. The group could make a pact that they will always do something from the action plan if they come across bullying online.
There are numerous organisations or sites on the Internet which deal with cyberbullying. Make sure that participants are aware of any support systems that they could turn to after the activity, if it prompts such a need. Use a search engine to find local initiatives, or look for general information on the following sites: www.stopcyberbullying.org and http://yp.direct.gov.uk/cyberbullying .

HANDOUT (FOR VOLUNTEERS)

INSTRUCTIONS

Prepare a short role play to illustrate the following scenario. It should begin at the moment when Jared and Derek approach Albert after school. Decide who will play the roles of Derek, Jared, Albert and Ahmed.

- Derek, Jared – popular boys in school. They start the bullying.
- Albert – a boy who has trouble making friends. He gets taken up by Derek and Jared.
- Ahmed – a new boy, originally from Ethiopia.

START THE ROLE PLAY HERE:

As Derek, Jared and Albert are walking home, they see Ahmed ahead of them, walking alone. Ahmed has recently joined the class and is from another country. He is teased by some of the children for speaking the language used in school badly, for being smaller than most people in the class, and for his shabby clothes.

Derek and Jared walk a bit faster so as to catch up with Ahmed. Then they start shouting insults at him, pulling his bag and asking whether everyone in Ethiopia wears clothes like him, and whether he should be in the baby class if he can't speak the language used in the school.

Albert feels very uncomfortable. Derek and Jared keep looking at him, encouraging him to join in and asking what he thinks. In the end, Albert makes what he thinks is a witty comment about people in Ethiopia living in trees and speaking monkey language. Derek and Jared laugh a lot but Albert can see that Ahmed is very upset and frightened of the three boys.

When Albert gets home, he feels bad. He knows what it's like to be teased by other children, and what he'd said to Ahmed had been far worse than anything people had said to him. But it had been good to laugh with Derek and Jared, and their friendship was worth a lot. He logged onto the Internet and 'friended' Derek and Jared. Then he posted his comment about Ethiopians onto his profile.

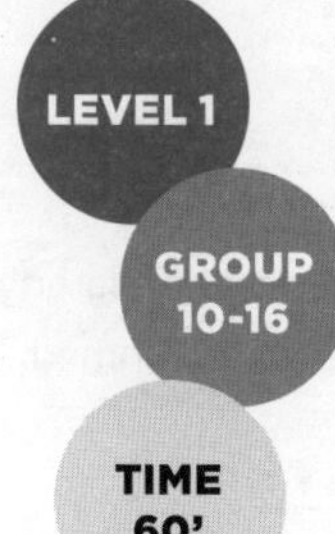

LEVEL 1

GROUP 10-16

TIME 60'

RACE FOR RIGHTS!

This activity provides a basic introduction to human rights through a team game. Participants have to depict different rights to members of their team using anything they like – except for words!

THEMES	Human Rights, Racism and Discrimination, Private Life and Safety
COMPLEXITY	Level 1
GROUP SIZE	10-16
TIME	60 minutes
OBJECTIVES	• To understand the rights contained in the Universal Declaration of Human Rights (UDHR) • To think about human rights protections in the online world • To discuss the links between human rights and hate speech online
MATERIALS	• Copies of the Rights Cards: make 1 copy for each team • Copies of the Guess Cards: make 5 copies of page 100 • Copies of the UDHR (summary): make enough copies for everyone • Flipchart paper and marker pens (optional) • Space for 2 or more teams to work separately, ideally in different rooms • 2 facilitators (ideally)
PREPARATION	• Cut up the Rights Cards and Guess Cards • You may wish to copy the 'Briefing card for Collectors', or put the text up on a flipchart / overhead projector

INSTRUCTIONS

OPTIONAL STARTER (FOR GROUPS UNFAMILIAR WITH HUMAN RIGHTS)

1. Ask participants what they understand by human rights. Write up suggestions on a flipchart and prompt with further questions, if necessary. For example:
   - Who has human rights?
   - Can you name any human rights?
   - Who has to make sure that human rights are respected?

- Where do they come from?
- Do human rights apply online?

2. Provide a brief summary of human rights, for example:

Human rights belong to *everyone*, and they are 'laws for governments'. Human rights mean that governments have to make sure that individuals are protected from unfair treatment, extreme abuse and violence – amongst other things. Human rights are important because they protect us, and because they mean we shouldn't behave towards others in a way that does not respect *their* rights.

MAIN ACTIVITY

3. Explain that the activity involves a team game to remind participants of the rights contained in the Universal Declaration of Human Rights. Outline the aim and rules of the game (page 99) and divide the group into teams of 5-8 people. Hand out the following to each team:
   - Copies of the UDHR summary
   - 2 Guess cards
   - Information for Collectors, or write this on a flipchart.
   - Sheets of flipchart paper for each team and marker pens (optional)
4. If participants are unfamiliar with the UDHR, give them some time to read the articles and ask questions if they do not understand any of the rights.
5. Run through the rules (page 99) and make sure everyone understands them. Then start the game!
6. When one team has guessed all the rights, or a team runs out of Guess cards, the game is over. Ask for feedback and allow participants to wind down after the heat of the competition! Use some of the following questions to debrief the activity.

DEBRIEFING

REFLECTIONS ON THE GAME:

- Which of the rights were most difficult to communicate? Why?
- What conclusions can you draw about communication: why is it often difficult to understand each other? Is it the fault of the 'communicator' or the 'listener', or both?
- What emotions do you feel towards your team now? What do you feel towards the other team?
- Think about competitive games: why do we often attach ourselves to one team rather than another? Is this attachment based on reason? Can you think of any parallels in real life?

REFLECTIONS ON HUMAN RIGHTS:

- Were any of the rights particularly difficult to understand?
- Do you think you could 'do without' any of these rights? If so, which ones?
- Do you think these rights should apply to the online world as well as the 'real' world? Can you think of examples where some of these rights are relevant to online activity?
- Do you think that human rights are respected on the Internet?

REFLECTIONS ON HATE SPEECH:

- Explain briefly that hate speech is any 'expression' of hatred towards a group or member of a group which is nasty, hurtful and likely to lead to violent reactions towards members of the group. Ask for a few examples to clarify.
- Which of the rights in the game might be relevant to hate speech? Why?
- If you were a target of hate speech online, which rights would you be most likely to need?
- What can be done about the proliferation of hate speech online?

TIPS FOR FACILITATORS

- The game will be more effective with 2 facilitators. The facilitators will need to make sure that Collectors do not respond to 'unofficial' guesses (for example by shaking the head or looking encouraging).
- Participants could work in pairs to convey the rights. This may be helpful to allow them to discuss what the rights mean, but it may also add time to the activity.
- When the Collectors come up to receive a new Rights Card, remind them that they must hand over any Guess Cards used. Check what is written on the cards and hand out any new Guess cards if necessary.
- You may wish to concentrate on one or two of the areas of 'reflection' in order to explore issues more fully. Do not try to cover all questions!
- The reflections on team 'affiliation' could be used to reflect on other affiliations, for example, on country or ethnic groups. You could explore the emotional attachments which people often have towards their 'own' group, and use that to explore questions relating to racism and discrimination.
- In case you have time to talk more about how human rights apply online, you and the participants could familiarise yourselves with the Council of Europe's *Guide to Human Rights for Internet Users*.

VARIATIONS

The activity could be run purely as a drawing activity, or purely as a drama activity, or both, as in the instructions above.

IDEAS FOR ACTION

Ask participants to identify an online news article which features a human rights abuse. Remind them that human rights abuses are not necessarily 'ordinary' crimes: they must indicate a failure on the part of a *government* to protect people.

HANDOUTS

TEAM GAME: RULES OF PLAY

Aim of the game: to guess all the human rights cards before the other team(s) – or to end up with the largest number of remaining Guess Cards

Rules:

- 1 person from each team (the 'Collector') collects a human rights card from the facilitator. Their task is to convey the right written on the card to the rest of their team without speaking. They are allowed to draw pictures, use gestures or mime, but cannot use any other props to communicate the right written on the card.
- The rest of the team has a list of the rights in the UDHR and need to guess which human right is on the card. This should be discussed and agreed by the whole team before an 'official' guess is made. When they have agreed on the team's guess, this should be recorded on one of the Guess cards and given to the Collector. The Collector then responds.
- For each right, a maximum of 2 Guess Cards can be used. After that, the right is regarded as 'not guessed' and the next Collector goes to fetch a new card from the facilitator. They should also hand over any Guess Cards they have used.

If the first guess was correct, the team will be given 2 new Guess Cards.
If the second guess was correct, they will be given 1 new Guess Card.
If the right was 'not guessed' (in 2 guesses), no additional Guess Cards are received.

- A different Collector should be sent up for each card. When everyone has had a turn, a second round begins.
- The game ends when one team has guessed all cards correctly, or when a team runs out of Guess cards.

Remember!

- Not all rights are included in the game: there are 30 different rights in the UDHR, and only 12 cards to guess.
- Each team starts off with only 20 guesses. They will need to be careful not to waste their guesses! If they run out of Guess Cards first, they will lose the game.

BRIEFING CARD FOR COLLECTORS

You are not allowed to speak when it is your turn to be a Collector! You can draw pictures and use gestures or mime to help your team guess what's on the card. Try not to use other props.
If your team makes an 'unofficial' guess – in other words, they don't write it on a card – you must not respond! You can encourage them and nod or shake your head if they ask questions about anything else, for example, 'are you sweeping the floor?', 'are you in prison?', 'is that an ice cream?', but NO SPEAKING!

HANDOUTS

GUESS CARDS

Guess card	Guess card
Write your guess here	*Write your guess here*

Guess card	Guess card
Write your guess here	*Write your guess here*

Guess card	Guess card
Write your guess here	*Write your guess here*

Guess card	Guess card
Write your guess here	*Write your guess here*

Guess card	Guess card
Write your guess here	*Write your guess here*

Guess card	Guess card
Write your guess here	*Write your guess here*

HANDOUTS

HUMAN RIGHTS CARDS

Article 1	Article 14
All human beings have the same human rights	Everyone has the right to ask for asylum in another country if they are being persecuted
Article 2	**Article 18**
No-one should be discriminated against	Everyone has the right to religious belief
Article 3	**Article 19**
Everyone has the right to life	Everyone has the right to freedom of expression (to say what they want)
Article 5	**Article 20**
Everyone has the right to be free from torture	Everyone has the right to join an association and to meet with others
Article 11	**Article 21**
Everyone has the right to be considered innocent until proven guilty	Everyone has the right to vote in elections and take part in government
Article 12	**Article 27**
Everyone has the right to privacy	Everyone has the right to take part in the cultural life of their community

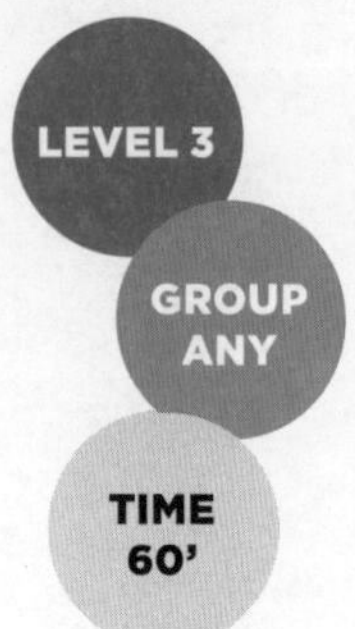

READING THE RULES

Participants discover the terms of use or community guidelines of a website and take steps to report inappropriate content to the website. Participants also discuss what the advantages and disadvantages of reporting are, particularly in relation to the possibilities of Web 2.0.

THEMES	Campaigning Strategies, Internet Literacy, Democracy and Participation
COMPLEXITY	Level 3
GROUP SIZE	Any
TIME	60 minutes
OBJECTIVES	• To understand some of the ways that Internet content is regulated, including rules which prohibit hate speech online • To examine the terms and conditions of some popular websites and assess their suitability • To discuss the effectiveness of using online reporting mechanisms to combat hate speech
MATERIALS	• Computers with access to the Internet • Pens and the questionnaires on pages 106-107
PREPARATION	• Copy the questionnaire on pages 106-107. You will need 1 copy for each small group (4 people).

INSTRUCTIONS

1. Ask participants who makes the rules for the Internet. *Are* there any rules? Where are they written down?
2. Use some of the information on pages 105-106 to explain that there are rules at different 'levels' on the Internet: there may be rules set by the owners of websites (or by hosting providers), there are rules set by national governments, and there are rules set by international law, in particular, human rights law. The activity will concentrate on the first level, the rules set by websites themselves.
3. Ask if anyone has ever looked at the 'rules' for websites they use! Has anyone ever made use of them, for example, reported an abusive comment or post to the website owner, where this is forbidden by the rules? Has anyone ever wondered whether this is possible, or how to do it?
4. Explain that the rules for users of websites are normally known as the 'terms and conditions', and most websites have them! The terms and conditions can often be a useful tool in combating hate speech online because many websites have provisions which do not allow it. The problem is that people do not always make effective use of the rules, and website owners do not always monitor content according to their own rules.

5. Divide participants into groups of about 4 people and give each group a copy of the questionnaire on page 106-107. Explain that each group should select a website that they use frequently, and try to work through the questionnaire. If necessary, run through the questions quickly with the group to make sure that participants know what they should be looking for.
6. Give them about 20 minutes to complete the task then bring them back for the debriefing.

DEBRIEFING

Begin by running through the questionnaire, comparing what participants found.

- Were there significant differences between your results, for example, in the kind of content that is permitted or the ease of reporting?
- Did anyone find a 'perfect' example of terms and conditions?
- Did any group feel that the terms and conditions were wholly inadequate, either because they did not address hate speech, or because the rules and reporting procedure were too complicated?
- Now that you have looked at the terms and conditions, do you think you would ever report an abusive post on a website? Why, or why not?
- What if no-one ever reported abusive posts!?
- Do you think that as users of a website you might be able to improve the terms and conditions, or ensure that they are more rigidly observed? How could you do this?
- What else can you think of that could make reporting more effective? For example, is there any difference if one user reports inappropriate content or if 1,000 users do it at the same time? What if a company, which uses this website for advertising, threatened to withdraw the advertising from the website unless the website took off the abusive information?
- Can you think of some other ways of responding to hate speech online, apart from using the reporting procedure? When might other methods be more appropriate?

TIPS FOR FACILITATORS

- You may want to run through an example with participants before asking them to do their own research. You could select a website and illustrate how to find the terms and conditions, and how to scan them quickly for relevant clauses. Note that not all sites will have terms and conditions, and sometimes these may be called something else, for example 'community guidelines' or 'posting guidelines'. Participants should make a note when this is the case.
- You can select sites for participants to make sure they all look at different sites, or you could give them a few minutes before they start the research to decide on their site. Try to make sure you have a good selection of sites, for example, a video sharing site, social media site, a central news hub, gaming site, and so on.
- The notes section in the questionnaire can be used to record any other relevant factors, for example, whether there is a link on the front page, whether there is a complaints form, whether sites state whether they will respond to complaints in a given amount of time, and so on.
- Remind participants that if the terms and conditions are long, they can use a search to look for key words, such as 'hate speech', 'abuse', 'racism', and other similar words and phrases.

- Going through the questionnaires as a group may be time-intensive, and boring for some participants! You could give them 5 minutes after they have done their research to pair up with another group and compare results. Or the questionnaires could be passed between groups so that they can look at them before the discussion begins.
- Emphasise to participants that it is important to know about a website's rules before making a complaint, but that does not mean they cannot complain about something which they find abusive, and which is not being dealt with properly by the website (or is not covered in the terms and conditions). As an example, you could refer participants to the Sexism Campaign against Facebook. See www.bbc.co.uk/news/technology-22689522 and www.bbc.co.uk/news/technology-22699761 .
- It is also worth reminding participants that reporting is not the only strategy for addressing hate speech online, and that it is often not the best strategy. Refer to the information in Chapter 5 on Campaigning Strategies for other ways of responding.
- It may also be interesting to learn more about how human rights apply online by using the *Guide to Human Rights for Internet Users*.

VARIATIONS

Participants could also spend some time searching the site they have chosen for examples of hate speech. This will give them an idea of how well the terms and conditions are actually working. They could perform searches on the site using key words such as 'nigger', 'fagot', 'whore' or other abusive terms. This will take a little longer, but would provide useful material for using the reporting procedure to make a complaint to the website.

Reporting inappropriate content to a website is only the first step one can take. Another step is to report the content directly to a state body dealing with discrimination, or to the police. You can run a variation of the activity by asking participants to file a complaint about abusive content on a website to the police or other equality bodies existing in your country. NGOs such as INACH are also active in several countries and use reporting procedures. You can also take the example of True Vision in the United Kingdom: www.report-it.org.uk .

IDEAS FOR ACTION

If the 'variation' above is not used in the activity, you could ask participants to explore further the websites they investigated in the activity. They could conduct an analysis of any examples of hate speech they come across, noting the number of cases, the target audiences, and how 'bad' the examples are. If they find a significant number of cases, suggest some of the following possible courses of action after they have conducted their analysis:

- Post the examples, and the analysis, to Hate Speech Watch and discuss with other activists what should be done about it. (www.nohatespeechmovement.org/hate-speech-watch)
- Send the worst examples and the analysis to the website owner, using the terms and conditions of the website to strengthen their complaint.
- If the site is a social media site, they could create a profile on the site and publicise their results there (see examples such as www.nohatespeechmovement.org/hate-speech-watch and https://en-gb.facebook.com/WOH247 .)

- Sort the examples according to how extreme they are (see 'Saying it worse' for some guidance). Then identify strategies for different cases, for example, responding to some of the posts or posters where these are based on false information.
- Check the online tool called EULAlyzer (www.brightfort.com/eulalyzer.html), which allows users to scan terms and conditions and will highlight any interesting language or terms as well as highlighting any key points that users should be aware of.

HANDOUTS

LAWS REGULATING INTERNET USE

Most of the Internet is owned by private companies. Even a private blog will normally be hosted on a private server. The company which owns the server may decide to restrict the type of things posted on the blog, or it may not! The rules that users of a website must observe will often be set out in the 'terms and conditions'. They may be very different from one website to another.

Apart from the terms and conditions, there may be laws established by governments which apply to users of the Internet and website owners. Some examples include laws relating to privacy and security, or laws covering extreme hate speech. Even if a government does not have specific laws to protect people's safety online, this is often covered by international human rights legislation (see the example below).

Much of the Internet is therefore a bit like a shopping mall or a nightclub! Even if there's no law against wearing jeans or looking scruffy, you can still be turned out of a nightclub if the rules say jeans are not allowed. In a similar way, websites can also make their own rules for their 'private space' on the Internet. However, their rules must also be compatible with the laws in the country as a whole.

Example: Governments must protect people online as well as offline

K.U. v. FINLAND

In March 1999 an advertisement was posted on an Internet dating site pretending to be from a 12-year-old boy. It included a link to the boy's web page and said he was looking for an intimate relationship with a boy of his age or older "to show him the way". The boy only found out about the advertisement when he received an e-mail from an interested man. The service provider refused to identify the person responsible for posting the advertisement, claiming it would constitute a breach of confidentiality. The Finnish courts held that the service provider could not legally be obliged to disclose the information.

The case went to the European Court of Human Rights. The Court said that the Finnish State had failed in its duty to protect children and other vulnerable individuals. The advertisement had made the child a target for paedophiles and had failed to protect his right to private and family life. (Article 8 of the European Convention)

HANDOUTS

LAYERS OF LAWS

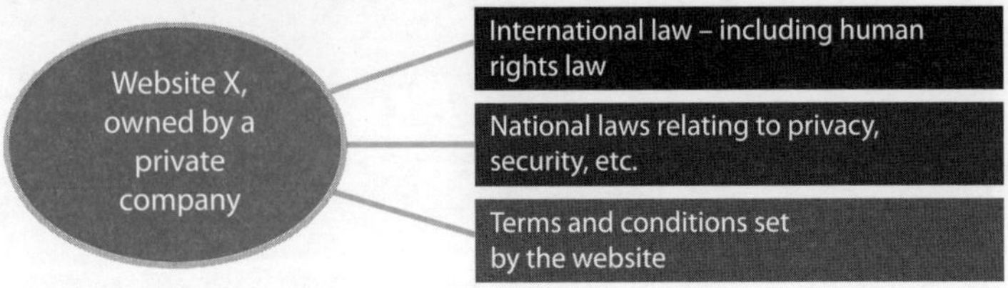

Website X, owned by a private company
International law – including human rights law
National laws relating to privacy, security, etc.
Terms and conditions set by the website

QUESTIONNAIRE

1. **How easy is it to find the Terms and Conditions (T&C)?**

Very easy	Quite easy	Difficult	Very difficult
O	O	O	O

Notes:

2. **How easy is it to understand the T&C?**

Very easy	Quite easy	Difficult	Very difficult
O	O	O	O

Notes:

3. **Is it clear what you can do to make a complaint?**

Very clear	Quite clear	Not very clear	Very unclear
O	O	O	O

Notes:

4. **Is it clear what they will do when they receive a complaint?**

Very clear	Quite easy	Quite difficult	Very difficult
O	O	O	O

Notes:

HANDOUTS

HATE SPEECH

5. **Is there anything in the T&C which relates to hate speech?**

Yes	No	Not sure / Something else
O	O	O

Notes: *If the T&C lists different types of abuse, for example racist abuse, homophobic abuse, and so on, make a note of this.*

6. **Is cyberbullying mentioned?**

Yes	No	Not sure / Something else
O	O	O

Notes:

INAPPROPRIATE CONTENT

7. **Do the T&C say anything else about inappropriate content, for example, is pornography allowed on the site?**

Yes	No	Not sure / Something else
O	O	O

Notes:

COMMUNITY GUIDELINES?

8. **Does the website include anything else which tells you what kind of content is encouraged? For example, a brief statement in a more accessible place, something in the 'About us' section, 'Posting guidelines', or something else?**

Yes	No	Not sure / Something else
O	O	O

Notes:

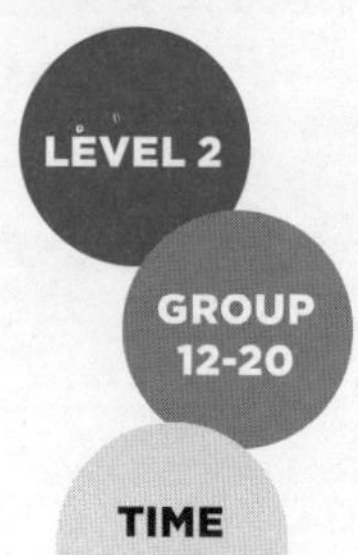

ROOTS AND BRANCHES

Participants explore the causes and effects of hate speech online using a 'problem tree' approach. This activity can be used as a follow-up activity to the activity Group X, or as a standalone activity.

THEMES	Racism and Discrimination, Human Rights, Campaigning Strategies
COMPLEXITY	Level 2
GROUP SIZE	12-20
TIME	45 minutes
OBJECTIVES	• To understand the causes and effects of online hate speech • To consider the connections between hate speech online and offline behaviour • To explore ways of addressing hate speech online by examining the roots of the problem
MATERIALS	• Flipchart paper and markers
PREPARATION	• Make copies of the 'Hate speech tree' (page 111) for participants, or draw onto a flipchart

INSTRUCTIONS

1. Provide a brief introduction to hate speech online and the Council of Europe Campaign, if this is the first activity you run. Use points 1 and 2 in the activity 'Saying it worse' to introduce hate speech, and some of the information from Chapter 2 to tell them about the Campaign.
2. Explain that in order to understand and respond to hate speech online, we need to see it as a problem with numerous connections to other issues, and to the 'real' world. In particular, when we are trying to combat hate speech, it can be useful to look at the underlying causes. Addressing these is often more effective than trying to address instances of hate speech itself.
3. Show participants the 'Hate speech tree' and tell them that they will be working in groups to identify some of the things which lead to hate speech online (the 'roots' of the tree), and some of the effects of hate speech (the 'branches').
4. Explain how the tree works. Every box which leads up the tree to another box is answering the question 'why?' This is true for the branches as well as the roots. You could take an example of hate speech to illustrate this in more detail (see the Tips for Facilitators).

5. **For the roots:** when participants work down the tree, starting from the hate speech itself, they are exploring answers to the question 'why does this happen?' They should fill the 'roots' with as many reasons as possible. Give them an illustration of how one 'cause' will have its own causes. For example, ask them why 'everyone says negative things' about certain groups. Prompt with questions about where we 'learn' the negative things we believe about particular groups (examples might include the media, public figures, strong prejudices or ignorance in society as a whole).
6. **For the branches:** here participants need to explore the possible consequences of items lower down the branch. Ask them what could happen to an individual or to a group which is targeted by hate speech. Ask them what might happen as a result of that.
7. Divide participants into groups and give them a piece of flipchart paper to draw their tree on. Tell them to write the following text, or an example of your own, in the 'trunk' of the tree and then to complete as many branches and roots as they are able to. They should imagine the text has been posted on the Internet:

   "[Group X] are dirty criminals. They steal and they don't belong here. Make them leave!"
8. Give groups about 15 minutes to complete their trees. Then ask groups to present their results, or display the trees around the room for people to walk around and look at.

DEBRIEFING

- Do you notice any interesting differences between the trees produced by groups? Do you have any questions for other groups?
- How easy did you find the 'roots' of hate speech? Explain any difficulties or differences in opinion within the groups.
- Did any of your roots or branches go into the 'real' world? What does this tell us about hate speech online?
- Did the activity give you a deeper understanding of the issue? How important do you think it is that we find ways to stop the spread of hate speech on the Internet?
- Does the activity help you to do that? How could you use your problem tree to make hate speech against [your target group] less likely?

To give the activity a more practical focus, you could take some of the roots and brainstorm ideas for addressing them. For example, if participants have identified 'prejudice' or 'ignorance of Group X' as an underlying cause, ask them how this problem could be tackled. Explain that campaign planning often uses a problem tree approach to identify ways of breaking the problem down, and finding ways to approach it.

TIPS FOR FACILITATORS

- A problem tree is a very common way of understanding a given issue at a deeper level. It is easier to explain with an example, so you could use a different statement to introduce the trees, for example: "Young people are idle and selfish. They should be hidden from society until they grow into normal human beings".

- When participants work on their own 'trees', you could provide them with a copy of the handout – photocopied to A3 – or ask them to draw their own on the flipchart paper. The second method will give them more possibility to extend the roots and branches further, but may appear more difficult than filling out a set number of boxes. Make sure that groups consider the effects on both individuals and on society.
- For the statement to be discussed by participants, you should replace 'Group X' by a group commonly targeted by society. You could also take a case of cyberbullying and have an imaginary individual named as the target.
- If participants appear to have missed out important causes or effects, you may want to prompt them to consider these. You could also provide them with the following list as prompts when they draw their trees. They could consider whether the factors or actors in the list have any relation to the problem, and where they might fit into the tree:
  - The media
  - Politicians / public figures
  - Hate speech offline
  - Little interaction between Group X and the rest of society
  - Peer pressure
  - Discrimination in the work place
  - Economic factors
  - Schools / education
- You can also find more information about how human rights apply online by having a look at the *Guide to Human Rights for Internet Users*. Specifically, the section 'Access and non-discrimination' gives an idea of what kind of rights apply online for those who are targets of hate speech.

IDEAS FOR ACTION

Participants could take one of the causes they have identified and develop a strategy to address this problem. The could select one online action and one offline action to carry out as a group.

Find out more about how to take action for human rights online, by visiting the No Hate Speech Movement website or by contacting your National Campaign Committee.

If you need more information about how to take action for human rights, have a look at *Compass*, the *Council of Europe Manual for Human Rights Education with Young People,* www.coe.int/compass, where a whole chapter is dedicated to the steps needed for taking action.

HANDOUTS

PROBLEM TREE

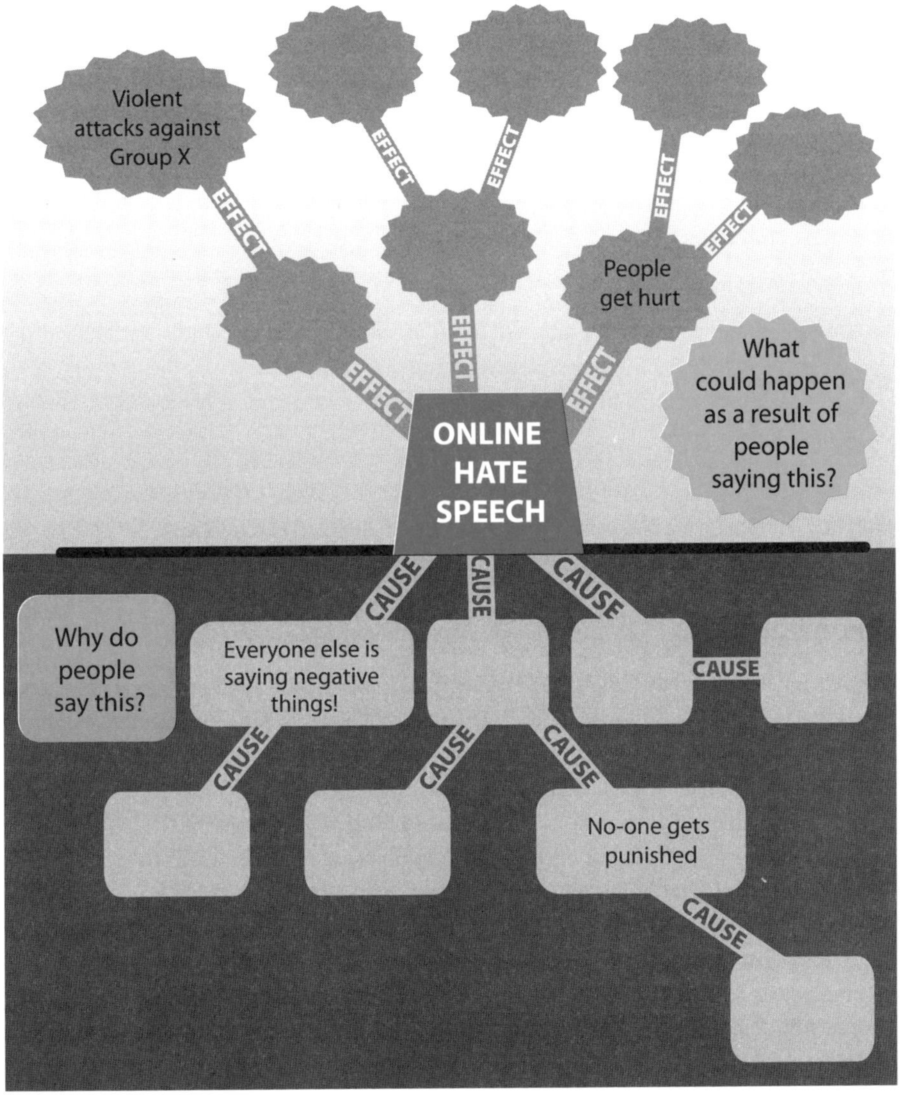

Violent attacks against Group X

EFFECT

People get hurt

What could happen as a result of people saying this?

ONLINE HATE SPEECH

CAUSE

Why do people say this?

Everyone else is saying negative things!

No-one gets punished

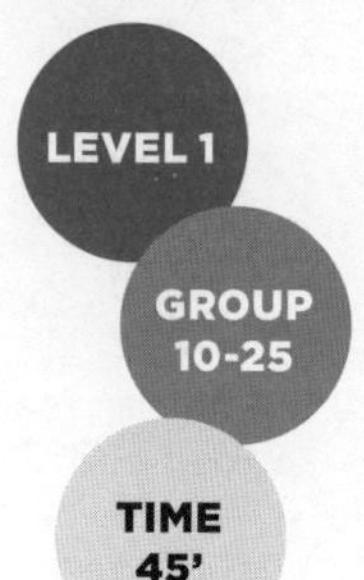

SAYING IT WORSE

This is an introductory activity to hate speech online. Participants rank different examples of anti-gay hate speech according to which they think are 'worse'.

THEMES	Racism and Discrimination, Democracy / Participation
COMPLEXITY	Level 1
GROUP SIZE	10-25
TIME	45 minutes
OBJECTIVES	• To understand the different forms of online hate speech and assess their impact • To address anti-gay stereotypes and prejudices • To consider appropriate responses to different instances of hate speech online
MATERIALS	• The cards on page 116 • Table or floor space to lay the cards out in groups
PREPARATION	• Make one copy of the cards for each small group (4-5 people). • Cut them into cards and select 11 of these for groups to discuss (remove one card).

INSTRUCTIONS

1. Ask participants what they understand by hate speech online. Ask whether anyone has encountered hate speech online, either directed towards an individual or towards representatives of particular groups (for example, gays, blacks, Muslims, Jews, women, etc.) What do people feel when they come across it? How do they think the victims must feel?
2. Explain that the term 'hate speech' is used to cover a wide range of content:
   - Firstly, it covers more than 'speech' in the common sense and can be used in relation to other forms of communication such as videos, images, music, and so on.
   - Secondly, the term can be used to describe very abusive and even threatening behaviour as well as comments which are 'merely' offensive. There may be no universal agreement on what constitutes hate speech but there is no doubt that it constitutes an abuse and violation of human rights.
3. Introduce the No Hate Speech Movement, the Council of Europe Campaign against hate speech online, and tell them that this Campaign is intended to address all forms of hate speech – from the very mild to the very abusive. Explain that knowing how to respond to hate speech often depends on being able to assess how 'bad' it is: although all hate speech is bad, some examples can be *worse* than others.

4. If participants are not familiar with the diamond ranking system, show them how this works (see the diagram and explanation in Tips for Facilitators). Explain that they will be given a number of examples of online posts against gay people and should try to rank these from 'least bad' to 'worst'. The 'worst' examples should be those that participants would most like to be completely absent from a future Internet.
5. Divide participants into groups and give each group a copy of the cards.
6. Tell them they have 20 minutes to discuss the cards and try to agree about how they should be ranked. After 20 minutes, invite participants to look at the 'diamonds' of other groups. Then invite them back to the group for the debriefing.

DEBRIEFING

QUESTIONS ABOUT THE ACTIVITY:

- How did you find the activity? Was it easy to assess the different examples?
- Were there any strong disagreements in your group, or have you noticed any significant differences between your diamond and that of other groups?
- Did you use any criteria in deciding which cases were 'worse'? For example, did you consider who was making the statement or the number of people likely to see it?

QUESTIONS ABOUT HOW HATE SPEECH ONLINE SHOULD BE ADDRESSED:

- Do you think statements like these should be allowed on the Internet? What are the arguments for and against?
- Do you think there should be different rules for 'worse' expressions of hate? Should any be banned completely?
- If you think some should be banned, where would you draw the line?
- What other methods can you think of for addressing hate speech online?
- How would you react if you found these kinds of examples of hate speech online?

QUESTIONS ABOUT HOMOPHOBIA

- Why are homosexuals a common target of hate speech? Can you think of ways of addressing the prejudice?
- Do you think it is fair to treat anyone like this, whatever your personal views may be?

TIPS FOR FACILITATORS

- You will need to be aware of any strong anti-gay feeling in the group as well as of any participants who might be upset by the activity (or by other participants). If you think there is a risk of this, try running the activity 'Checking the facts' in this manual first, or look at some of the activities in Gender Matters or in Education Pack (www.coe.int/compass).
- You can find more information about the Campaign against hate speech online in Chapter 2, or on

the campaign website (www.nohatespeechmovement.org). Background information on Hate Speech Online can be found in Chapter 5.

- You can find more information about human rights online in the *Guide to Human Rights for Internet Users*. Specifically the part 'Access and non-discrimination' gives more detailed information about the right to a discrimination-free Internet.
- The diamond ranking system is a method used to compare different cases according to 'best' and 'worst' (or least bad, and worst). Cards should be arranged as in the diagram below, according to the following scheme:
  - The least bad example should be placed at the bottom of the diagram (position 1) and the worst example should be placed at the top (position 5 in the first diagram, position 6 in the second). Remaining cards should be placed in the other rows with cards in a higher row worse than those in the row below (cards in row 4 are worse than those in row 3).

A normal diamond (using 9 cards)

A 'fat' diamond (using 12 cards)

- The information on Hate Speech Online in Chapter 5 contains some 'criteria' for assessing cases of hate speech. These include the following:
  - The **content** or **tone** of the expression: this covers the type of language used
  - The **intent** of the person making the statement, in other words, whether they meant to hurt someone
  - The **target audience**. This is less relevant to this activity as the target audience is the same (gays).
  - The **context** of the utterance. In this case this might include the fact that anti-gay legislation is being proposed (Card 6) or the fact that there is strong anti-gay feeling in the country.
  - The **impact**, in other words, what effect the statement might have on individuals or on society as a whole.
- You may also want to provide some information about freedom of expression when discussing what should be done about the examples. You can find more background material in Chapter 5. You can also find more background information from the *Guide to Human Rights for Internet Users*, specifically in the section on 'Freedom of expression and information'.

VARIATIONS

The ranking could be done in a straight line instead of as a diamond – in other words, only one card is allowed in each 'row'. This is slightly harder and may take more time.

You can use all 12 cards but this will need more time, and the diamond will be a bit mis-shapen! Alternatively, you can select 9 cards, removing those you think are least appropriate or useful for your group. The two diagrams above show how the diamond ranking works for either selection.

IDEAS FOR ACTION

In discussing methods of addressing hate speech online, you could show participants the site 'Wipe out homophobia on facebook' (https://en-gb.facebook.com/WOH247), which uses humour to respond to hate speech. This site has has built a strong solidarity movement for gays online.

Join the No Hate Speech Movement to report any examples of hate speech online. You can use Hate Speech Watch for this, www.nohatespeechmovement.org .

HANDOUTS

1. Said in a private email to a friend - as a 'joke'.

We should just wipe out gays!

2. Petition posted on a Facebook page with over 1,000 'friends'

Ban gays from public life. Sign here to tell our politicians

3. Comment on a neo-Nazi site, voted up by 576 people

Hitler was right to send gays to the gas chamber

4. Refrain in an anti-gay song. The online video has had 25,000 views.

Wipe out gays!

5. An online newspaper editorial complaining about a decision of the European Court

It's a sick society that regards it as 'natural' to be homosexual

6. An interview with the Home Secretary talking about a proposal for new legislation

We need to concentrate on curing gays, not tolerating them

7. Comment at the bottom of an article by a journalist known to be homosexual

F* you and f*** your mother. You're a sick b********

8. Caption to an image of a celebrity known to be gay; on a personal blog with few readers.

Gay or retarded? Most gay people are retarded

9. Popular website 'outing' gays; accompanied by a photo and the name of the school.

This person is GAY. And he's been teaching children! Complain here

10. Anti-gay video suggesting being gay is more dangerous than smoking (because of AIDS)

You'll die earlier

11. Tweet sent by a politician to 350,000 followers

No gays from my old school have been successful in life

12. Cartoon showing a stereotypical 'gay' with horns and a tail

Homosexuals are possessed by demons

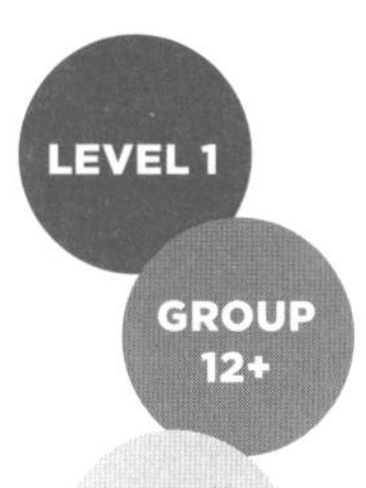

TALKING IT OUT

The activity uses a 'fishbowl discussion' to explore common prejudices about particular groups in society, and engages participants to think critically about commonly held beliefs and develop arguments against hate speech.

THEMES	Campaigning Strategies, Racism and Discrimination, Internet Literacy
COMPLEXITY	Level 1
GROUP SIZE	12 upwards
TIME	45 minutes
OBJECTIVES	• To reflect on personal prejudices and negative stereotypes towards certain groups • To develop arguments and explore responses to expressions of hate online • To fill gaps in understanding and develop empathy towards groups often misunderstood by society
MATERIALS	• 3 chairs • Space for participants to sit in a circle and move around • Small slips of paper and pens • A hat (or small container)
PREPARATION	• Cut up a number of small pieces of paper – about 2 for everyone in the group (with a few in reserve). • Be aware of any representatives in the group who may fall into a common 'target group'. If you think there may be difficulties, take individuals aside beforehand and explain the activity to them. Let them know that they can be a useful resource for the group, and make sure they do not feel uneasy about the activity. • It may be useful to prepare a few responses to some of the common concerns or misconceptions the group are likely to raise.

INSTRUCTIONS

OPTIONAL STARTER

1. Put the following made-up statements, with the heading 'True Facts', on a flipchart / slide so that all participants can read them. You can also make up and add some of your own.

True Facts:

- If all immigrants went back to their own country, there would be enough jobs for everyone.
- Girls are less good at online games than boys.
- Scientific studies have shown that Europeans have smaller brains than Asians.
- Being gay is a disability which can be cured.

2. Ask for participants' reactions. After a few responses, tell them that these statements are completely made up! Each statement is actually false. Ask for reactions again, and explore briefly why participants believed these statements (if they did!).
3. Ask participants whether they have ever read anything online and either known it was untrue, or wondered if it might be untrue. Did they do anything about it?

MAIN ACTIVITY

4. Explain that a lot of hate speech and many racist attitudes are driven by ignorance. People believe or they are made to believe things about groups of other people that they may never have met! Or they believe things about whole communities on the basis of information about just 1 person! When these beliefs are discussed widely, and go unchallenged, they start to be accepted as 'fact'. We can forget where we heard something, and forget that it may have been false, or just someone else's opinion, and start believing it ourselves.
5. Tell participants that everyone on the Internet can play an important role in questioning 'facts' or opinions that they come across. Asking why – or explaining why not – is one of the most important things we can all do to stop the spread of false or malicious ideas. It is also the best way of arriving at reliable opinions for ourselves!
6. Explain that the activity will explore some of the negative 'facts' or opinions about certain groups which have become widely accepted today. Participants will try to develop arguments and 'debunk' common myths using the knowledge and expertise of the group. They should see this as an opportunity to gain a better understanding, and an opportunity to share their own knowledge / experience.
7. Hand out the pieces of paper, two for each participant, and put the remaining pieces in a general pile, explaining that they can take extra slips if needed. Ask participants to write down any negative opinions or statements of 'fact' which they have seen expressed about particular groups, and which they would like to discuss. Give a few examples:
   - People should live in their own countries and not move around the planet!
   - A woman's place is in the home: women should stop taking jobs away from men.
   - The Roma need to start living according to the customs of the country they're in.
8. Tell participants they don't have to believe in the statement themselves; they may just want to explore responses to commonly held 'beliefs'. The papers should not be signed, and should all be placed in a hat or other container when ready.
9. Place the three chairs in a semi-circle in front of the group. Only those sitting on one of the chairs will take part in the discussion; the rest of the group are observers.

10. Explain that you will begin by inviting three volunteers to join in a conversation. If at any point someone else would like to join then they may do so, but as there will only be 3 conversationalists at any one time, someone will have to change places with them. Anyone who wants to join the conversation should come forward and gently tap one of the 'conversationalists' on the shoulder. These two people exchange seats and the original conversationalist becomes an observer.
11. Encourage participants to come forward to express their own opinions, but also to express other opinions, which are not necessarily their own. In this way points of view that are controversial, 'politically incorrect', or unthinkable can be aired and the topic thoroughly discussed from many different perspectives. Offensive or hurtful comments directed at individuals in the group are not allowed.
12. Ask a volunteer to pick a question from the hat and start discussing it. Let the discussion run until participants have exhausted the topic and points are being repeated. Then ask for three volunteers to discuss another question and start another round of conversations under the same rules as before.
13. Discuss as many questions as you have time for. Allow a small amount of time at the end to 'wind down' after the discussion and reflect on the activity as a whole.

DEBRIEFING

Use the following questions to allow participants to reflect on whether the activity has altered their views, or given them arguments to counter examples of prejudice:

- Has anyone found out anything they didn't know before?
- Has anyone's opinion changed on a particular group or issue?
- Do you feel more able to engage in discussion with prejudicial views? Do you think you might do this, either online or offline? Why or why not?
- How could you engage in a similar discussion online? What would be similar? What would be different?
- What can one do when having doubts about a belief they are not sure about?

TIPS FOR FACILITATORS

- You will need to be very aware of different sensitivities or affiliations in the group, and should encourage participants to keep this in mind in their discussions.
- There may be a number of questions or statements that participants, or you, feel unable to address directly. Write these up on a flipchart and either look into them yourself, to feed back later, or allocate to participants to research and feed back.
- If the 3 conversationalists do not appear to be finding arguments against prejudicial statements, feel free to enter the conversation yourself. Avoid doing this too often: it might be worth stopping the conversation from time to time and asking if others in the group feel able to offer an alternative opinion.
- It is important to keep the discussion open, and for participants to feel free to express views which they may themselves hold, or which are viewed as controversial but are commonly expressed in the media or in society as a whole. At the same time, the conversation should not deteriorate into a series of unkind and unjustified repetition of negative stereotypes. Encourage participants to adopt an enquiring tone, and to phrase their comments in as sensitive a way as possible, even when they

express a negative opinion about certain groups. Provide them with a few formulations, if necessary, for example:
- "I have heard it said that ..."
- "Some people seem to think that ..."
- "Can you help me to understand ...?"
- "Why might this view be wrong?"

- Try to encourage everyone to enter the conversation at some point!

VARIATIONS

After gathering questions from participants, you may want to allow time for them to research some of the comments before engaging in the discussion. The questions / statements could be distributed and participants asked to prepare brief arguments to address the issue. The discussion would then take place against a better level of general awareness.

This activity can also be organised as a series of activities, for example choosing to look at prejudice affecting a specific group in society in each one of them. Each time you could prepare or ask a group of volunteers in the group to prepare information about the situation of that specific group in your country.

Participants can produce informative videos that provide alternative information by comparison to commonly held beliefs. Use the No hate Speech Movement website to share these video messages and inform other people as well about the reality.

IDEAS FOR ACTION

Participants could be encouraged to research issues which were not fully addressed in the discussion, and then feed back to the group.

They could begin drawing up a 'myth-busting' list. This could consist of some of the more common prejudices about particular targets of hate together with arguments, information or statistics which undermine these prejudices. The list could be posted to the No Hate Speech Movement website to help other online activists.

You could also start developing with the group a list of counter-arguments participants can use when they see prejudices or racist speech online. It is also important to discuss how they could present these arguments online, through humour, information or links sharing, and so.

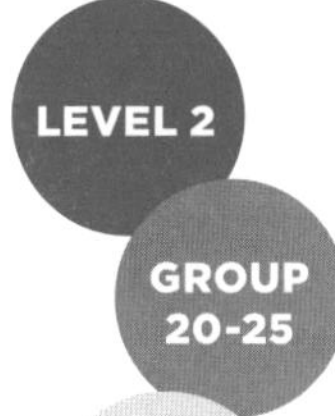

THE STORIES THEY TELL

Participants work in small groups to analyse a news publication, focussing on the portrayal of immigrants and immigration. Results are presented as a collage.

THEMES	Racism and Discrimination, Human Rights, Freedom of Expression
COMPLEXITY	Level 2
GROUP SIZE	20-25
TIME	60 minutes
OBJECTIVES	• To look at the way immigrants are represented by the printed media and discuss how this may affect society's attitudes towards them • To identify less obvious forms of racism, such as 'hidden' messages, selective reporting or the use of images and how they feed hate speech • To discuss / research 'positive' stories relating to immigrants and immigration
MATERIALS	• About 3 copies of 5 different newspapers / magazines (depending on group size) • Several sheets of flipchart paper • Marker pens, glue, scissors • Plenty of space for 4 or 5 groups to work at producing a large collage • Access to the Internet (optional)
PREPARATION	• Stick 4 sheets of flipchart paper together for each working group. • Provide each group with marker pens, glue, scissors, and copies of one of the selected news publications. • Make copies of the checklist on page 124 for each group.

INSTRUCTIONS

1. Ask participants what they understand by the following terms:
   Stereotype, racism, discrimination
2. Explain the terms briefly (refer to the background information on pages 166-170 if necessary), making it clear that:
   – Broad generalisations about groups of people ('stereotypes') are very rarely true of everyone!

- When such generalisations become commonly accepted, they are often used to justify discrimination, victimisation, abuse – and worse.
3. Ask whether participants can name any particular groups which are unfairly stereotyped, and are often the target of discriminatory practices, harassment or hate speech. Explain that the activity will look at the way the media commonly represents one such group, that of immigrants.
4. Show participants the publications you have selected and explain that they will be working in groups to analyse the way that immigrants are represented by the media. Tell them that they will need to think about whether the different publications represent immigrants …
   - in a generally positive light
   - in a generally negative light, or
   - in a neutral manner.
5. Go through the checklist (page 124) and make sure that participants understand what they will be looking out for when they conduct the analysis. Encourage them to include any other information they think may be relevant!
6. Divide participants into groups of 5 or 6 people and give each group 2 or 3 copies of the same newspaper, the large sheets of flipchart paper, and pens, glue, scissors, and so on. Explain that they are asked to use the checklist to identify any possible bias and should then present the results of their analysis in the form of a collage. They should cut up the newspapers, annotate them, and include their own images or text. Explain that all the collages will be displayed at the end of the activity.
7. When the groups have finished, display the posters and give everyone time to walk around and look at what each group has done. Then bring them back for the debriefing.

DEBRIEFING

- Ask participants for their general impressions about the activity: did they find it useful / surprising? What is their general impression about the way immigrants are represented by the media, and do they believe this representation is 'fair'?
- If groups did not address this in their collages, ask what kind of 'good news' stories might be included to provide an alternative view. Were there, for example, good news stories about 'non-immigrants'?
- Why do participants think that immigrants have become targets of discrimination, harassment and hate speech in countries across the globe? How much of a role do the media play in reinforcing negative stereotypes?
- Have participants come across similar biases or intolerant attitudes on websites they visit? Ask for examples.
- What is likely to be the impact on immigrants themselves, their families and children, and on society as a whole of a culture where they are "blamed" for many of society's problems? How does this reflect on hate speech targeted at immigrants?
- Is there anything young people can do to promote a more positive view of immigrants? Have they come across Internet sites and pages with positive news about immigrants?

TIPS FOR FACILITATORS

- Try to select newspapers or magazines which represent a good range of political / cultural views. It is probable that even those most sympathetic to immigrants will not be attempting to challenge or counterbalance strong negative feelings in society, for example, by reporting 'good news' about immigrant communities or individuals.
- It is likely that many in the group will share the negative attitudes apparent in the publications, and they may feel that such attitudes are justified. Encourage participants to voice their own opinions so that these can be addressed by the group. You may find it useful to research beforehand a few 'good news stories' that could have featured in the publications, or to look at some of the conditions in countries the immigrants have arrived from. Ask participants, for example, to imagine they were young people in Iraq or Afghanistan, where war has damaged much of the country.

VARIATIONS

Participants could also undertake an investigation of online news outlets instead of printed publications. It may be necessary to suggest particular pages, for example, the front page over a period of 5 days, in order to limit the amount of possible material. A similar approach could be used with television news.

IDEAS FOR ACTION

Help participants to set up a website or social media profile which demonstrates positive stories about immigrants. They could research some of the particular immigrant communities in their locality, looking at conditions in the native countries or regions, some of the reasons for migration, and some of the everyday stories about immigrants living in a new country. Send the website link to journalists at the newspapers which were part of the review, and tell them the site was inspired by the negative image portrayed in their publication!

You may consider, if you have access to the Internet, looking at the main news websites and running the exercise directly online. In this case, you can also raise the question related to the role of online forums linked with online articles, where users can make comments. Sometimes these comments can be of a racist nature. In this case, you can discuss with your group whether these forums should be acceptable, and under what conditions.

You can also make variations to the exercise, by changing the group it refers to, according to your context.

HANDOUTS

CHECKLIST FOR GROUPS

Are there any photos / images representing immigrants?

- Are any of them 'positive'?
- Are any 'negative'?

How many stories does the paper contain which relate to immigrants?

- Are there any 'good news' stories where immigrants are shown in a positive light?
- Are there any negative stories?

What words are used to describe (any) immigrants in your paper?

- Are these mostly positive, mostly negative or mostly neutral?

Are there any openly racist statements?

- If so, are these made by public figures, or are they the 'opinion' of the journalists?

What would you feel if you were an immigrant and reading this paper? Is there anything you might want to add or change?

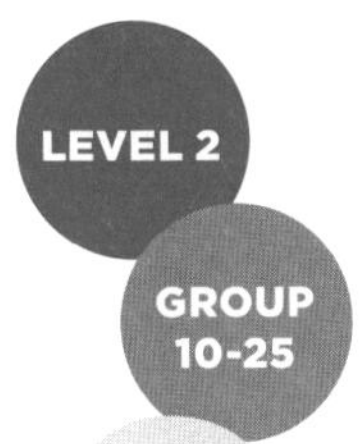

UNDERSTANDING HATE SPEECH

Participants look at examples of hate speech and discuss its possible consequences for individuals and society.

THEME	Human Rights, Racism and Discrimination
COMPLEXITY	Level 2
GROUP SIZE	10-25
TIME	60 minutes
OBJECTIVES	• To understand different forms of hate speech online and their consequences for victims and society • To explore possible responses to hate speech online
MATERIALS	• Photocopies of the examples of hate speech • Papers and pens • Flipchart paper
PREPARATION	• Make copies of the examples of hate speech. • Prepare two flipchart papers, with the titles 'Consequences for victims' and 'Consequences for society'.

INSTRUCTIONS

1. Ask participants what they understand by hate speech online. Ask whether anyone has ever seen hate speech online, either directed towards an individual or towards representatives of particular groups (for example, gays, blacks, Muslims, Jews, women, etc.) What do participants feel when they come across it? How do they think the victims must feel?
   Explain that the term 'hate speech' is used to cover a wide range of content:
   - Firstly, it covers more than 'speech' in the common sense and can be used in relation to other forms of communication such as videos, images, music, and so on.
   - Secondly, the term can be used to describe very abusive and even threatening behaviour, as well as comments which are 'merely' offensive.
2. Explain to participants that they will analyse some real examples of hate speech online, looking particularly at the impact on the victims themselves and on society.

3. Divide participants into groups and give each group one example of hate speech online from the case studies (pages 127-130).
4. Ask them to discuss their case and answer the questions. Tell them they have 15 minutes for the task.

DEBRIEFING

Go through each of the examples asking for the groups' responses. Make a note of responses to the questions on a flipchart. If groups give similar answers, indicate this by underlining the first instance, or put a number next to it to indicate that more than one group arrived at the same answer. After all the groups have presented their results, review the two flipchart sheets, and use the following questions to reflect on the activity with the whole group:

- What did you think about the activity? What were your feelings about the example you analysed?
- What were the most common 'consequences' of hate speech listed by groups?
- Did the groups targeted by hate speech in the examples have anything in common?
- Were there any similarities in the consequences, regardless of the target group of hate speech?
- What might some of the consequences be if this behaviour spreads online, and no-one does anything to address the problem?
- What tools or methods can you think of for addressing hate speech online?
- What can we do if we come across examples like these online?

TIPS FOR FACILITATORS

- You can find more information about the Campaign against hate speech online in Chapter 2, or at the campaign website (www.nohatespeechmovement.org). Background information on hate speech online can be found in Chapter 5.
- You can also give participants more information about human rights online by using the *Guide to Human Rights for Internet Users*.

VARIATIONS

If time allows, participants can be asked to develop solidarity messages for the victims affected by hate speech in each of the examples.
You can use the case studies to look also at the links between hate speech and freedom of expression. In this case, you could discuss with participants the limitations (or lack of) that could be applied in every case.

IDEAS FOR ACTION

Invite participants to discover the No Hate Speech Movement and join the movement in order to show they are against hate speech online. They can use the campaign website to share statements regarding the consequences of hate speech and the importance to stand against it in solidarity with the victims.
If participants have encountered examples of hate speech online, report them to Hate Speech Watch on the campaign website and discuss these examples with other users. You can also browse together with

participants Hate Speech Watch and discuss the examples posted by other users. Participants could develop a 'Charter' against hate speech online for their school or youth centre. They could also organise a school day against hate speech and use the existing human rights celebrations to raise awareness about the problem. They could use 21 March, the International Day against Racism and Discrimination, to organise events against hate speech online.

HANDOUTS

EXAMPLE 1:

A young man displays a huge nationalist party flag on his social media profile and posts comments such as "Islam out of my country – Protect our people". He posts photos with the symbol of a crescent and star in a prohibition sign. He spreads this information through social media and his personal website.

- Who are the victims of hate speech in this example? What consequences does hate speech have on them?
- What consequences can this example of hate speech have on the people identifying with the communities where this happens, and society in general?

EXAMPLE 2:

A. writes a publication in which he not only demonstrates that the Holocaust "never happened", but also makes abusive and racist remarks about Jewish people. A. shares the publication on his personal blog and on several anti-Jewish websites. A. also includes the content on online wikis, presenting it as 'scientific information' about the Holocaust.

- Who are the victims of hate speech in this example? What consequences does hate speech have on them?
- What consequences can this example of hate speech have on the people identifying with the communities where this happens, and society in general?

HANDOUTS

EXAMPLE 3:

An article by a leading journalist in a newspaper close to the leading political party calls Roma people "animals" and calls for their elimination by any means. In the forum connected with the online version of the newspaper, many comments are made agreeing with the journalist's remarks. The newspaper fails to explain or apologise for the remarks. Other articles appear online which take the same position and use a similar tone, and an increasing number of people begin commenting in the forum.

- Who are the victims of hate speech in this example? What consequences does hate speech have on them?
- What consequences can this example of hate speech have on the people identifying with the communities where this happens, and society in general?

EXAMPLE 4:

An online campaign is organised suggesting that the economic crisis in the country is the fault of immigrants and refugees. Posts begin to circulate on social media platforms: photographs portraying refugees as aggressive, images with refugees in humiliating situations, and comments about how they steal jobs from local people. A great deal of misinformation spreads through social media sites, including false statistics showing that immigrants are violent and cause problems.

- Who are the victims of hate speech in this example? What consequences does hate speech have on them?
- What consequences can this example of hate speech have on the people identifying with the communities where this happens, and society in general?

EXAMPLE 5:

Abusive comments are posted on various news sites claiming that foreigners have no right to be in the country. Some of the comments call for violence against non-white foreigners.

- Who are the victims of hate speech in this example? What consequences does hate speech have on them?
- What consequences can this example of hate speech have on the people identifying with the communities where this happens, and society in general?

HANDOUTS

EXAMPLE 6:

Videos appear online suggesting that LGBT people are "deviant" and "sick" and should be kept away from society because they destroy the traditions and continuity of the nation. The videos make reference to 'scientific research' but the references are often misquoted or selective. Some of the videos show pictures of LGBT families with their children.

- Who are the victims of hate speech in this example? What consequences does hate speech have on them?
- What consequences can this example of hate speech have on the people identifying with the communities where this happens, and society in general?

EXAMPLE 7:

A football game is interrupted because of insults and chants by supporters against one of the players seen as "black". A video of the chanting and game being stopped goes online and is spread widely. Racist comments are echoed on several websites. When complaints are raised, a number of people supporting the comments claim they have been victims of censorship.

- Who are the victims of hate speech in this example? What consequences does hate speech have on them?
- What consequences can this example of hate speech have on the people identifying with the communities where this happens and society in general?

EXAMPLE 8:

An advertisement for blue jeans has been circulating on the Internet for some time. It shows a scene where a woman is surrounded by men. The scene has sexual implications but the overall impression given is one of sexual violence and rape. In one country, several organisations complain. The news about the case on the Internet attracts a lot of comments, many of them reinforcing the idea that women are things men can play with and be violent with.

- Who are the victims of hate speech in this example? What consequences does hate speech have on them?
- What consequences can this example of hate speech have on the people identifying with communities where this happens, and society in general?

HANDOUTS

EXAMPLE 9:

A politician accuses Muslims of being the main cause of crimes against girls. He appeals to 'common knowledge' and provides a few 'telling examples'. The video linked to the article attracts many comments, some of a racist and violent nature. The speech is quoted by other people who support the same view and is presented as a respectable and informed opinion.

- Who are the victims of hate speech in this example? What consequences does hate speech have on them?
- What consequences can this example of hate speech have on the people identifying with the communities where this happens, and society in general?

EXAMPLE 10:

Videos about violent conflicts in the past between two countries remain on a video channel online. Many comments are added, using racist language about people in one of the countries. The racism and abuse between representatives of the two communities continues over a long period.

- Who are the victims of hate speech in this example? What consequences does hate speech have on them?
- What consequences can this example of hate speech have on the people identifying with the communities where this happens, and society in general?

EXAMPLE 11:

Music with nationalist content is spread through an online music channel. Some songs are posted by members of two ethnic communities which had a violent conflict in the past. The songs often encourage violence against people of the other ethnic group.

- Who are the victims of hate speech in this example? What consequences does hate speech have on them?
- What consequences can this example of hate speech have on the people identifying with the communities where this happens, and society in general?

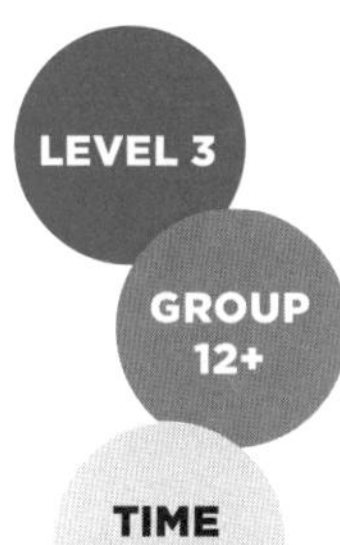

VIRTUAL ACTION

This is an activity during which participants will be inspired by some anti-racism actions and reflect together on how they could develop similar actions online.

THEMES	Campaigning Strategies, Racism and Discrimination, Human Rights
COMPLEXITY	Level 3
GROUP SIZE	12 upwards
TIME	60 minutes
OBJECTIVES	• To understand the role of the Internet as a space for young people to act for respect and freedom • To be aware of the limits of the Internet and its links with offline spaces in the mobilisation of young people for human rights values and principles
MATERIALS	• Paper and pens • Access to the Internet (optional)
PREPARATION	• Visit the websites of the organisations carrying out the initiatives participants will look at during the activity to familiarise yourself with anti-racist youth work • Photocopy the handouts for the participants

INSTRUCTIONS

1. Ask participants if they know of any initiatives or actions where people have taken action against racism and other forms of discrimination. Discuss their examples briefly.
2. Tell participants that what they will be looking at some examples of anti-racist actions and will think about how these actions could be translated into online activities.
3. Divide participants into small groups (up to 5 participants per group) and give each group one of the case studies on the handouts. Ask them to read their case study and discuss the following questions:
   - What is the problem the project is tackling?
   - What is the aim of the project?
   - What methods does the project use to achieve their aim?
4. Give the groups about 10 minutes to discuss the questions. After 10 minutes, give them a new task: ask them to discuss how they could address a similar issue using the Internet rather than working offline. Ask them to think of the kind of actions which could be taken online which would mirror the offline

activities described in the case studies. They need to address the following questions:
   - What online methods could they use to achieve their aim?
   - What are the limits of using the Internet to achieve their results?
5. Give participants about 20 minutes for the task and then invite them to share their ideas with other groups in plenary.

DEBRIEFING

Use the debriefing to review the results of the working groups with participants and to reflect on the advantages and disadvantages of using the Internet to address racism and discrimination. Use some of the following questions:

- Do you think the suggestions of the groups could be implemented successfully?
- Do you think they would help in achieving the aim?
- What are the advantages of using the Internet as a campaigning tool?
- What are the disadvantages or limits of online campaigning?
- Are you aware of other online tools or initiatives which could support campaigns like the ones in the case studies?
- Are you aware of any online campaigns against racism and discrimination?
- How could you use the Internet to campaign against racism and discrimination?

TIPS FOR FACILITATORS

- If participants have a very basic understanding of hate speech and Racism and Discrimination, you could begin the activity by brainstorming these concepts.
- If participants have difficulties in imagining these initiatives online, provide them with a few examples about how the Internet can be used for taking action.
- You can find more information about campaigning strategies and online participation in the manual's background information, chapters 5.6 and 5.7. You can also find the Ladder of Participation on page 86.
- You can also familiarise yourself with the *Guide to Human Rights for Internet Users*, and specifically the section 'Assembly, association and participation'.

VARIATIONS

You could adapt the case examples to reflect your local or national reality and could choose other examples of action which may be more suitable for your group. Remember to select a variety of initiatives so that participants see that there are many ways of taking action.
You could also perform the activity in reverse: online actions could be selected for the groups to consider. The task would then be to transform them into offline activities.

IDEAS FOR ACTION

Make contact with local organisations carrying out anti-racist work and invite them to talk to participants about what they do and how they work.

Discuss with participants whether any of the ideas they came up with could be put into practice and encourage them to do this! You could also set up a blog for your group and invite them to post information about groups often targeted by racism in order to correct commonly held prejudices, as well as to raise awareness of their harmful effects.

Encourage the group to join the No Hate Speech Movement in order to show solidarity with the victims of hate speech online! This can be done at the campaign website: www.nohatespeechmovement.org. Participants can submit examples of hate speech and share examples of good practice with other activists from different countries.

HANDOUTS

EXAMPLE 1. RACISM IN SPORT

"It was nightmarish. Before I went, I couldn't imagine that I would be that emotionally affected"

A 22-year-old football fan

German football fans regularly chant antisemitic slogans and songs during football matches. The initiative Dem Ball Ist Egal Wer Ihn Tritt (The ball doesn't care about who kicks it) aims to address this, and takes fans from various soccer clubs to visit to the former concentration camp of Auschwitz.

Why Auschwitz? The initiative was triggered by fans singing the song 'We're going to build an underground train from Mönchengladbach to Auschwitz'. The 'Auschwitz Song' has now established itself nationwide and can be heard in all soccer stadiums and in clubs across the country.

The organisation started a pilot project where fans from 18 to 28 from various clubs took part in a three-day trip to the death camps in order to trigger a deep discussion about antisemitism and racism in soccer. Fans were strongly affected by the experience and many went on to share their impressions with larger audiences. Flyers were produced to go on club websites and the initiative was accompanied by a broad media campaign.

(Inspired by the initiative of the Amadeu Antonio Organisation)

www.amadeu-antonio-stiftung.de/eng/we-are-active/topics/against-anti-semitism/football

EXAMPLE 2. PAINTING OUT RACIST GRAFFITI

The anti-racist organisation 'Never Again', based in Krakow, has organised local actions against hate graffiti under the campaign motto, Let's Paint The Walls Of Krakow! Over the course of a year, Never Again worked with local partner organisations to involve as many activists and citizens as possible:

- Young people gathered to remove and paint over racist stickers and graffiti.
- Home owners were invited to engage in white washing actions.
- Anti-racist graffiti was sprayed inside schools with the help of teachers and pupils.
- Journalists were invited to report on the campaign and published articles in local newspapers and magazines.

In this way, many single activities became one big action and managed to spread a powerful message: "Make Krakow free of hate graffiti".

www.unitedagainstracism.org/pages/thema05.htm, www.nigdywiecej.org

HANDOUTS

EXAMPLE 3. LIVING LIBRARY

The Living Library is an idea developed by the Council of Europe which seeks to challenge prejudice and discrimination. A living library works just like a normal library: visitors can browse the catalogue for the available titles, choose the Book they want to read, and borrow it for a limited period of time. After reading, they return the Book to the library so other people can read it. If they want, they can then borrow another. The only difference is that in the Living Library, 'books' are people, and reading consists of a conversation with a 'book'.

The Living Library attempts to challenge prejudice by facilitating a conversation between two people: Books and Readers. Books are volunteers who have either been subjected to discrimination themselves or they represent groups or individuals within society who are at risk of suffering from abuse, stigma, prejudice or discrimination. 'Books' often have personal experiences of discrimination or social exclusion that they are willing to share with Readers. Most importantly, Books give Readers permission to enter into dialogue with them, in the hope that their perspectives and experiences will challenge commonly held perceptions and stereotypes and therefore affect the attitudes and behaviours of wider society.

Don't Judge a Book by its Cover, available at http://eycb.coe.int

EXAMPLE 4. LOVE MUSIC HATE RACISM

"Our music is living testimony to the fact that cultures can and do mix."

Love Music Hate Racism (LMHR) aims to create a national movement against racism and fascism through music. It was set up in 2002 in response to rising levels of racism and electoral successes for the extreme right wing party, the British National Party (BNP). The organisation uses the energy of the music scene to celebrate diversity and involve people in anti-racist and anti-fascist activity as well as to urge people to vote against fascist candidates in elections.

There have been many hundreds of LMHR events, from large outdoor festivals to local gigs and club nights. Top artists have performed at LMHR events, including Ms Dynamite, Hard-Fi, Babyshambles, Akala, Get Cape Wear Cape Fly, Estelle, The View, Lethal Bizzle, Roll Deep and Basement Jaxx. Many up-and-coming bands, DJs and MCs have also performed or organised their own local LMHR nights.

http://lovemusichateracism.com/about

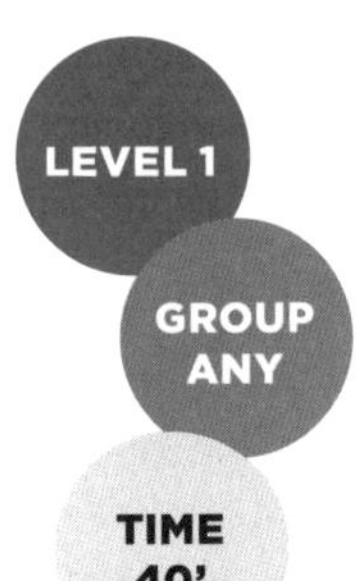

WEAR AND SHARE

Participants fill out a diagram to show their preferences in sharing particular information online and discuss ways of being more cautious when sharing personal information online.

THEMES	Private Life and Safety, Internet Literacy, Cyberbullying
COMPLEXITY	Level 1
GROUP SIZE	Any
TIME	40 minutes
OBJECTIVES	• To consider different online 'relationships' • To arrive at personal 'benchmarks' for online sharing and communication • To raise awareness of privacy concerns online, and learn about precautions we can take to protect our privacy and human rights online
MATERIALS	• Copies of the diagram on page 137 • Flipchart and marker pens
PREPARATION	• Make enough copies of the diagram for every participant.

INSTRUCTIONS

1. Ask participants what precautions they take to protect their privacy with people they don't know, for example, in a shopping centre. Prompt with questions, if necessary:
   - Do you wear the same clothes as you wear on the beach?
   - Do you write your mobile phone number on your face?
   - Do you tell people your password for online activity?
2. Explain that these things can seem obvious in 'real' life, but we don't always take the same precautions online. Ask participants whether they believe they are as careful online as offline about protecting personal information. Explain that the activity will explore the kind of information we feel ready to share with different people online.
3. Put up a copy of the diagram on page 137 (or draw on the flipchart) and run through a few examples with participants to indicate how they should approach the task. Explain that responses should be individual because different people may have different things about themselves that they feel ready to share.
4. Give them about 15 minutes to complete the task, and then ask them to share their diagram with

two or three other people. Participants can either walk around, showing their diagram to others, or you may want to put them into small groups, depending on time / space and the size of the group.

5. After they have compared their diagrams with a few others, bring the group together for a general discussion.

DEBRIEFING

Begin by asking a few general questions:

- Was there any information you weren't prepared to share with anyone? Ask for reasons.
- Was there any information you were prepared to share with everyone? Explore any differences in opinion within the group.
- Did you notice any differences when you compared your diagram with other people's, and can you explain these differences?
- Why do you think it might be important to be cautious about sharing information about yourselves with strangers? What could some of the consequences be?
- Why do you think it might be important to be careful about sharing information about 'others'?
- Has anyone ever shared information about you which you did not want them to share? Could that be a violation of your human rights? Could that be used for hate speech online?

Close the activity by asking participants whether the activity has made them more aware of the way they interact online. Does anyone intend to make any changes? What could participants identify as some of the things to always take into account before sharing personal information online?

TIPS FOR FACILITATORS:

- There may not be a 'correct' answer for many of the connections in the diagram; this will partly depend on individual preferences. However, it is important to alert participants to some of the dangers of not taking precautions to protect privacy online. If they do not raise the issues themselves, you should warn them about the risks of cyberbullying and financial exploitation. A lack of attention to personal privacy and safety can greatly increase these risks. See Chapter 5 for more information on Cyberbullying and Private Life and Safety.
- In the debriefing, you may want to point out that protecting our privacy online is important partly for safety reasons and partly for reasons to do with personal integrity / dignity. We may not endanger ourselves (if we are lucky) by walking around half-naked or making silly / unkind comments about others; however, we may come to regret it later on! Content we post on the Internet is much more 'permanent' than things we do in the non-virtual world and we often are not able to remove it.
- The *Guide to Human Rights for Internet Users* gives more information about everyone's right to privacy and data protection.

VARIATIONS

Although the focus in the activity is on protecting our own privacy, you could also use it to explore issues around respecting the privacy of others. For example, you could ask whether participants ask permission before sharing information about other people, and why it might be important to do so. Use some of the information on Private Life and Safety in Chapter 5 to talk about the human rights aspects of this.

IDEAS FOR ACTION

Participants could keep a log of their 'sharing' over the course of a week: what sort of information did they share, and with how wide an audience? They would not need to provide exact details of content but could monitor the kind of things they made available to the groups identified on the diagram (parents, friends, teachers, etc). They could record the information they share about themselves and the information they share about others.

HANDOUTS

YOUR SHARING RELATIONSHIPS:
WHO WOULD YOU TELL?

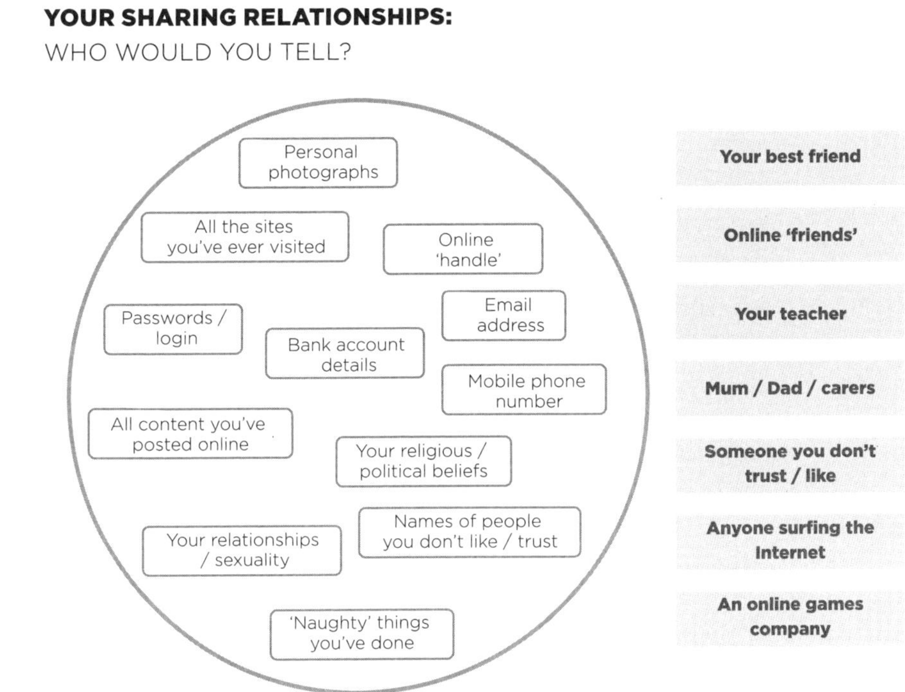

Connect each textbox in the circle to the textboxes on the right side, using arrows.

Example:

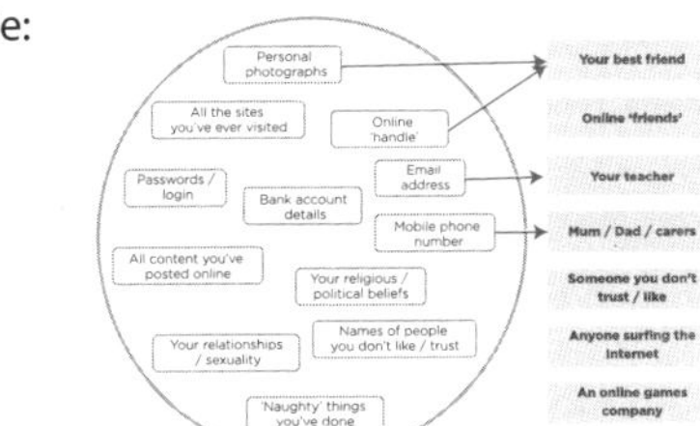

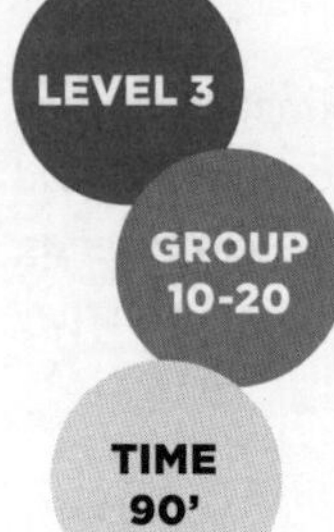

WEB ATTACK

Participants redesign a (fictional) campaign website to cope with a flood of racist comments from the local community.

THEMES	Internet Literacy, Campaigning Strategies, Racism and Discrimination
COMPLEXITY	Level 3
GROUP SIZE	10-20
TIME	90 minutes
OBJECTIVES	• To consider key messages for addressing racism • To explore ways of campaigning against racism and hate speech online • To develop skills of presentation, persuasion and online communication
MATERIALS	• Flipchart paper and coloured pens / markers • Access to the Internet (optional)
PREPARATION	• Photocopy the handouts (pages 140-141). • Ask participants to identify some of their 'best' and 'worst' websites before the activity (optional).

INSTRUCTIONS

1. Explain that the activity will involve redesigning the website for a school campaign. Give participants the following background information:

> Your school is based in an area with a large immigrant community. The school is proud of its efforts to create good ethnic relations and there are few instances of racism among pupils. However, relations outside the school grounds continue to be very troubled. Ethnic minorities are often the victims of abuse and violence from the majority 'white' population and neo-Nazi groups have been on the rise.
> The school's management decided to try to address this problem by launching an Internet campaign to raise awareness about why it is important to include everyone in the community. A quick website was set up with a forum for comments and questions from the public. However, people were not asked to register on the forum and it was quickly flooded by racist comments.

2. Show participants the 'campaign page' and ask them what they think of it. Prompt with a few questions:
   - Is the campaign message clear?
   - What do you think about the general layout and the way the information is presented?

- Is it a good campaign page? Why, or why not?

3. Explain that the activity will involve redesigning the website, and rethinking the online forum policy, if necessary. Hand out the task sheet (page 140) and divide participants into groups (maximum 6 people in each group).
4. Give the groups about 20 minutes to discuss the questions, and then give each group a piece of flipchart paper and some coloured pens.
5. After 20 minutes, hand out a piece of flipchart paper and coloured pens to each group. Tell them they have a further 15 minutes to produce a mock-up of their front page. Suggest that they divide up the different tasks and allocate some members of the group to work on content, and others to work on design (see Tips for Facilitators).
6. When the groups have finished, display the 'websites' around the room and bring participants back together for the debriefing.

DEBRIEFING

- How easy did you find the task? What was most difficult, and what went well within your group?
- Were you happy with your finished product?
- How much did you consider your target audience when designing the website: did you do anything to appeal to this particular group? (For example, adopting a specific writing style?)
- Did you find anything that visitors to the website could do to engage with the campaign or interact with the website? How important do you think this is?
- Compare the different forum policies among the groups. Ask them why they chose the policy they did. What were the most important considerations?
- Do you think racism is a problem in your community? (Ask for reasons)
- Have you ever come across racist abuse on the Internet? Would you do anything if you did come across it?

TIPS FOR FACILITATORS

- Try to record participants' views on what they think is lacking in the school's 'campaign page'. You could write the points on a piece of flipchart paper, with a line drawn down the middle: 'pluses' could be recorded on one half of the page, 'minuses' on the other.
- If there are differences of opinion, make sure that these are also recorded: a website can appeal to some people and not to others. This may also be worth drawing out when they are thinking about their target audience and working on their own sites.
- The group work could benefit from more time. At the design stage, you could allow participants to use the Internet to look at 'real' sites. This will give them an idea of how much content they can fit on the page, and different ways of presenting information.
- When groups start working with the flipcharts, encourage them to divide up the tasks among members of the group. For example, some could work on improving the campaign message, some could work on proposing links to other sites (or pages), and some could work on the actual design. Remind them that content and style are at least as important as design!
- You can find more information and examples about campaigning strategies in Chapter 5.7.
- You can explore the No Hate Speech Movement youth campaign website at www.nohatespeechmovement.org for examples and ideas of online campaigning.

VARIATIONS

You could alter the campaign to address different targets of hate, for example, women, young disabled people, a religious minority, or Roma people.

If members of the group have good IT skills, the website design could be done either using a word processing programme or a free blogging service such as Wordpress or Blogger. This would demand more time.

Depending on how much time you have available, after this you could ask participants to name some of their favourite websites, and some of their least favourite. This might bring out other points that they think are important in designing the campaign page.

The discussion on forum policy could be started in the whole group, if there is time available. You could draw up a list of the advantages and disadvantages of a policy which allows all comments and does not require registration.

You could use the No Hate Speech Movement campaign website and analyse it during the activity, as if your group were the group running this Campaign.

IDEAS FOR ACTION

After the debriefing, provide some information about the Council of Europe's No Hate Speech Movement and encourage participants to browse the website and sign up to the Campaign in their country.

The groups' website plans could be used as the basis for a real campaign website. The ideas would need pooling so that the final product was the work of the whole group and participants would have to work on producing content for the site. This could be a longer-term project and would require people competent to put the content online. They could also set up a group page on a social media site.

Participants could research the real state of ethnic relations in their own community. Local NGOs are a good place to start.

HANDOUTS

TASK SHEET

Discuss the following in your group:

1. Who is your main target audience? E.g. young people, all members of the local community, members of ethnic minorities, members of the 'white' majority, … the world?
2. What is the aim of your campaign, and how can people engage with it?
3. What is your policy on posting comments?

- Should people be required to register before posting a comment?
- What is your forum 'policy': can people post anything at all, or are certain comments unacceptable?

HANDOUTS

CAMPAIGN PAGE

Siddlefield High School

Campaign to further long-term inter-ethnic understanding and human rights

The Forum

You can say anything you like on this forum. We believe in free speech!

Top discussions:

• Do you like what we do?	7,345 post
• Clean up our schools (sign here)	3,231 posts
• Get your **** back home	3,123 posts
• Whites against mixed education	2,898 posts
• Congratulations, Siddlefield!	1,002 posts
• *** off. We didn't ask you to come here	976 posts
• How can you learn without a brain	535 posts
• Parents' petition against racism	812 posts

Click here to join the discussion!

Our blog

Siddlefield High School places great emphasis on intercultural understanding in a healthy learning environment. Read more

Siddlefield submits an interim report for the Commission for Racial Equality's latest Consultation on Affirmative Action in Places of Higher Education.
Read more

Other sections

- Statement from the Head Teacher
- Statement from the local authority
- Official documentation
- Economic indicators
- Statistics and evidence base

About the campaign

Our campaign is designed to further inter-ethnic understanding within the school and local community. We adopt a proactive approach to developing a positive learning environment for all pupils, irrespective of race, ethnic origin, religious affiliation or cultural identity. Read more

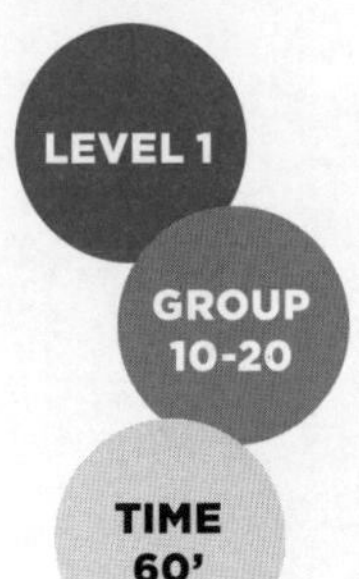

WEB PROFILES

The activity takes place in an imaginary Internet forum. Participants are asked to greet each other according to common stereotypes about particular groups. They use the activity to draw up a set of guidelines for interacting online.

THEMES	Racism and Discrimination, Internet Literacy, Democracy and Participation
COMPLEXITY	Level 1
GROUP SIZE	10-20
TIME	Part I: 35 minutes Part II: 25 minutes
OBJECTIVES	• To discuss prejudice and hate speech about certain groups • To consider the differences between online and offline interaction • To establish guidelines for interacting online
MATERIALS	• Sticky tape • Paper and pens (and clipboards, or something to rest the paper on) • Flipchart and markers • Space to move around
PREPARATION	• Make enough 'profiles' for everyone in the group (use those on page 146 or create your own). • Write each profile on a piece of paper (about A5 size) and prepare pieces of sticky tape to tape the papers to people's backs. • Photocopy the Council of Europe's definition of hate speech for each participant. • You will need enough space for participants to walk around.

INSTRUCTIONS

PART I. IN THE FORUM (15 MINUTES)

1. Ask participants to imagine they are in an Internet forum on football (or ice hockey or some other sport). Explain that everyone will be given a new 'profile' and they are to represent that person. However, no-one will know what is written on their own profile!

2. Tell participants that the activity will involve participants introducing themselves and greeting others. Discussions should be brief: participants should try to greet as many other visitors in the forum as they can in the time available.
3. Explain that the purpose of the activity is to explore common perceptions and prejudices about different groups in society. When meeting others, participants should think about the kind of things that people *might* say (online) to someone with their identity, for example, to a disabled person in a sports group, a black African, an older woman, and so on. People should not necessarily interact with others as they would in their real identity, but should think about the kind of opinions that exist online and try to represent these. Nasty comments are permitted: no-one will be held responsible afterwards for a comment they make in the course of the activity.
4. Stick an identity on the back of every participant without letting them see it. Give everyone a piece of paper and pencil to record the words used by others in relation to their identity.
5. Now, Invite them to move around the room. Allow about 10 minutes for meeting and greeting. Ask participants while they are moving around to note down some of the words that others use when greeting them. After 10 minutes, ask participants to stop, take off their given identity and proceed with the debriefing.

DEBRIEFING (20 MINUTES)

Make sure participants are out of role before debriefing the activity: begin by asking them all to give their real names, and say one thing about themselves. Then use some of the following questions.

- Was anyone able to guess any aspects of their profile? Ask them to give reasons and to list some of the words which were used to greet them.
- Did anyone enjoy the activity? Did anyone dislike it? Why?
- Invite participants to look at their own profile
- Was anyone surprised by any of the words used to greet them?
- Do you think the profiles were 'realistic'? Would people put this kind of information on a public profile?
- How easy was it to say nasty things to others? Was it easier to find nasty things for certain profiles?
- Do you think it would have been easier to say nasty things if you had been online, in other words, if the 'person' had not been before you? Why might this make a difference?

PART II. ESTABLISHING GUIDELINES (25 MINUTES)

1. Tell participants about the Council of Europe's Campaign against online hate speech, and give them the definition of hate speech below.

> Hate speech covers all forms of expression which spread, incite, promote or justify racial hatred, xenophobia, Antisemitism or other forms of hatred based on intolerance, including: intolerance expressed by aggressive nationalism and ethnocentrism, discrimination and hostility against minorities, migrants and people of immigrant origin.
>
> (Committee of Ministers, Council of Europe)

2. Ask for a few opinions on the following questions, and explain that these will be discussed further in groups:
   - Do you think that hate speech should be allowed online?
   - Why do people post hate speech about others?
   - What can *you* suggest as ways of monitoring your own posts, so that they are not offensive to others?
3. Explain that participants will work in small groups (4 – 5 people) to establish a set of guidelines for online activity. Give them about 10 minutes for this task, and then bring the groups together to look at the different suggestions.

DEBRIEFING

- Do you have any comments on the different proposals? Have people remembered things you may have forgotten?
- Do you think it would be possible to stick to your guidelines?

TIPS FOR FACILITATORS

- The choice of identities is important in this exercise: you may want to adapt the names or some of the profiles so that are more suitable for your group. Make sure, when you allocate profiles to people, that you do not give anyone a profile that is close to their real identity.
- You may want to tell people their names when you give them the profiles. Do not give them any other information, and prompt them not to ask others to tell them what is written on their label.
- When briefing participants for the forum, encourage them to mix a few positive or neutral greeting with some negative ones. Tell them that the comments must only be triggered by what is written on the profile, not by anything they know about the real person. It may be useful to give a few examples before starting the activity, for example:
  - "Hello, sporty!"
  - "Sorry, this is not for people like you!"
  - "You alien - what are you doing in here?"
- After the activity, make sure that no-one has been hurt or offended in their 'real' identity by anything said to them during the activity. It may be important to address some of the negative comments directly: for example, by asking anyone who used offensive greetings whether they really think this about the person.
- It may be useful to have some tables around the room in case participants find it difficult to write notes while moving around. Alternatively, you could have a number of observers who do not take part in the activity, but take notes on what people say (and people's reactions).
- When groups have developed their guidelines, these could be posted around the room so that others can walk around and look at them.

VARIATIONS

The activity could be carried out as a writing activity. You would need to make 3 or 4 copies of the profiles on page 146 and cut them into cards. After giving people their own profile (on their back), hand them 3 or 4 random cards. They should write their greetings on the back of each card. The cards will then be given to the person with that profile.
This method may more closely mirror the relative anonymity that people have online, but will take slightly longer.

IDEAS FOR ACTION

Participants could work further on the guidelines and develop a single set for the group as a whole. You could return to the guidelines at a later date and ask how people have been managing to observe them. You can share the guidelines on the website of the No Hate Speech Movement. You can also discuss them online with other young people on the "Join the Discussion" page of the Campaign, www.nohatespeechmovement.org.
If you noticed strong prejudices against particular groups, you may want to address these through more targeted activities. Have a look at the *Education Pack* and *Compass* to identify activities that combat prejudice and discrimination. More information: www.coe.int/compass

HANDOUTS

Alla (F) **Age: 19** **Lesbian**	**Pierre (M)** **Age: 9** **Likes online gaming**	**Miguel (M)** **Age: 16** **National maths champion**
Stephen (M) **Age: 33** **Football coach**	**Hugo (M)** **Age: 21** **From Venezuela**	**Chris (M)** **Age: 43** **Traffic warden**
Dafne (F) **Age: 65** **Owns her own business**	**Amlin (M)** **Age: 27** **From Somalia**	**Sonia (F)** **Age: 33** **Unemployed**
Hanzi (M) **Age 23** **Roma**	**Slava (M)** **Age: 26** **Hairdresser**	**Lisa (F)** **Age: 30** **Cook**
Rebecca (F) **Age: 28** **Learning disabled**	**Johann (M)** **Age: 31** **Jehovah's Witness**	**Steffi (F)** **Age: 12** **Deaf**
Liana (F) **Age: 13** **Plays for school football team**	**Ricardo (M)** **Age: 72** **Gay**	**Sam (M)** **Age: 21** **Professional tennis player**
David (M) **Age: 26** **War veteran (disabled)**	**Leon (M)** **Age: 29** **Imam (Muslim "priest")**	**Joe (M)** **Age: 37** **Charity worker**

CHAPTER 5

BACKGROUND INFORMATION

5.1 HATE SPEECH ONLINE

(...) the term "hate speech" shall be understood as covering all forms of expression which spread, incite, promote or justify racial hatred, xenophobia, antisemitism or other forms of hatred based on intolerance, including: intolerance expressed by aggressive nationalism and ethnocentrism, discrimination and hostility against minorities, migrants and people of immigrant origin.

Council of Europe, Committee of Ministers, Recommendation No. (97) 20

DEFINING HATE SPEECH

Hate speech is rarely a black-and-white, yes-or-no concern. Opinions differ both over how it should be classified and over what we should do about it. Part of the reason for the difference of opinion is that these questions are seen by most people as related: if something is classed as hate speech, it seems to warrant some action. If it is not, we assume it is acceptable, or at least, that it should be tolerated. That means that the definition we use also seems to tell us when we should act.

Some people are reluctant to 'act' against hate speech because they see this as an unacceptable limit on freedom of expression. For that reason, they use the term 'hate speech' to refer only to the very worst instances, for example, when immediate threats are made to someone's life or security.

This manual is based on the Council of Europe's definition, which takes a much broader view of hate speech. The approach taken in these pages also agrees with the idea that 'something must be done' about anything which falls under that definition. However, it is important to remember that 'doing something' does not have to mean restricting speech, or banning it: there are many other ways we can respond! The background information on campaigning strategies deals with this question in more detail.

The last section of this chapter looks at ways of classifying and assessing instances of hate speech. Prior to that, however, is the question of why or whether online hate speech needs addressing. Some people believe that "the Internet will sort itself out" and that we should let speech roam free, at least in this realm!

The Council of Europe's definition of hate speech covers "all forms of expression", in other words, not only through speech, but also by means of images, videos, or any form of online activity. Cyberhate is therefore also hate speech.

WHY DOES HATE SPEECH ONLINE NEED ADDRESSING?

HATE SPEECH HURTS

Words hurt, and hate hurts! Hate speech is a serious problem and can constitute a violation of human rights. Hate speech online is no less serious than the offline form but is often more difficult to identify and challenge.

ATTITUDES FEED ACTIONS

Hate speech is dangerous not only because it is damaging in itself, but also because it can lead to more serious human rights violations, including physical violence. If unchecked, hate speech online feeds back into the offline world, inciting further racial tension and other forms of discrimination and abuse. The potential for hate to spread quickly in the virtual world increases its potential damage.

ONLINE HATE SPEECH CONSISTS OF MORE THAN MERELY 'WORDS'

The Internet allows us to communicate quickly, and in numerous ways, including for example through social media and online games, and very often also anonymously. Online hate can be expressed through videos and photographs, as well as in its more familiar 'text' form. The visual or multimedia forms can often have a greater impact on conscious and subconscious attitudes.

How many ways can people 'hate' online?
A song, a video, a tweet, a cartoon, a manipulated image…

HATE TARGETS BOTH INDIVIDUALS AND GROUPS

Online hate may be directed at groups, and the targets tend to be those groups which are already vulnerable in some way, such as asylum seekers, religious minorities, or those with disabilities. Individuals, however, are also increasingly becoming the targets of online hate. The impact is sometimes fatal, as in cyberbullying, which has led to suicides in a number of reported cases. Hate speech also threatens the safety and self-confidence of anyone identifying with the targets of hate speech.

Have you said things online you wouldn't say in person?
Might you do so if you thought you couldn't be identified?

THE INTERNET IS NOT EASILY MONITORED

Online hate speech is tolerated more than offline hate speech, and is less subject to control. It is also easier (and less risky) for 'haters' to be abusive online than offline, not least because people can often hide behind a mask of anonymity.

THE ROOTS OF ONLINE HATE SPEECH ARE DEEP

The attitudes and social tensions which give rise to online hate speech lie deep in society, and are generally the same as those which lead to hate speech offline. By addressing online hate, we are also working to reduce instances of offline hate.

THE INTERNET IS NOT AN ISLAND

Online activity is a huge, and growing, feature of modern society but it should not be seen as a realm where normal rules of human behaviour need not apply. People's virtual existence is strongly related to their 'real' existence. The two areas of our lives are not disconnected: the virtual world has simply become an important part of the 'real' world. Online hate speech often has consequences in everyday life: the people, the feelings, the experiences and the dynamics are the same, online and offline.

THE INTERNET IS STILL YOUNG!

Our understanding of the virtual world is in many ways less advanced than that of the non-virtual world; and so too, importantly, are the laws and regulations which relate to what is generally regarded as acceptable or unacceptable. Online activity needs to be viewed through the same prism of general values that guide us in our offline activity. It also needs to be subject to the same legislation: in particular, it needs to be regulated by existing human rights laws.

THE INTERNET *CAN* BE BETTER!

The Internet is no more, and no less, than what human beings make it. Just as in real society, if certain modes of behaviour become 'acceptable', that is, the norm, they are likely to prevail. We need a vision of what we would like the accepted modes of online behaviour to be. What's more, we need to work to make *those modes* accepted, rather than other modes. This means that we, as citizens and young people of all ages, also need to take an interest in how the Internet is governed, and why some things are allowed and others not.

Some forums or websites have their own 'culture'.

How can young people help to create their preferred 'Internet culture'?

THE MYTHS OF ANONYMITY AND IMPUNITY

Hate speech online is propagated and amplified by underestimating its devastating effects on people, and by two myths about online social interaction: impunity and anonymity. Anything done online can ultimately be traced to its author or agent; it depends how far law enforcement is willing to go. The impression, however, that one can post or re-post hate speech content without leaving a trail makes it easier to express hate speech than if the perpetrator knows that their name will be accessible to everyone.

Together with anonymity comes the feeling of impunity: the agents of hate speech may be aware that their actions are illegal, unfair or immoral, but they are convinced that nothing will happen to them. Impunity is also a myth, because hate speech can indeed give reasons for prosecution in many member states.

Both myths of anonymity and impunity need to be addressed and also demystified.

CLASSIFYING HATE SPEECH

BAD HATE, WORSE HATE

Any response to hate speech needs to recognise that 'hate' falls along a spectrum: although all expressions of hate may be bad to some extent, one case can still be *worse* than another, for example, it may be more offensive, it may affect larger numbers of people, be more inflammatory, potentially more damaging, and so on. Any attempt to respond to hate speech needs to take account of this, because differences in the degree of hate expressed will make a difference to our response. An appropriate response to hate speech will not be overly restrictive of freedom of expression, but it will acknowledge and attempt to address the damage it causes (or is likely to cause). The following list offers some useful things to consider when assessing individual instances.

THE CONTENT AND TONE OF THE EXPRESSION

Some expressions of hate are more extreme, use more abusive words, and perhaps even call for action by others. At the other end of the spectrum there are mild insults or broad generalisations which show particular groups or individuals in a bad light (and may be false).

You can find more information on freedom of expression, including its legitimate restriction, on page 160.

A *provisional* classification, based only on content and tone, might rank the following expressions from bad to worse:

Immigrants have, historically, had an evil influence.	Disabled people are scrounging off the state.	A nigger is not a human being, it's an animal.	You're a **** slut. I will rape you tomorrow.

Increasingly abusive or threatening

In practice, it is very difficult to isolate the content or tone from the general *context*. Consideration of other factors (below) might alter the way these statements are arranged, for example the impact of the comment about immigrants might be a great deal more damaging precisely because it uses more measured language.

THE INTENT OF THE PERSON RESPONSIBLE FOR THE EXPRESSION

People say things, particularly online, without properly weighing them up. We often cause offence without meaning to, and then regret it, and perhaps even retract our words. In the following two examples, both statements are intolerant and nasty, but one is said with the intention to hurt. At the very least, the two cases would require a different response.

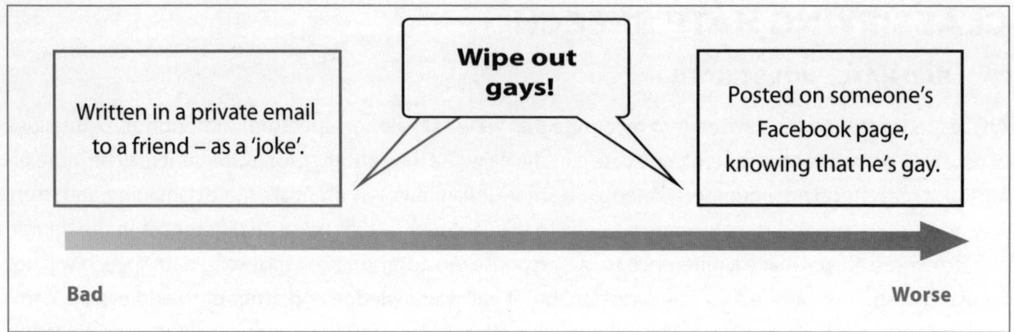

THE TARGETS OR POTENTIAL TARGETS

Some groups, or individuals, may be more vulnerable than others with respect to certain criticisms. That may be because of the way they are generally viewed by society, or the way they are represented by the media, or it may be because their own circumstances make them less able to defend themselves. A slur against Muslims, for example, is likely to be far more damaging in a country where the overwhelming majority is non-Muslim; Christians may feel more threatened where *they* are in the minority. Children are regarded as in need of particular attention and protection in almost every society.

The groups most commonly targeted by hate speech are identified in the definition given at the start of this section, but *anyone* might be a target of hate speech, even if they do not fall under one of the forms of intolerance listed.

The following example illustrates how the same expression applied to different groups may have a very different impact. The second is likely to be far more damaging.

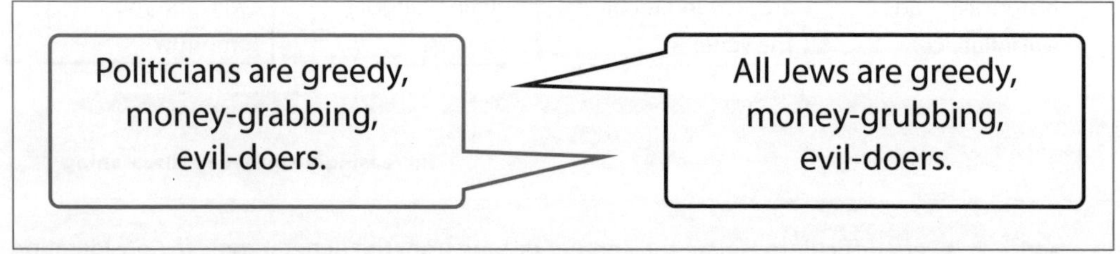

THE CONTEXT

The context of a particular expression covers the historical and cultural circumstances surrounding an expression of hate. It may also include other factors such as the medium and the likely target audience, existing tensions or prejudices, the 'authority' of the person responsible for the expression, and so on.

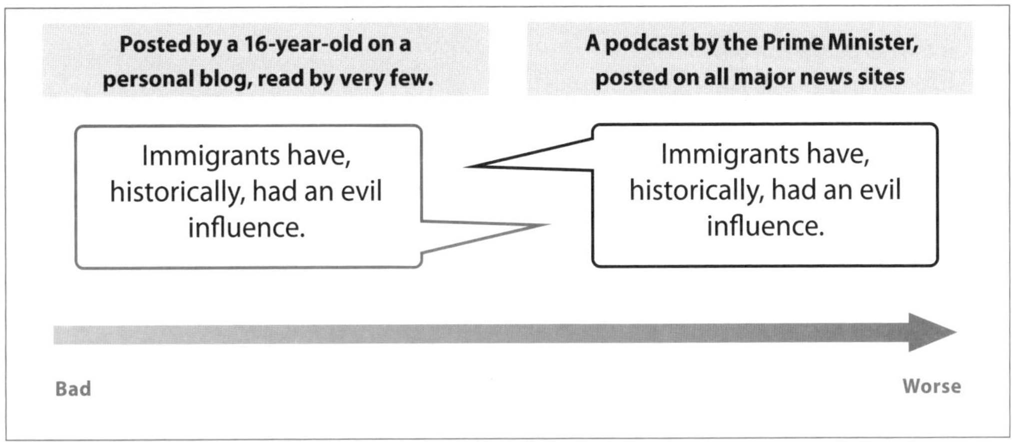

THE IMPACT OR POTENTIAL IMPACT

The actual or potential impact on individuals, groups, or society as a whole is one of the most important considerations in assessing an expression of hate, and in weighing up our response. How a person or group was in fact affected is often more important than how outsiders feel they *should* have been affected. For example, if a child is severely troubled by comments that others claim to be making in a 'friendly' way, the actual pain will probably be more important in simply allowing those others to 'express their opinions'.

HATE, CYBERHATE AND INTERNATIONAL LAW

Although the emphasis in this manual is not necessarily on using legal means, it is worth mentioning some of the legal prohibitions on hate speech which also apply in a virtual world.

> Further information on human rights and human rights law can be found in section 5.2 on Human Rights.

- Article 20 of the **International Covenant on Civil and Political Rights** states that "any advocacy of national, racial or religious hatred that constitutes incitement to discrimination, hostility or violence shall be prohibited by law".
- Article 4 of the **International Convention on the Elimination of All Forms of Racial Discrimination** declares all propaganda activities which promote and incite racial discrimination illegal.
- Article 10 of the **European Convention on Human Rights** protects freedom of expression, but allows for it to be limited "for the protection of the reputation or the rights of others", as well as for some other purposes. This article makes it possible for member states to ban certain instances of hate speech in their own countries.
- Article 17 of the Convention forbids any actions "aimed at the destruction of any of the rights and freedoms [contained in the Convention]". This article has also been used to legitimise government restrictions on some forms of hate speech.

> *Do you know which forms of hate speech are banned in your country?*

Another relevant international law instrument of the Council of Europe is the Convention on Cybercrime (also known as Budapest Convention, 2001). The Convention on Cybercrime of the Council of Europe is the only binding international instrument on this issue. It serves as a guideline for any country developing comprehensive national legislation against Cybercrime and as a framework for international co-operation between State Parties to this treaty.
The Additional Protocol to Convention on Cybercrime concerning the criminalisation of acts of a racist and xenophobic nature committed through computer systems (2003) is an optional protocol to be signed by States Parties to the convention. It defines 'racist and xenophobic material' as "written material, any image or any other representation of ideas or theories, which advocated, promotes or incites hatred, discrimination or violence, against any individual or group of individuals, based on race, colour, descent or national or ethnic origin, as well as religion if sued as a pretext for any of these factors". The protocol requires member states to take certain measures tending to prohibit and criminalise acts of racism and xenophobia. The Committee on Cybercrime gather together the representatives of the parties to the Convention for consultation on the implementation of the Convention in member states and support measures to be taken.

In 2014, the Committee of Ministers of the Council of Europe adopted the *Guide to Human Rights for Internet Users* (CM/Rec(2014)6). The Guide contains information about what rights and freedoms mean in practice in the context of the Internet, and how they can be relied and acted upon, as well as how remedies can be accessed. The guide provides an overview, for example, on how non-discrimination and freedom of expression apply online. In Chapter 5.2 you can find more information about human rights and human rights online. In Chapter 5.3 you can find more information about how freedom of expression applies on the Internet. Here is a link to the Guide www.coe.int/en/web/internet-users-rights/guide.

5.2 HUMAN RIGHTS

> All human beings are born free and equal in dignity and rights.
>
> *Article 1, Universal Declaration of Human Rights*

Human rights are relevant to hate speech in a number of ways. From a legal point of view, certain human rights may be engaged both by particular instances of hate speech and also by attempts to ban or limit it. From the point of view of attitudes or values, nearly all hate speech derives from attitudes which are racist or discriminatory, and both of these are human rights concerns. From the point of view of education, in its broadest sense, human rights offer one of the most effective frameworks for understanding and addressing online hate speech.

This section contains basic information about human rights principles, human rights law, and how human rights apply to hate speech online. Some of the specific rights which are most directly relevant to hate speech online are addressed in other sections.

WHAT ARE HUMAN RIGHTS?

Key facts

- Human rights are internationally agreed standards, based on a set of universal values which have been agreed by every government around the world.
- Human rights are based on the idea that all human beings are worthy of respect and that no-one should have to suffer to such a degree that they are made to feel *less than human*. All human beings are *equal* in this respect; their *dignity* should be treated as a fundamental value.
- Human rights have been embodied in *international law*, creating obligations for governments around the world. Governments have a duty to ensure that the basic needs of every individual are met, including the need for personal dignity.
- Human rights do not ensure a life of luxury, free from all harm or hurt. They provide a baseline, a set of *minimum standards* which define what is required for people to lead a life of dignity.
- Most human rights can be *restricted* under certain circumstances if this is necessary in order to protect the rights of others, or is necessary for society as a whole. Some human rights, for example, the right to life and the right to be free from inhuman and degrading treatment, can never be restricted.

HUMAN RIGHTS AND THE LAW

Human rights have been incorporated into various legal systems, creating obligations for governments at a number of levels. Key human rights instruments, together with some of the rights they cover, are shown in the diagram on the page 157.

HUMAN RIGHTS AT INTERNATIONAL LEVEL

The **United Nations (UN)** has developed a number of human rights treaties which define government obligations with respect to individuals. The most important are:

- The **UN Declaration of Human Rights** (UDHR). The UDHR was drawn up in 1948, immediately after the Second World War. It has been accepted by every government around the world and sets out the basic rights and fundamental principles to be found in every successive human rights treaty.
- The **International Covenant on Civil and Political Rights** (ICCPR) was adopted by the UN General Assembly in 1966. It expands many of the rights set out in the UDHR, as illustrated by the diagram on page 157.
- The **International Covenant on Economic, Social and Cultural Rights** (ICESCR) was adopted by General Assembly at the same time as the ICCPR. It covers the remaining rights in the UDHR.

All European governments have agreed to respect, protect and fulfil the rights contained in the International Bill of Rights. They have also signed up to various other international human rights treaties, including the UN Convention on the Rights of the Child.

AT REGIONAL LEVEL

The European human rights framework was created, and is monitored, by the Council of Europe, and to a lesser extent, by the European Union.

The two key treaties at European level divide the rights in the UDHR in a similar way to the two International Covenants mentioned above, although these treaties of the Council of Europe were adopted earlier.

- The **European Convention on Human Rights** was adopted in 1953 and contains nearly the same rights as those in the ICCPR. The **European Court of Human Rights** was established in 1959 to oversee Council of Europe member states' observance of the Convention.
- The **European Social Charter** was adopted in 1961 and contains almost identical rights to those found in the ICESCR. These rights are monitored by the European Committee of Social Rights which considers reports submitted by the government (and sometimes other actors, such as trade unions and other NGOs).

AT NATIONAL LEVEL

Many countries also have human rights protections built into their own national legislation. Where this is the case, potential human rights violations can be heard in national courts.

WHICH RIGHTS DO WE HAVE?

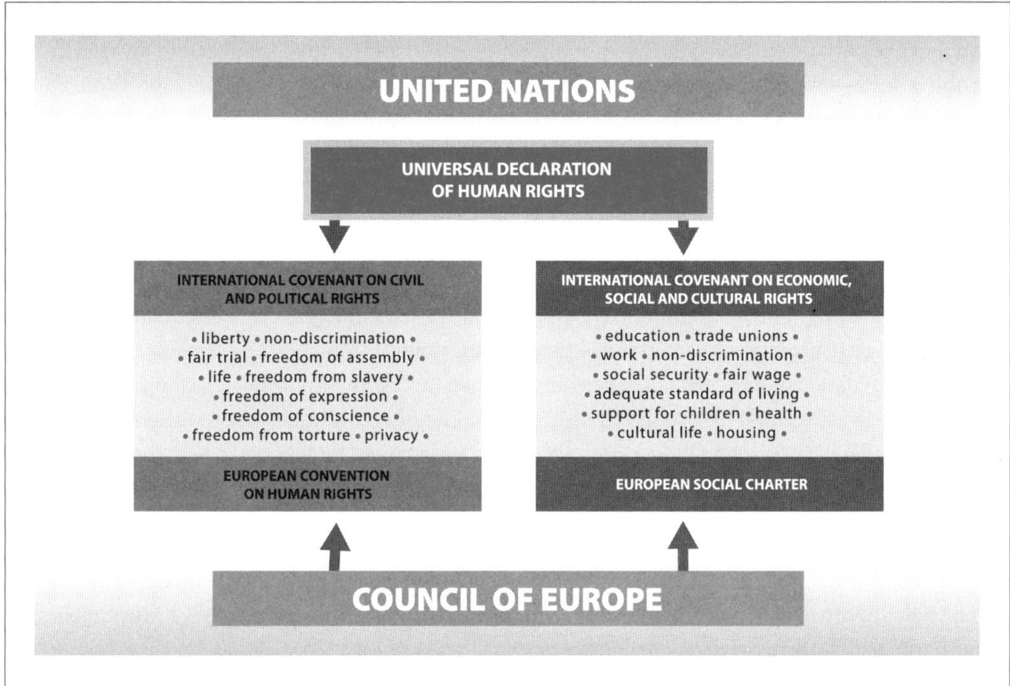

HUMAN RIGHTS AND HATE SPEECH

Human rights are relevant to hate speech at a number of different levels:

UNDERLYING CAUSES

Hate speech is driven by negative stereotypes which see some groups, or individuals, as inferior, different, and less worthy of respect. Human rights view human beings as *equal* in terms of human rights, and equally worthy of respect. Non-discrimination is a fundamental principle. Developing respect for human rights is a way of ensuring that the attitudes which drive hate speech are not allowed to flourish.

IMMEDIATE IMPACT

The worst expressions of hate speech are themselves a form of discrimination, and an abuse of human rights. Hate speech alienates, marginalises, and undermines personal dignity, often of those who are already vulnerable in other ways. Where the target of hate speech is individualised, for example in instances of cyberbullying, hate speech may also infringe the right to private life and can even constitute inhuman and degrading treatment. However, hate speech also undermines the confidence, dignity and security of *anyone* identified with the groups targeted by hate speech.

THE CONSEQUENCES OF HATE SPEECH

If hate speech is unchallenged, it drives human rights abuses further: negative stereotypes are disseminated throughout society, groups become increasingly marginalised and isolated, conflict and division grows, and abuse or threats increase as new boundaries are tested. In the worst cases, mere 'expression' begins to translate into physical abuse. Hate speech can lead to hate crime, engaging human rights relating to personal safety and security. Hate crimes, including genocide, are always accompanied by hate speech. Not all hate speech results in hate crimes, but hate crimes always involve hate speech.

FREEDOM OF EXPRESSION?

Actions taken to combat hate speech may also engage certain human rights, because freedom of expression is a fundamental human right, and so is the right to freedom of thought, conscience or religion. Those who are accused of promoting 'hate' often appeal to *these* rights.

A proper understanding of human rights can help in resolving this apparent conflict. One of the key challenges in working to combat hate speech is being able to identify the best balance between allowing free expression, while still protecting other rights which may be engaged by its more violent forms.

USING HUMAN RIGHTS TO ADDRESS HATE SPEECH

Human rights education provides a powerful tool to address hate speech online by developing young people's knowledge, skills and attitudes to tackle hate speech from a human rights-based approach. A human rights approach helps not only with developing empathy and respect for others; it also encourages active participation and a sense of individual agency.

You can find more information on Human Rights in Chapter 4 of *Compass:* www.coe.int/compass

HUMAN RIGHTS AND THE INTERNET

KEY FACTS

- Human rights and their protection are always more important than rules and regulations set by private companies.
- While exercising human rights on the Internet, everyone should be protected from unlawful interference or harassment.
- Everyone whose rights and freedoms are violated on the Internet has the right to seek help and support.

The Internet is mostly "owned" and controlled by private companies. This makes the protection of human rights more complicated, because human rights are really 'rules for governments', not private companies. If a shopping mall or private nightclub wants to forbid people from wearing jeans, protesting, or distributing information about another company, all of which are forms of 'expression', you cannot plead freedom of expression and take them to the European Court of Human Rights! In the same way, private companies can mostly set the rules that people must abide by when using parts of the Internet owned by them. If people do not like the rules, they can complain, but the ultimate sanction is simply not to use the service.

However, this does not mean that those parts of the world which are owned by private companies, including the Internet, are not regulated by human rights laws! Human rights impose (at least) two different types of obligation on governments:

1. They set limits on what governments are *actively* allowed to do, for example, they are not allowed to ban all political dissent, engage in torture, or deprive someone of their liberty without proper reason.
2. They oblige governments to take positive action to ensure that rights are properly protected. This may mean passing laws which prohibit discrimination, making sure that violent acts are prosecuted (and punished), or ensuring that victims receive proper protection.

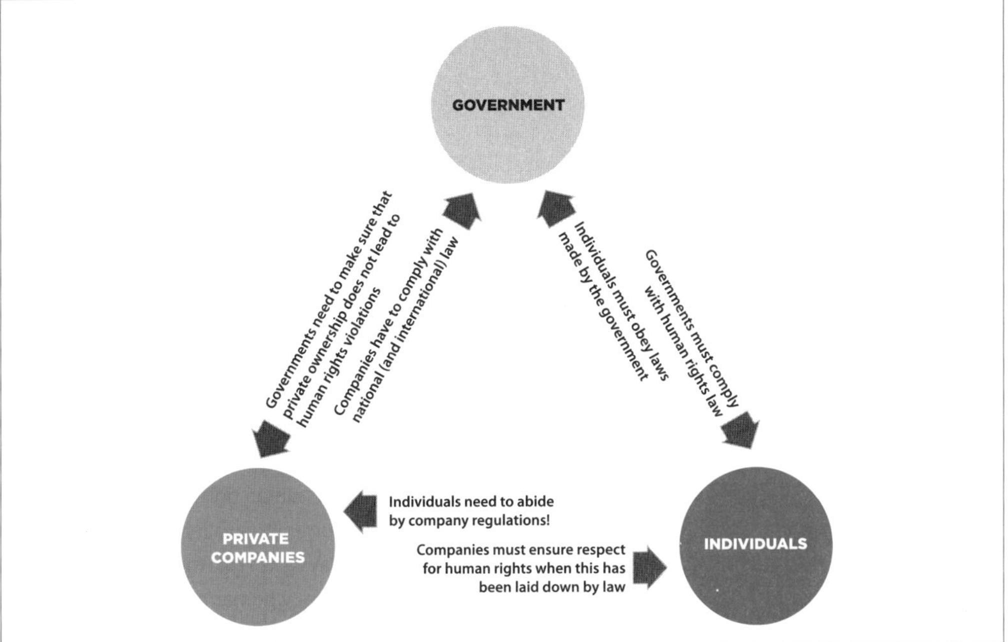

In other words, governments also have to ensure that 'private' spaces do not lead to human rights violations. There are an increasing number of judicial cases related to human rights violations on the Internet.
The European Court of Human Rights has affirmed in its judgments that States are obliged to protect the fundamental rights and freedoms of individuals on the Internet. Specifically freedom of expression, the protection of children and young people, the protection of morals and the rights of others should be protected through combating racism, xenophobia and other forms of discrimination.
Furthermore, the distinction between private and public space is blurred and merits discussion. Not all sites are privately owned, and even when they are, the question of public accountability remains relevant. Is a social network that brings together 500 million people a purely private enterprise?
The No Hate Speech Movement has been called for by youth representatives in the Council of Europe to claim the Internet as public space with interests that extend far beyond the interests of Internet businesses.

Remember: Just because there are relatively few 'laws' regulating expression on the Internet, that does not mean that individuals are encouraged to say and do whatever they like! The Internet will become whatever users of the Internet decide to make it, and young people should have as much possibility to influence this as anyone else!

5.3 FREEDOM OF EXPRESSION

Everyone has the right to freedom of opinion and expression; this right includes freedom to hold opinions without interference and to seek, receive and impart information and ideas through any media and regardless of frontiers.

Article 19, Universal Declaration of Human Rights

FREEDOM OF EXPRESSION AND HATE SPEECH

Freedom of expression is of fundamental importance in any work to protect human rights and address hate speech. Although all forms of abuse or hate are unpleasant, and many may be racist, any attempts to limit or eliminate expressions of hate must take into account the rights of both sides. This includes the rights of those expressing the 'hate'. This may seem strange, but respecting human rights is nearly always a question of balancing *different* claims to rights. However much we may dislike abusers, criminals, or even those who injure others through their words, there are human rights protections which apply to them as well.

Free speech, or the right to free expression, is regarded as a fundamental human right for two key reasons: firstly, because it is important to individuals, and secondly because it is important to society. Freedom of expression is one of those 'basic needs' essential to human dignity, and it also plays a key role in democratic society. Without freedom of expression, democracy cannot function; without democracy, human rights are unprotected.

> Freedom of expression "constitutes one of the essential foundations of [democratic society], one of the basic conditions for its progress and for the development of every man".
>
> *European Court of Human Rights: Case Handyside v. United Kingdom*

In everyday language, people generally refer to the right to 'free speech'. In fact, freedom of expression covers all forms of human expression, including the written word, visual images, drama, videos, music, and so on. It is therefore particularly relevant to online activity: everything online is an 'expression' and is potentially covered by this right.

WHY IS FREEDOM OF EXPRESSION IMPORTANT?

PART OF BEING HUMAN!

People's thoughts, opinions and beliefs are an important part of their identity. Preventing someone from 'expressing' themselves cuts off a part of their personality, diminishing their identity. Human rights are to a large extent about retaining personal control – autonomy – over our own lives.

Limiting people's freedom of expression also limits their opportunity to participate in society. Participation

is itself a key human right, both as a form of social interaction and as a way of influencing decisions which may be made on our behalf. Participation is central to democracy and citizenship.

IMPORTANT FOR DEMOCRACY

Debate and discussion are an essential part of democratic society. Ideas are born through sharing them with others, refining them, joining them, matching them against other interpretations. Creativity and 'truth' depend on the interchange of ideas and a 'free' exchange of ideas adds to the richness of society. Debate and discussion are also ways of facilitating better human interaction. We understand others by listening to their thoughts, perhaps disagreeing with them, but finding a common way of living together which allows both parties to co-exist. That too is important for a cohesive society.

So freedom of expression is important both because it allows society to develop and flourish, and because it allows individuals to develop and flourish. Cutting off expression is recognised as something we need a very good reason for doing.

WHAT THE LAW SAYS

THE LIMITS TO FREEDOM OF EXPRESSION

All expression
Cannot be restricted
Can be restricted
Expression which undermines safety, health morals, reputation, etc.
Individual harm
Teachers stink like pigs
Hassan's a gay cripple
'Mild' hate / intolerance
Extreme hate
Violent expression which undermines other human rights
Kill all gypsies!
Hate speech

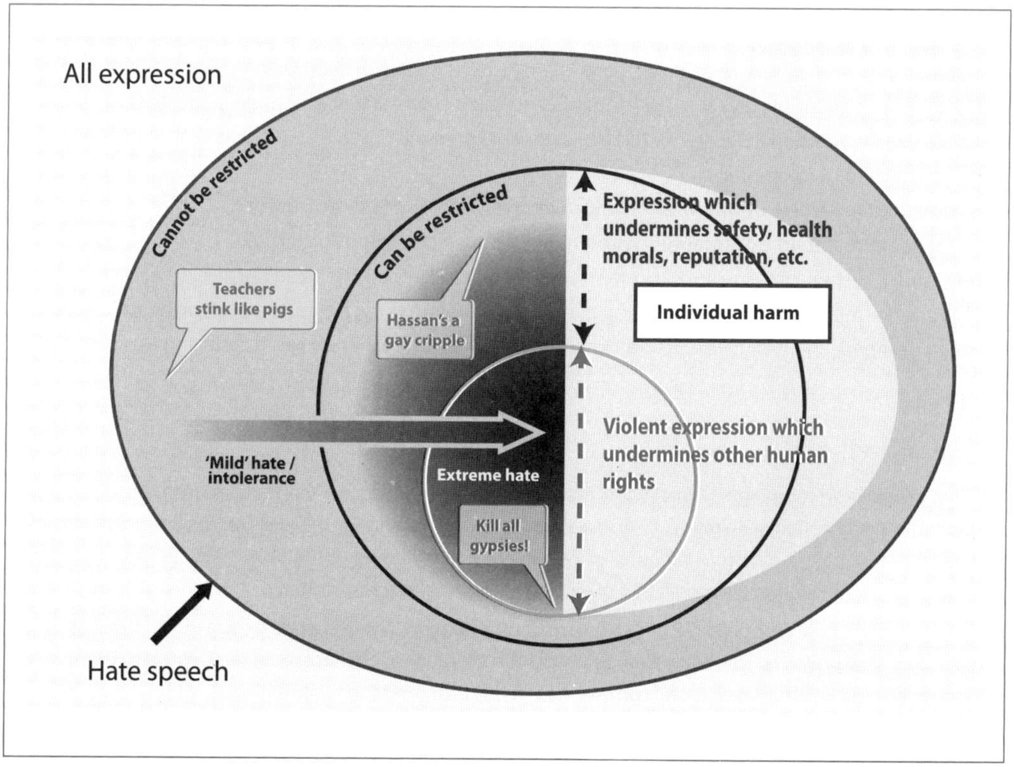

The diagram shows the broad forms of expression which may be restricted or which *must* be restricted under international human rights law. Do you agree with these boundaries and restrictions? Do you think more (or less) speech should be restricted?

Despite the strong reasons for protecting free speech, human rights treaties also recognise that speech itself is an 'act' which has the potential to harm others, and can even threaten society as a whole. For this reason, freedom of expression is one of the rights which can be restricted in certain circumstances, and which occasionally *should* be restricted. There needs to be a balance between allowing people to express their inner thoughts, and ensuring that this does not undermine the rights of others, or cause greater damage to society.

Article 19 in the UDHR and Article 10 in the European Convention on Human Rights (ECHR) both protect freedom of expression. Article 10 lays out the conditions which must be satisfied if a government wishes to impose limits on free speech or punish unacceptable expression. These conditions must be met, otherwise any restriction will be regarded as a violation. However, there is some flexibility for a broad interpretation of the conditions so that different countries can respond to specific concerns in the most appropriate way.

WHAT DOES THE EUROPEAN CONVENTION OF HUMAN RIGHTS SAY?

> Everyone has the right to freedom of expression. This right shall include freedom to hold opinions and to receive and impart information and ideas without interference by public authority and regardless of frontiers ...
> *ECHR. Article 10, paragraph 1*

First of all, the Convention says that freedom of expression is important and must be protected.

Secondly, the Convention includes within freedom of expression:

- Freedom to hold opinions
- Freedom to receive information "without interference by public authority"
- Freedom to impart information "without interference by public authority"

Thirdly, under certain circumstances, when there is a 'socially pressing need', Article 10 allows for some restrictions on freedom of expression. However, any restriction must be *necessary* in order to meet a particular social need, and it must be proportionate to that need; in other words, it must not be excessive.

> **ARTICLE 10**
>
> *Féret v. Belgium*
>
> During the election campaign, several types of leaflets were distributed carrying slogans including "Stand up against the Islamification of Belgium", "Stop the sham integration policy" and "Send non-European job-seekers home". Because of this, a Belgian member of Parliament and chairman of the political party Front National/ Nationaal Front in Belgium was convicted of incitement to racial discrimination.
>
> He complained to the European Court of Human Rights, claiming that there had been a violation to his right to freedom of expression. The Court found no violation of freedom of expression; the Court also found that his message, conveyed in an electoral context, was clearly incitement to racial hatred.

This requirement of 'proportionality' means that censorship, as a *general* restriction, is not seen as compatible with people's right to free expression. Cases must be assessed on their particular merits, and wherever possible, expression should be permitted. Alternative methods should be found to protect those who may be affected by specific instances.

ARTICLE 17 OF THE ECHR

Apart from the right to freedom of expression, the ECHR also includes an article which prohibits any act "aimed at the destruction on any of the rights in the Convention". This may include extreme cases of hate speech (and hate speech online).

Article 17 means that anyone calling for violent action against certain groups will not be able to appeal to the right to freedom of expression. There is no right to be able to call for people to be attacked or killed.

ARTICLE 17

Norwood v. the United Kingdom

A British citizen was convicted in the United Kingdom of hostility towards a religious group. He had displayed in his window a large poster of the BNP (British National Party), showing a photograph of the Twin Towers in flames, with the words "Islam out of Britain – Protect the British People" and the symbol of a crescent and star in a prohibition sign. He complained at the European Court of Human Rights arguing that his right to freedom of expression had been violated. The European Court declared his request inadmissible and found that such a general, vehement attack against a religious group, linking the group as a whole with a grave act of terrorism, was incompatible with the values proclaimed and guaranteed by the Convention, notably tolerance, social peace and non-discrimination and that the applicant could not claim the protection of Article 10 (freedom of expression).

Garaudy v. France

The author of a book entitled *The Founding Myths of Modern Israel* was convicted in France of the offences of disputing the existence of crimes against humanity, defamation in public of a group of persons – in this case, the Jewish community – and incitement to racial hatred. He argued that his right to freedom of expression had been violated. The European Court declared his application inadmissible, and considered that the content of the applicant's remarks had amounted to Holocaust denial, and pointed out that disputing the existence of clearly established historical events did not constitute scientific or historical research; the real purpose was to rehabilitate the National Socialist regime and accuse the victims themselves of falsifying history. As such acts were manifestly incompatible with the fundamental values which the European Convention sought to promote, the Court applied Article 17 (prohibition of abuse of rights) and held that the applicant was not entitled to rely on Article 10 (freedom of expression).

WHO USES ARTICLE 10?

Although governments may have obligations to restrict freedom of expression when the expression is likely to be harmful, the cases brought before the European Court under Article 10 are not normally about governments *failing* to act. Instead, they are about challenging instances when a government has taken

action to restrict freedom of expression, perhaps in order to protect certain groups or individuals, and where this restriction is thought to be excessive. The right to freedom of expression is important for hate speech because it helps us to see why certain (mild) forms of intolerance may need to be 'tolerated' in democratic society, and it provides certain limits to what people should be allowed to say.

Victims of hate speech normally need to raise concerns about their rights under a different article, for example the right not to suffer discrimination or the right to private life.

FREEDOM OF EXPRESSION AND THE INTERNET

Ensuring that human rights are respected in the virtual world is a developing area, and the problem of online hate speech adds particular urgency to the debate. The Council of Europe has published a *Guide to Human Rights for Internet Users* to help people understand their rights online. The Guide is based on the European Convention on Human Rights (ECHR), and it is a good reminder that human rights apply offline and online. The Guide also explains in more detail how the right to freedom of expression and information applies on the Internet.

You can find further information on how human rights law applies to the virtual world in the section on human rights, page 155. As far as freedom of expression is concerned, the following highlight some of the key issues:

THE 'NON-GEOGRAPHICAL' NATURE OF THE INTERNET

Many service providers and many of the most popular social networking sites and search engines are located in the USA or in other countries with limited means of prosecution. The USA's views on freedom of expression differ from those contained in European human rights law, and in particular, from the interpretation given to these laws by the European Court. It is much more difficult to restrict freedom of expression under US law, even when the expression is openly racist or calls for violence. This means that hate sites which are based on US servers cannot easily be removed, and advocates of hate cannot always be prosecuted.

THE DIFFICULTY OF CONTROLLING CYBERSPACE

The Internet is a vast space, much of which is user-driven and not subject to external monitoring or governance. Even when there is good reason to remove a site, perhaps because it advocates violence against a particular community, it is relatively easy for the owners or site managers to open a new location, and re-post the original content.

THE NEED TO PRESERVE THE BENEFITS OF THE INTERNET

Many people feel that this aspect of the Internet – the ease with which people can use it to communicate as they wish – is one of the key strengths. Stricter monitoring, and censorship, might be successful in reducing the volume of hate speech in the virtual world, but setting up such a system would have significant

repercussions for the way that people have become accustomed to using the Internet. It would reduce its important role as a forum for free discussion and debate.

OWNERSHIP: THE ROLE OF PRIVATE COMPANIES

The fact that most sites are the 'property' of private individuals or companies means that without laws regulating how they should respond to hate or calls for violence, they are relatively 'free' to allow any content they wish. Human rights are laws that governments need to comply with: private companies only need to obey the laws that governments decide are necessary!

Of course, private companies also obey the 'law of the market' and it is often pressure from those who use their services that is most likely to lead to a change in their policies. This makes it particularly important for young people to communicate their own views about hate speech online to those responsible for the sites they use. Successful online campaigns, such as the one carried out in 2013 by various NGOs to remove content from Facebook that legitimised violence against women, highlight, nonetheless, that the borders between private and public space online are increasingly blurred. Additionally, such campaigns emphasise that it is not possible for the states to rely only on self-regulation. Online space is also public space.

5.4 RACISM AND DISCRIMINATION

[T]he term 'racial discrimination' shall mean any distinction, exclusion, restriction or preference based on race, colour, descent, or national or ethnic origin which has the purpose or effect of nullifying or impairing the recognition, enjoyment or exercise, on an equal footing, of human rights and fundamental freedoms in the political, economic, social, cultural or any other field of public life.

Article 1, Convention on the Elimination of Racial Discrimination

THE CONNECTION WITH HATE SPEECH

Hate speech is nearly always the result of racist or discriminatory attitudes. It is also nearly always discriminatory in itself.

Discrimination is best viewed as the 'opposite' of equality. Under human rights law, people are equal in rights. When someone's rights are impaired just because of how they are viewed by other people or how they view themselves, this is discrimination. Abusing someone either online or offline because they are seen as 'foreign', disabled, gay, female, or for any other such reason, counts as discrimination.

Discrimination is often racist in nature. When hate speech targets someone because of their 'race', national or ethnic origin this is an example of both discrimination and racism.

ATTITUDES AND ACTIONS

Hate speech needs to be addressed not only when it shows its face, but also at the roots, in other words, at the level of attitudes. Hate speech thrives on racist attitudes and negative stereotypes and it also helps to strengthen them. If it is unchallenged it can feed back into society, reinforcing the stereotypes and making further abuse more likely, including, in some cases, physical violence. It has been noticed that mass violations of human rights, such as genocide and ethnic cleansing, are always preceded or accompanied by hate speech.

DEFINITIONS

STEREOTYPES

Stereotypes are shared beliefs or thoughts about particular groups and may be positive or negative (or neutral). Although they can be useful, stereotypes become damaging when they are applied rigidly to individuals and are used as a reason for different treatment or behaviour. Stereotypes are generalisations, and will not always be true of every individual case!

Examples of stereotypes include "men are stronger than women", "footballers can run fast than other people", and "all swans are white".

PREJUDICE

A prejudice is a particular class of stereotype, one which contains an evaluation or judgement. Many stereotypes which appear to be neutral in fact contain an element of judgement. For example, "women aren't good at computer games" appears to be a statement of fact but it is really making a judgement about women's technical ability.

Even when stereotypes or prejudice seem positive they nearly always have a negative aspect. The statement "Australians are the most generous people in the world" is positive about Australians, but it contains the judgement that people in other countries are less generous! The statement "Africans are good at sport" can be interpreted as "Africans are only good at sport". Nationalism and patriotism appear to be positive in nature but they can easily turn into racism.

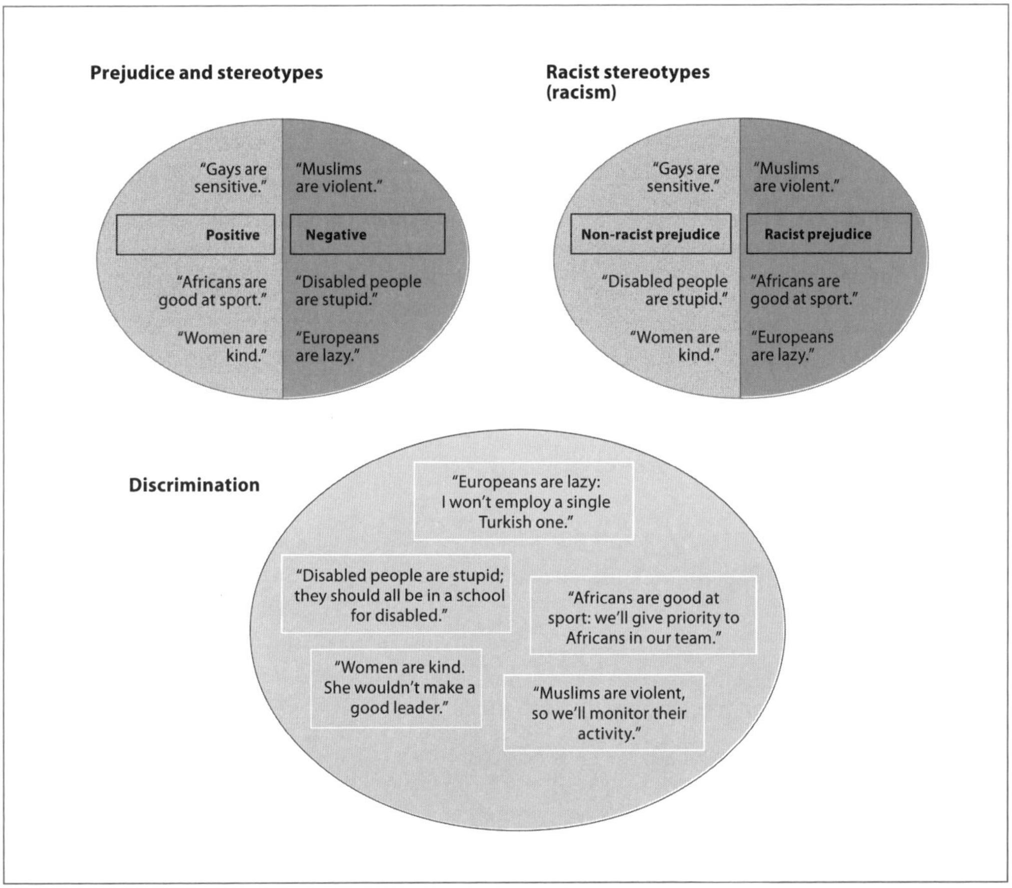

Prejudice and stereotypes

Positive	Negative
"Gays are sensitive."	"Muslims are violent."
"Africans are good at sport."	"Disabled people are stupid."
"Women are kind."	"Europeans are lazy."

Racist stereotypes (racism)

Non-racist prejudice	Racist prejudice
"Gays are sensitive."	"Muslims are violent."
"Disabled people are stupid."	"Africans are good at sport."
"Women are kind."	"Europeans are lazy."

Discrimination

"Europeans are lazy: I won't employ a single Turkish one."

"Disabled people are stupid; they should all be in a school for disabled."

"Africans are good at sport: we'll give priority to Africans in our team."

"Women are kind. She wouldn't make a good leader."

"Muslims are violent, so we'll monitor their activity."

RACISM

When a stereotype or prejudice is based on someone's skin colour or national or ethnic origin, it is likely to be racist, whether or not it is positive or negative. Racism is an ideology which involves discriminatory or abusive behaviour towards people because of their imagined 'inferiority'. It is important to note that 'race' is now considered to be a social classification, not a biological one. No physical or genotypical traits have been found which are common to one 'race' and not shared by another.

DISCRIMINATION

When negative attitudes towards a particular group result in that group being unable, or less able, to enjoy their human rights, this constitutes discrimination. Discrimination is itself a violation of human rights and may be the result either of racist attitudes, or of other prejudices which are non-racial in nature but are just as negative in their consequences for the direct victims and for society as a whole.

CONNECTING UP THE CONCEPTS

HATE CRIME is an unlawful act against a group or individual based on a prejudice about their perceived identity.

HATE SPEECH is a negative *expression* – about an individual or group – often based on prejudice, spreading, inciting, promoting or justifying racial hatred and intolerance. Specific instances may or may not be a crime depending on the laws of the country and the context of the speech.

DISCRIMINATION is unfair treatment resulting from *any* prejudice, including non-racial prejudice.

RACISM is a prejudice based on the idea of 'race' or ethnicity or any other characteristic connected to these, often leading to someone being treated unfairly.

A PREJUDICE is a generalisation containing a judgment which is usually negative about other people or social groups.

STEREOTYPES are generalisations about other groups of people, which may or may not contain judgments.

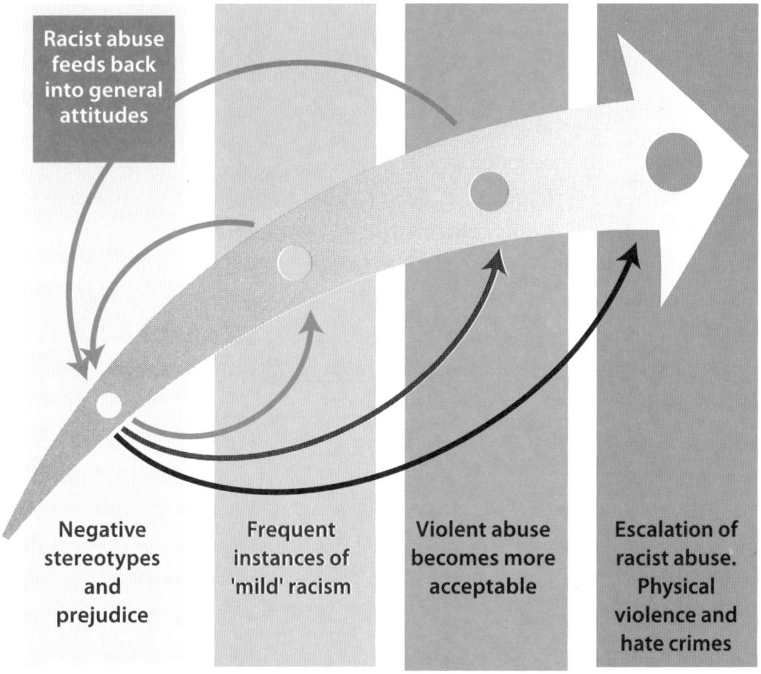

Racist abuse feeds back into general attitudes

Negative stereotypes and prejudice

Frequent instances of 'mild' racism

Violent abuse becomes more acceptable

Escalation of racist abuse. Physical violence and hate crimes

HUMAN RIGHTS AND DISCRIMINATION

The recognition of the inherent dignity and of the equal and inalienable rights of all members of the human family is the foundation of freedom, justice and peace in the world.

Preamble of the Universal Declaration of Human Rights

Everyone is entitled to all the rights and freedoms set forth in [the UDHR], without distinction of any kind, such as race, colour, sex, language, religion, political or other opinion, national or social origin, property, birth or other status …

Article 2, Universal Declaration of Human Rights

Discrimination is a human rights violation and is prohibited by nearly all the major human rights instruments, as is racism. Certain groups may also be protected against discrimination by specific national or international laws.

- Article 14 of the European Convention on Human Rights (ECHR) forbids discrimination relating to any other rights – and all Council of Europe member states are bound by this. This also means that

What are the laws against discrimination in your country? Has your government signed Protocol 12 of the ECHR?

in interactions with public authorities, internet service providers and providers of online content and services, or in interaction with other users or groups of users, no-one can be discriminated against on any grounds such as gender, race, colour, language, religion or belief, political or other opinion, national or social origin, association with a national minority, property, birth or other status, including ethnicity, age or sexual orientation.

- Many member states have also signed a more extensive ban on discrimination contained in an (optional) Protocol to the ECHR (Protocol 12). This prohibits discrimination with respect to *all* laws, not just those which relate to the rights contained in the Convention.
- There are other human rights treaties, both at European level and at the level of the UN, which address discrimination against certain specific groups because of their vulnerability, for example, women, children, people with disabilities, and representatives of different national or ethnic groups.
- Many countries also have specific national legislation which protects specific groups, or any group against discrimination.

5.5 PRIVATE LIFE AND SAFETY

THE CONNECTION WITH HATE SPEECH

Hate speech only takes place when people think that they know something about a target group or individual. Completely anonymous identities do not become targets of hate speech, except perhaps when being 'anonymous' becomes identified with certain 'personal' characteristics! For many groups, revealing core aspects of their identity can easily lead to their becoming targets of hate speech. Such is often the case for women, disabled people, ethnic minorities, and so on. If someone falls into such a target group, revealing information about themselves online, and allowing connections to be made to their *offline* identity, can even become a safety risk.

Private or personal information can present a particular risk in cases of cyberbullying and online hate speech. Many people place personal information about themselves online, including personal photos, information about relationships, or details about where they live or study. If they become a target of cyberbulling, this information may often be used to harm them.

PRIVACY IN THE VIRTUAL WORLD

The Internet is a public space. It is public in the same sense as the street or a shopping centre: other people are 'around' and can see what we do. There are particular features of life in the virtual world, however, which make privacy of more concern than it is in the street.

On the street, we mostly know that other people are looking, or could see if they chose to look. On the Internet, there is very little awareness of what it means for other people to 'look' at us and there is even less awareness of how we can protect ourselves against their gaze. That lack of awareness can leave people open to threats or exploitation, both physical and psychological. Those who wish to bully, torment, threaten or exploit will find it much easier to do so if they have information about their 'victims'. Issues of privacy are therefore particularly relevant to cyberbullying.

KEY MESSAGES

- Young people need to remember that the Internet is a public space, where people can see what we are doing and what we are like, even when we think they can't.
- The Internet has its own dangers: there are people who might use personal facts or information to cause offence or harm. Young people should try to limit that possibility by taking certain precautions.
- Whatever is posted on the Internet stays there forever! Young people need to be aware of this, and think about whether the personal details they reveal today might be something they might later regret.
- Young people should remember to respect the private life and safety of *others*. This does not only mean they should not engage in harmful or abusive behaviour themselves; it also means they should be careful about sharing information about other people which could be used to harm them.

- There are human rights protections which apply in cases where others either access information about us that we have not given them authority to do, and when things are posted about us online which harm our sense of personal integrity.
- There are many organisations and public institutions which can help in such cases, particularly when they concern young people. Young people should feel empowered to report cases when they are being abused or exploited online.
- There is no anonymity. Anything done online can be traced back to the person who posted it. There is also no impunity; many forms of hate speech online and cyberbullying are punishable by law.

PRIVATE LIFE, PRIVATE LIFE ONLINE AND HUMAN RIGHTS

Everyone has the right to respect for his private and family life, his home and his correspondence; this applies also to the Internet.

Article 8, Part 1, European Convention of Human Rights

1. No child shall be subjected to arbitrary or unlawful interference with his or her privacy, family, or correspondence, nor to unlawful attacks on his or her honour and reputation.
2. The child has the right to the protection of the law against such interference or attacks.

Article 16, UN Convention on the Rights of the Child

THE RIGHT TO PRIVATE LIFE

The right to private life is protected by various human rights treaties. 'Private life' under human rights law covers a great deal more than mere privacy and includes those aspects of someone's personal life which are most important to their identity and sense of dignity. When it comes to the Internet, private life encompasses correspondence including email in the workplace, one's own photographs and video-clips. These areas of our life are supposed to be free from interference from state authorities, and the state is also supposed to protect us against interference from other people. The European Court of Human Rights uses the idea of someone's 'physical and psychological integrity' to assess many of the claims brought under Article 8. This also applies to online life and relationships.

Governments are supposed to ensure that people are able to go about their normal lives, according to their personal preferences, without others either forcing them into a mould that 'fits all' or persecuting them for having different needs from others. What matters is how something that the state has done, or failed to do, impacts on an individual: our private life is a personal matter!

However, the right to private life is not an 'absolute' right; in other words, state authorities need to balance one person's private life against other demands from society, or from other individuals. Very occasionally, it may be justifiable for the state to access people's personal data, perhaps in order to protect others; and sometimes it may decide not to protect someone's privacy, either because the risk to the individual concerned is not sufficiently serious, or because the cost to others is too high.

Striking the right balance is not always easy. In the case of *Copland v. UK*, the European Court of Human Rights considered whether it was a violation of Article 8 for a higher education college to monitor all emails and telephone conversations of employees. The Court decided this was a violation of the right to privacy. In the case of *K.U. v. Finland*, the Court decided that protecting the private life and safety of a minor was more important than protecting the private life of someone who had posted a false advertisement in his name.

In general, and as with all human rights, the onus is on the state authorities to ensure that people's private lives and personal dignity are not interfered with, either by the state, or by other parties. This applies as much online as it does offline.

PRIVACY AND HUMAN RIGHTS

Privacy is a particular aspect of 'private life', and is also protected by Article 8 of the ECHR. Privacy concerns those areas of our physical, social or emotional life which we do not wish to share publicly. Unless we give our express permission, or unless there are very strong reasons to do with protecting other people's rights, those things we wish to keep private should be *kept private!* No-one, and no organisation, has the right to know things about our private life that we do not wish them to know.

However, the default settings on many Internet forums or websites are not always easy to understand, and are not always designed primarily to protect the privacy of users. Ensuring that private details are indeed kept private demands care and attention, and a general awareness of potential dangers.

Issues relating to privacy can also be important in relation to sharing content online. Young people need to be aware that just as their own privacy is important, so is the privacy of others. The ease of sharing photos, videos, messages, or other information can lead to carelessness, sometimes resulting in harm to others. The key message for young people is that material which relates directly to someone else should only be shared if it is either already in the public domain (and is not harmful or abusive) or if the person has given their permission for it to be shared.

It is also worth noting that in most cases of online communication, material is never really private. Email messages and anything that has been posted online can almost always be accessed by others. It can also never be fully removed from virtual space.

Weak passwords or inadequate security precautions can make it possible for other people to access information stored in 'private' sections of user profiles or in email boxes. Even a strong password cannot provide a full guarantee against intrusion by hackers, or intrusion by state security agencies!

Young people need to be aware of such risks, and need to exercise care and responsibility to protect details of their lives that they would not want others to know. They also need to be aware that if they *do* take adequate precautions, but someone manages to gain access to their private information, this is very likely to be illegal, and a violation of their right to privacy.

The section on cyberbullying addresses some precautions that young people can take to ensure their private details do not fall into the public domain.

5.6 DEMOCRACY AND PARTICIPATION

THE CONNECTION WITH HATE SPEECH

FREEDOM OF EXPRESSION AND DEMOCRATIC DIALOGUE

The connection between democracy and hate speech can be looked at from two different perspectives. From one point of view, democracy might be seen to make hate speech more likely, or perhaps more difficult to combat. The best way of seeing this is to imagine a non-democratic society with severe censorship: in theory, it might be possible to eliminate hate speech, and hate speech online, in such a society. Anything deemed offensive to others could be banned, and any infringements could be severely punished. Such a society, however, would have a lot of disadvantages due to the lack of freedom of expression.

In a democracy, where people are free to express their opinions, it is likely that we will have to listen to views with which we do not agree. Some will be irritating, some may be harsh or upsetting, and some may cross the line and be deeply offensive and even dangerous. A small amount of hate speech may be an inevitable consequence of being able to express our opinions freely, and have them taken into account. No democracy is perfect!

INVOLVEMENT AND PARTICIPATION

However, one of the advantages of democracy and free speech is that it also provides us with the tools to address hate speech, possibly in a more effective way, and certainly in a way that better preserves other freedoms. So from another point of view, democracy itself offers the most promising hope for combatting hate speech while still protecting human rights.

In a properly functioning democracy, where people play an active role in protecting the rights and freedoms that everyone values, society's defence against hate speech can be much more refined, and potentially much more comprehensive than it would be with a strict form of censorship. If the task of 'monitoring' hate speech and dealing with its worst examples is not regarded as solely the task of government, or the task of an Internet 'police', and if 'monitoring' extends to monitoring our own behaviour as well as others, it should be possible to preserve the right to freedom of expression while still ensuring that individuals are protected from abuse.

An effective response to hate speech depends on a full understanding of the benefits, challenges and demands of democratic society, and it depends on the active participation of the individuals who make up that society. Many of the skills which are necessary for democracy to function effectively are also skills that are needed to combat hate speech, and an awareness of the value of diversity and democratic discussion can help to prepare participants in reacting to particular expressions of intolerance or hate.

DEMOCRACY, PARTICIPATION AND HUMAN RIGHTS

> (1) Everyone has the right to take part in the government of his country, directly or through freely chosen representatives.
> (3) The will of the people shall be the basis of the authority of government...
>
> *Article 21, UDHR*
>
> The High Contracting Parties undertake to hold free elections at reasonable intervals by secret ballot, under conditions which will ensure the free expression of the opinion of the people in the choice of the legislature.
>
> *Article 3, Protocol 1, ECHR*

Although human rights create similar obligations on all governments of the world, this does not mean that the laws and form of government in every country must be identical. Human rights allow for a variety of different systems and different ways of ensuring that basic human right are respected.
However, Article 21 of the UDHR (and Optional Protocol 1 of the ECHR) indicates that not *every* form of government is acceptable. States have an obligation to ensure that those who make the laws are representative of "the will of the people". In other words, only a democratic system is consistent with human rights. One of the reasons for this being the case relates to the importance of autonomy and participation as fundamental human rights values.

THE RESPONSIBILITIES OF DEMOCRACY

A democratic form of government allows those not in a position of authority to retain some control over the laws that they are supposed to live under. It is easy to see the connection with human rights, since human rights are in large part about being able to retain personal autonomy in our actions, in other words, about not being subjected to arbitrary interference or having to live under a system which is detrimental to our fundamental needs.
However, and despite its many advantages, democracy is in some ways a more demanding form of government than the alternatives. It makes demands both in terms of what we should do, and in terms of what we should tolerate, or how we should behave when we do not agree with decisions or views. This applies as much to decisions or actions made by those in authority as it applies to the behaviour of other individuals. In a democracy, we are all 'responsible' to some degree for the way the system works.
The following list includes the main skills or areas of understanding which are needed in order for democracy to function effectively. Each item in the list is also important in addressing hate speech.

ACTIVE PARTICIPATION

A government cannot represent the will of the people if 'the people' do not express their will! We can only have representative governments if everyone makes their wishes known. This obviously does not just mean voting when there are elections; it also means making sure we respond to new initiatives, alert members of parliament – or other authorities – when things are unsatisfactory, propose changes, lobby for better protection, demand more openness, and so on.

If participation is essential to democracy from the side of citizens, the government also has an obligation to ensure that people's *views* can be heard. For this reason, freedom of expression must be guaranteed, at least as long as forms of expression do not undermine other basic values or threaten groups or individuals.

Participation can be exercised both offline and online. The Internet has become a significant tool for citizens to use for playing an active role in building and strengthening democratic societies. Even without leaving their home, people can take part in political debates, drafting legislation, signing petitions, controlling politicians and running online campaigns.

Each person can play different roles participating online: from spectator to creator.

BEING INFORMED

In order to be able to react and respond to decisions made on their behalf, people must also be informed about those decisions, as well as about the ways that exist to make their voices heard. This also creates demands both on the part of individuals and on the part of governments: governments need to make sure that information is available, which is why the right to information is an important part of freedom of expression. Individuals, in turn, need to make sure that they keep themselves informed, and press those in authority to release any details which have not been made public.

One important area where an informed public is essential is awareness of human rights. Observance of human rights is not something which can be left either to 'professional' human rights activists, nor is it something that governments should always be trusted to respect! Every individual needs to be aware of basic human rights standards, and needs to play a part in ensuring they are always respected.

TOLERANCE

A representative government is unlikely to mean that all the wishes or demands of every individual are met! Human rights are supposed to ensure that the *basic* needs of every individual are provided for, but there will clearly be a variety of different opinions relating not only to other needs, but also to the best way of meeting the set of basic needs. In a democratic society there is bound to be disagreement.

The extent to which we should 'tolerate' decisions with which we do not agree is not easily defined. When people's human rights are at stake, 'tolerance' is undesirable and it is vital that those responsible are held to account. But there will be numerous occasions, and numerous publicly expressed views with which we may be unhappy, but may, in the end, need to live with, and tolerate. This balance is explored further in the section on freedom of expression.

INTERNET GOVERNANCE

Our existence in the 'real' world is governed by rules or laws at different levels. In the workplace or in 'spaces' owned by private companies there will be one set of rules; local and national governments impose further laws and regulations; and international or regional organisations, such as the UN or the Council of Europe,

have established a further set of laws which governments themselves must abide by.

As different forms of human activity increasingly take place online, questions are beginning to be asked about the 'rules' which govern *this* activity. Every website has its own rules or code of conduct, and so do hosting providers; these are comparable to the laws regulating private spaces offline. Some governments have laws which apply to online activity, and certain international laws, particularly those relating to human rights protections, also extend to the Internet. However, there is now increasing recognition that there may be a need for general principles and regulations which ensure that Internet users are properly protected in their online activity. The question of what these principles should be and how they should be implemented is described as 'Internet governance'.

Internet governance is particularly relevant to the question of hate speech online because some countries, in particular the USA, have strong protections relating to freedom of expression. Since many Internet sites are hosted in the USA, it can be very difficult to challenge even the most violent and abusive examples of hate speech online.

THE COUNCIL OF EUROPE'S WORK ON INTERNET GOVERNANCE

> Protecting and preserving the Internet by "doing no harm" to its functioning is … vital to secure the online exercise of Articles 10 and 11 of the European Convention on Human Rights. At the same time, with freedom comes the need for citizens to be adequately informed, enabling them to deal responsibly with services offered via the Internet. For people to trust the Internet, the protection of personal data and respect for privacy on the Internet are indispensable…
>
> *From the Council of Europe's Internet Governance Strategy*

The Council of Europe has taken up the question of Internet governance. In 2007, the Committee of Ministers issued a Recommendation which referred to "people having a legitimate expectation that Internet services be accessible and affordable, secure, reliable and ongoing" (CM/Rec (2007)16In). In 2012, the 47 member states of the Council of Europe adopted an Internet Governance Strategy "to protect and promote human rights, the rule of law and democracy online". The Strategy proposes a framework of co-operation for member states to preserve a global, stable and open Internet as a means of safeguarding freedom of expression and access to information.

A special section in the Strategy is devoted to protecting and empowering children and young people. The security, dignity and privacy of children and young people on the Internet are identified as being "of paramount importance".

The Council of Europe promotes a vision of human rights and fundamental freedoms which apply equally offline and online. In 2014, the Committee of Ministers adopted the *Guide to Human Rights for Internet Users*. The Guide contains information on how human rights and freedoms can be exercised in the Internet. It also indicates possible means of protection if the rights are violated.

THE ROLE OF USERS

The role of users themselves is also of central importance in determining how the Internet works. A 'democratic' Internet needs a community of Internet users who are 'online citizens', participating in establishing norms and rules of communication and having an influence over how the Internet should function. An example of how this might work can be seen in the role that NGOs and citizens' movements played in stopping the adoption in the European Parliament of ACTA, an international agreement which would have reinforced intellectual property rights. The agreement was opposed on the basis that it threatened many civil liberties and human rights.

MESSAGES FOR YOUNG PEOPLE

To ensure that young people take on an active role in influencing the way the Internet works, the following principles are important:

- Internet users are more than consumers! They possess influence, and they can activate this by taking a more active role in shaping how the Internet should safeguard human rights: this can be done through campaigning and also through the way young people as users of the Internet behave towards one another online.
- Internet users need their human rights to be protected online. Knowing their rights and challenging any abuses is important in making sure that this happens.
- The Internet is a space whose dynamic architecture is still an unsettled terrain. On the one hand, it can allow for violations of human rights. On another, however, it can be a tool for fulfilling rights and freedoms, a vehicle for mobilising communities to ensure their protection.
- Children and young people, and other users, need support through educational programmes which will help to develop the understanding and skills necessary for effective use of the Internet.
- Children and young people should be afforded special protection from interference with their physical, mental and moral well-being when using the Internet.
- Although there are powerful economic and political forces which play a significant role in shaping the Internet, those who use it should assert their right to make the online world a public space where human rights principles, values and practices apply.
- Children and young people should be able to know and learn how and who governs the Internet, as part of their learning of democratic citizenship. Transparency and accountability of Internet governance are thus important, including the ways in which young people can effectively influence Internet governance, at least the public space that is also part of the Internet.

5.7 CAMPAIGNING STRATEGIES

The Council of Europe's Campaign against hate speech online depends on the active engagement of as many young people as possible. There are numerous ways that you and your groups of friends can work to combat hate speech and become part of the Campaign. Some of these are listed in this section.

The list has been divided into the following categories:

1. Education and awareness raising
2. Addressing the hate speech already existing online
3. Mobilising others
4. Expressing solidarity with victims or common target groups
5. Longer term strategies

These categories often overlap, and where they do not, it is often possible to strengthen an activity by adding items from another section.

For example:

- Addressing hate speech directly by providing an alternative narrative will also have an educational effect. If the alternative narrative or dialogue is publicised through social media, it may also be used to mobilise others
- An awareness-raising action designed to inform others about the problems of hate speech online is also a powerful expression of solidarity with victims of hate speech. It could be used to add signatures to a petition calling on politicians to engage with the problem
- Reporting an example of hate speech and blogging about the response of the website manager can motivate others to be alert to similar examples, and to make their own complaints.

The list below is not comprehensive and should be used only as a source for possible ideas. Your group will almost certainly be able to come up with others!

Some of the suggestions may not be appropriate in all cases. For example, reporting a comment or post may sometimes be excessive: it may be easier to send a question to the author of the original post to see if they will alter their language or retract the comment. In other cases, engaging directly with someone who has posted an abusive comment may often be inappropriate. Judgement should always be used to select the most appropriate or effective action.

You can use the suggestions to supplement activities in the manual and encourage your friends or group to engage with the No Hate Speech Movement.

- Make sure you involve your group or friends in selecting and planning any actions. They will be more likely to engage if they have chosen the focus and methods themselves!
- Remind them that creative actions are more likely to attract attention: grabbing people's attention online is like trying to stand out from the crowd!
- Remind them that information can be disseminated through images, videos and music, as well as by the use of words alone. The medium can be as important as the message.

- Make sure you look at the No Hate Speech Movement site (www.nohatespeechmovement.org) for other ways to engage with the Campaign!

LIST OF POSSIBLE ACTIONS

EDUCATION AND AWARENESS RAISING

- Use blogs and social media sites to raise awareness about what people can do if they are victims of hate speech or if they witness examples
- Use the language of human rights: raise awareness of the rights which protect us online and offline, and how human rights relate to hate speech online
- Create a 'mythbusting' sheet for groups commonly targeted by hate speech. Post it to social media sites or create leaflets to distribute offline
- Share sites or posts which highlight positive characteristics of common target groups
- Tell stories about individuals who have been the victims of hate speech online or offline. Use this to disseminate information about the problem and build empathy for those targeted by hate speech
- Set up your own website or social media profile. Use it to provide alternative information, properly sourced, about common target groups
- Organise offline actions, training sessions or awareness-raising events. These could look at:
  - the general problem of hate speech online and offline
  - prejudices relating to a particular target group
  - methods of dealing with hate speech online and offline
  - the impact of hate speech
  - the need for people to take responsibility for their own actions as well as for the actions of others
  - initiatives being taken by other youth groups – including the No Hate Speech Movement
  - something else!

ADDRESSING THE PREJUDICE OR HATE SPEECH ALREADY ONLINE

- Edit Wikipedia entries or other free content sites which offer inadequate or false information about common target groups of hate speech
- Post comments on sites which contain incorrect, biased or racist content. Send questions or complaints to the authors of any posts which show intolerance or racism
- Engage with individuals using abusive language: try to show them the impact of their behaviour on others
- Encourage others to ignore 'trolls' if they are engaging in abusive behaviour
- Use online reporting mechanisms or complaints procedures to alert website owners to examples of hate speech
- Report cases of hate speech through national reporting systems or through the media networks concerned
- Report cases of hate speech to moderators by using online reporting mechanisms
- Report examples of hate speech to organisations working on the problem – or to Hate Speech Watch
- Boycott hate sites – and call on others to do so. Report the sites using the legal mechanisms existing in your country or organisations, such as INACH, the International Network Against Cyber Hate

- Collect information about hate sites registered in your country. Send this to your parliamentary representative.

MOBILISING OTHERS

- Call on others to condemn or report hate speech, express solidarity with victims, or engage in other actions
- Use social media to draw followers to useful websites or exciting campaign initiatives
- Publicise successful cases of getting hate speech removed from particular sites
- Raise awareness about the No Hate Speech Movement. Link to your social media profile or add the logo to your signature
- Organise training or awareness sessions with representatives of common target groups. Show them how they can protect themselves – and others – by engaging with the Campaign
- Use online and offline actions to publicise any of the actions you may take in other sections!

SUPPORTING OR EXPRESSING SOLIDARITY WITH VICTIMS OR COMMON TARGET GROUPS

- Send private messages to individuals being publicly targeted by hate speech: express your solidarity and tell them what they can do
- Help to dispel prejudice or false ideas about common target groups. Build up an alternative narrative and publicise it wherever you are able
- Inform young people about their rights, and the methods they can use to protect themselves
- Organise a public action in solidarity with groups targeted by hate speech
- Publicise any examples of racist or discriminatory expression by politicians, the media or public figures. Call them to account!
- Work with groups commonly targeted by hate speech: encourage them to become involved in the Campaign.

LONGER TERM STRATEGIES

- Organise your own campaign at local level, or on the Internet; create a campaign video, song or fun action, and post it online
- Set up an online petition against hate speech online, or against the policy of a particular website in relation to hate speech online
- Contact web-based organisations working on the problem: tell them what you are doing and find out how you can become involved in their work
- Contact local organisations working on racism and discrimination, or other similar issues. Alert them to the problem of hate speech online and encourage them to join the Campaign
- Monitor the problem, either on a particular site or as it affects particular groups. Send the results of your research to Hate Speech Watch, to NGOs working on the problem, to politicians or to other people with influence
- Call on government officials to address the problem: contact your parliamentary representative.

5.8 INTERNET LITERACY

Internet literacy [is] the ability to access, understand, critique, and create information and communication content online.

Sonia Livingstone, 'Internet Literacy: Young People's Negotiation of New Online Opportunities.' [1]

THE NEED FOR INTERNET LITERACY

The Internet is probably the main source of information for many young people in Europe. Sometimes it is used directly as a reference tool; at other times information is picked up in the course of 'socialising' or engaging in other activities. In both cases, it is important that users are able to understand, analyse, assess and verify both the explicit content and any implicit messages. When it comes to encountering expressions of hate, the matter is even more relevant.

The body of skills and areas of knowledge that young people need to be able to find and process information are one aspect of media literacy or, as it applies specifically to the online world, Internet literacy. However, Internet literacy extends beyond the area of information gathering and processing, and there are many other skills and tools which are particularly relevant when preparing young people to address the problem of online hate. Among these are those which relate to the more technical aspects of the Internet and those required when posting and sharing content.

Key points (based on the *Guide to Human Rights for Internet Users*)

- Children and young users should be able to use the Internet in safety and with due regard for their privacy.
- Children and young people should receive training and information from teachers, educators and parents.
- Children and young people should be provided with information appropriate to their age and circumstances about the different types of illegal content and behaviour.

LEARNING BY DOING

In general, anyone using the Internet picks up the methods and rules needed to operate online in the course of their activity: they become sufficiently 'Internet literate' to be able to find their way around and satisfy most of their needs. However, if young people are not merely to replicate some of the 'bad' aspects and bad habits which result in online hate speech, and if, in particular, they are to learn to challenge particular instances, a greater degree of online literacy becomes important. The lists included in this section include some of the more relevant skills and areas of knowledge needed for the task.

1 *Digital Youth, Innovation, and the Unexpected (2008), MIT Press*

DIFFERENT TOOLS FOR DIFFERENT ROLES

It is important to note that in relation to hate speech, young people may at different times find themselves assuming a variety of roles. Each role requires a different set of skills, and any educational work should try to keep this in mind.

BYSTANDERS / OBSERVERS

Whenever we come across content which is harmful to others to some degree, we become a participant in the dialogue. We may ignore it, we may disseminate it further by sharing it, or we may decide to take a stand against it. Many of the activities in this manual are designed to move young people from the passive position of 'seeing-but-not-acting' to a position where they engage with the problem, in whatever is the most appropriate way. This demands skills of judgment and critical analysis, and it requires an awareness of the possible forms of action.

VICTIMS

People who are either directly targeted by online hate speech or who fall into one of the common target groups for abusive or racist expression or cyberbullying need to be given strategies for protecting themselves and coping with expressions of hate. They also need skills and knowledge which will help them to address the problem, for example, by holding the responsible person to account, reporting the abuse, encouraging others to take a stand, and so on.

'HATERS' AND POTENTIAL HATERS

This group includes those who disseminate hate speech online or are tempted to do so, whether by creating their own content or by sharing that of others. We should remember that just as there are some forms of hate speech which are 'worse' than others, so too can people's role as 'hater' be more or less damaging. Those who share content which is mildly racist also contribute to the general problem, even if their action is not illegal and does not directly incite others to violence. It is still a first step in a chain of harmful expression.
Many people contribute to the dissemination of hate speech online simply by sharing content which they do not recognise as harmful, abusive or fake. Avoiding this requires an ability to perceive prejudice or bias in online content and a greater degree of responsibility in creating or sharing it with others.

ACTIVISTS AND CAMPAIGNERS

The Campaign against hate speech online sees all young people, and all Internet users, as potential campaigners! Part of the aim is to encourage 'bystanders' of hate speech to respond and join a movement of people around the world in standing up against hate speech. Campaigning on the Internet demands a particular set of skills, including those of publicising, promoting, building support and constructing different messages and narratives.

USING THE INTERNET TO COMBAT ONLINE HATE

The following list outlines some of the more important areas of Internet literacy which relate to the activities in this manual, and to the Campaign more generally. A deeper understanding of these areas will help young people to play a more effective role in the Campaign. It will also help them in modifying their own online behaviour.

RECOGNISING HATE SPEECH ONLINE

The first task in the battle against hate speech online is being able to identify it when we come across it. This requires knowing what constitutes hate speech and knowing how to assess the possible impact, but it can also demand a deeper awareness of underlying messages and the ability to spot bias and prejudice where these are only implicit.

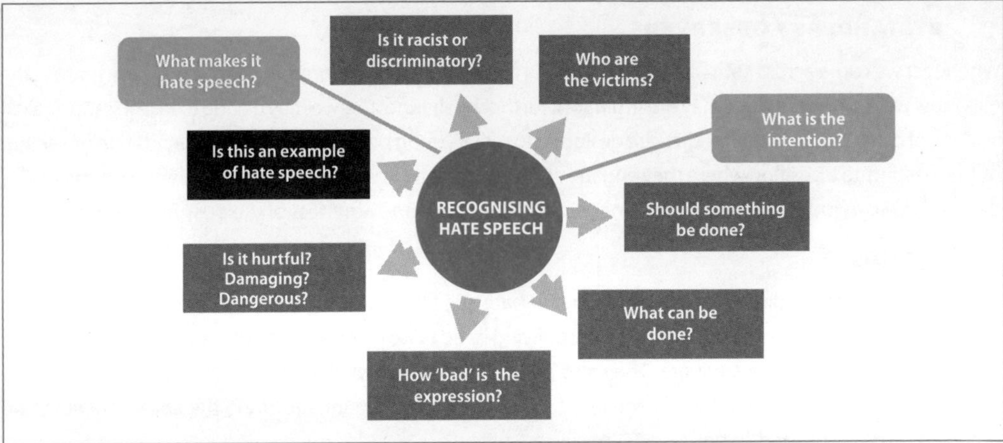

CRITICAL THINKING AND INFORMATION PROCESSING

There is a huge volume of information to be found online, and young people need the skills to ensure that they do not always take what they see at face value. This applies in particular to some of the false information, or inadequately sourced information, which feeds prejudice against particular groups. Users need to be able to identify possible errors in arguments and they need to be aware of the importance of checking the facts and 'hearing the other side', at least in cases where someone may be hurt.

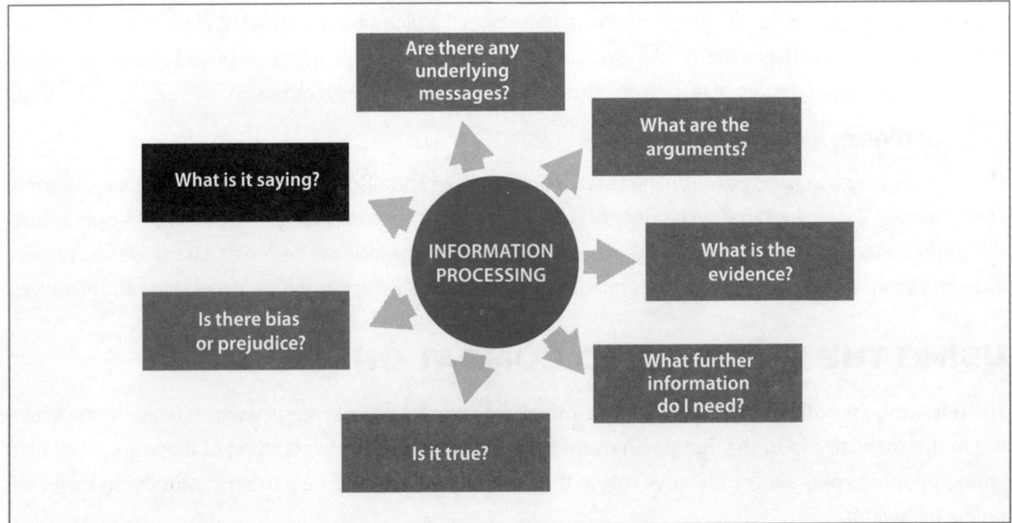

Useful tips: checking the argumentation

- Were sources given for the claims made, or were the arguments based on 'common sense'?
- Are the sources named and recognised as authorities on the subject?
- Were the arguments conclusive or are there other possible outcomes?
- Did the arguments rest on 'facts' or did they appeal to emotions, traditional beliefs, or only *probable* outcomes?
- Could the 'facts' presented or the arguments be tested?
- Were generalisations made about individuals or groups?
- Were any generalisations racist or discriminatory?
- Are other perspectives possible and would they falsify the argument?
- Do the claims use 'ad hominem' arguments, in other words, arguments attacking the opposing side because of who they are, not what they say?
- Is the argument made more persuasive by the *style* of presentation, for example, by the use of striking images or multimedia?

FINDING INFORMATION

Looking for other sources and knowing how to search effectively is part of 'checking the facts' and 'hearing the other side'. Most people know how to use a search engine, but there is less general awareness about *how* search engines work, and how additional tools can be used to refine searches and bring up different results.

Tips for searching

- Try to use different search engines rather than only relying on one.
- Try blocking cookies and clearing history before performing a search! The results will normally be different because many search engines show what they believe the user wants to see (based on what they 'know' about that user).
- Carry out a number of searches using different terms, even when researching one issue.
- Try performing more sophisticated searches, for example, limiting a search to one website, making sure that content including certain terms does not show up in the results or using the 'and' operator to ensure that *all* terms are included. The instructions for doing this are given by each search engine.
- Check the authority of websites before using a search result to identify relevant content.
- Be aware of 'cloaked' websites. These are sites which are recorded by a search engine as being one thing, while really containing content which is unrelated. Their aim is often to mislead the user and provide what they term as 'knowledge', which is actually ideologically biased information.

CHECKING THE AUTHORITY

People can post almost anything they like online! Given the amount of content and the unregulated nature of much of the Internet, it is also relatively easy to present opinion as 'fact' and to make false claims without being challenged. A great deal of hate speech can appear to the casual observer to be well-substantiated and properly argued. Apart from using critical thinking skills to check the facts and argumentation, an awareness of the type of site and authority of the author can also be useful in alerting young people to the possibility of hate speech.

There are thousands of websites which exist in order to promote racism or other forms of discrimination. Such 'hate sites' are often interlinked and may use the authority of other hate sites to back up racist claims. Many racist sites today are more subtle and may even try to hide their racism, for example, by claiming to be "promoting national values" while putting out racist statements. Some basic checks can help with identifying whether websites are trustworthy.

Useful tips: checking the authority

- Is the site well-respected as a source of information or opinion? Do other sites link to it?
- Are the site owners and authors clearly identified? Why should they be trusted?
- What does the site say it is trying to do?
- Is the site likely to have any biases, because of its location, the identity of the authors, or what it says about its mission?
- Is more than one point of view presented on the website?
- How often is it updated, and is there recent content?
- Can you find similar content on other (respected) websites?
- Are there any possible conflicts of interest, for example, connected to commercial interests or political affiliation?
- Are references and sources provided for content posted on the website?
- Does it have a policy on racist or discriminatory content?
- How does it deal with such content, and how does it respond to complaints?

PRODUCING AND SHARING CONTENT

The possibilities for creating online content, easily accessible by others, has opened up many possibilities for the 'ordinary' user, but also creates certain responsibilities. In relation to hate speech, the responsibilities and the need to take care when posting online are particularly important: it is here that users can easily become actors in disseminating hate, either knowingly or unknowingly.

For campaigning purposes, there are other important considerations relating to posting material. Successful campaigning needs strong messages which are likely to have a broad appeal, and are easily understood. Young people need to be aware of the different technical possibilities for reaching large numbers of people – in particular, through social media – and they need to be able to shape their messages so that others will find them convincing and want to pass them on. Effective use of multimedia can be a useful tool in helping to transform a serious message into something which has more popular appeal.

Useful tips for sharing content

- Make sure any content you share does not contain any examples of bias, prejudice, racism or hate.
- Make sure the information is reliable so that you don't spread misinformation.
- Do not share anything about other people that might compromise their privacy or safety. Always ask if you are unsure!
- Be careful about reposting information that may be copyright protected.
- Check the terms and conditions of any websites when you post material. They may contain restrictions on the type of content you can post, and they may also assume rights over your content, or relating to your private information.
- Consider whether others might be able to 'misuse' information you post to give a false image or harm others. Check your content is not ambiguous.
- Remember that content posted on the Internet can easily be misunderstood and may cause offence if it is not carefully phrased. Try to read back anything you post 'with the eyes of someone else'.

UNDERSTANDING THE RULES

A better awareness of some of the policies and laws which apply to Internet activity can be helpful in regulating user's own behaviour, and is essential in the battle to combat hate speech online. The awareness of, and involvement in, the processes of Internet governance and how it affects Internet users is therefore part of Internet literacy and of education for democratic citizenship altogether. The role of the Internet in shaping contemporary forms of citizenship, and participation cannot leave the issues of governance in the hands of business and experts alone.

LAYERS OF LAWS

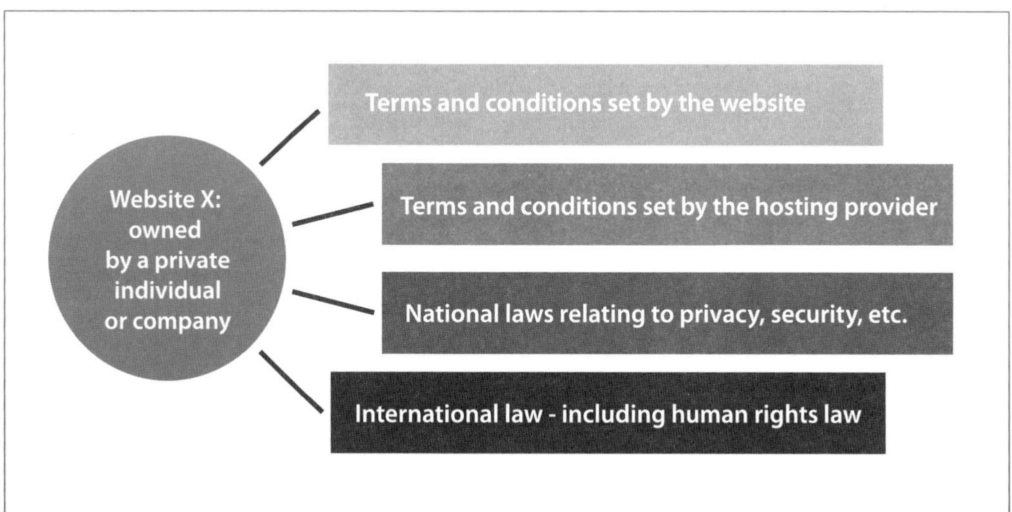

Most of the Internet is 'owned' by private companies. Even a private blog will normally be hosted on a private server. The company which owns the server may decide to restrict the type of things posted on the blog, or it may not!

Normally, the rules that users of a website must observe will often be set out in the 'terms and conditions'. They may be very different from one website to another. But apart from the terms and conditions, there may also be laws established by governments which apply to users of the Internet and website owners. Some examples include laws relating to privacy and security, or laws covering extreme hate speech. Even if a government does not have specific laws to protect people's safety online, this is often covered by international human rights legislation, as in this example.

Example: Governments must protect people online as well as offline

K.U. v. Finland

In March 1999 an advertisement was posted on an Internet dating site pretending to be from a 12-year-old boy. It included a link to the boy's web page and said he was looking for an intimate relationship with a boy of his age or older "to show him the way". The boy only found out about the advertisement when he received an e-mail from an interested man. The service provider refused to identify the person responsible for posting the advertisement, claiming it would constitute a breach of confidentiality. The Finnish courts held that the service provider could not legally be obliged to disclose the information.

The case went to the European Court of Human Rights. The Court said that the Finnish State had failed in its duty to protect children and other vulnerable individuals. The advertisement had made the child a target for paedophiles and had failed to protect his right to private and family life.

(Article 8 of the European Convention of Human Rights)

Much of the Internet is therefore a bit like a shopping mall or a nightclub! Even if there is no law against wearing jeans or looking scruffy, someone can still be turned out of a nightclub if the rules say that jeans are not allowed. In a similar way, websites can also make their own rules for their 'private space' on the Internet. However, their rules must also be compatible with the laws in the country as a whole and with international law.

Human rights, which are universal and indivisible, and related standards, prevail over the general terms and conditions imposed on Internet users by any private sector actor.

What this means for users

Young people should be aware of the laws or policies which apply on websites they use, particularly as these relate to hate speech online. Often hate speech can be challenged using the site's own guidelines and procedure for submitting complaints. Where these are inadequate, campaigners can sometimes challenging the policies themselves!

REPORTING ABUSIVE BEHAVIOUR

RESPONDING AND CAMPAIGNING

Reporting an instance of hate speech is not the only way of responding when we see it. It is important that young people are aware of other approaches to the problem, and that they are able to assess which of these will be most appropriate in particular instances.

The first diagram below illustrates some of the possible responses to individual expressions of hate. There are further examples of different ways of approaching the problem as a whole in the section on Campaigning Strategies.

When deciding on a particular response or strategy, the most appropriate response will often be dependent on the seriousness of the case. A 'mild' example of bias or prejudice is often best addressed by approaching the author directly and pointing out the potential harm; a regular 'troll' on a site which is mostly used by anti-hate speech campaigners should sometimes be ignored completely; and, at the other end of the spectrum, a hate site which incites violence against particular groups may need to be reported to the police.

One of the most important considerations in selecting the most appropriate response is the likely impact of the particular expression, or the site as a whole. Some of the questions to be explored in assessing the impact are shown in the second diagram below.

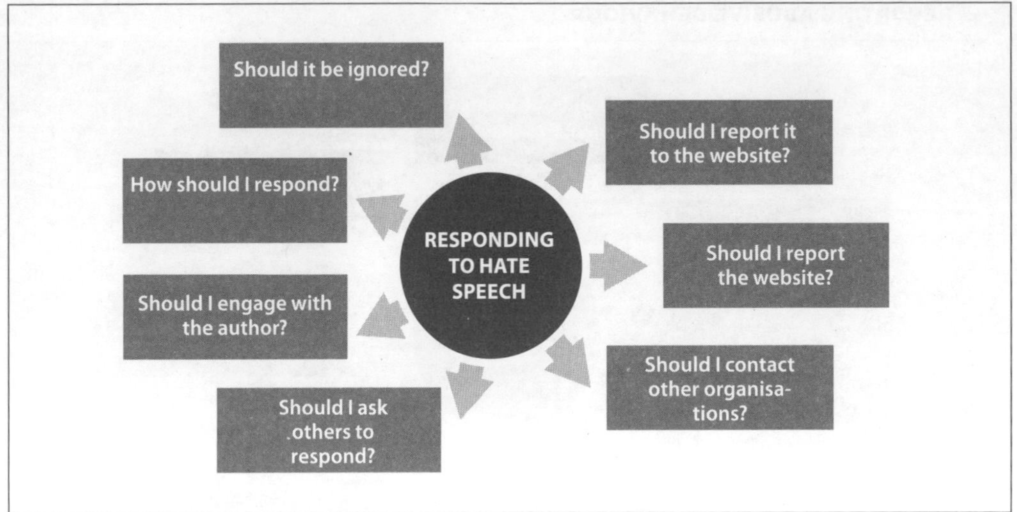

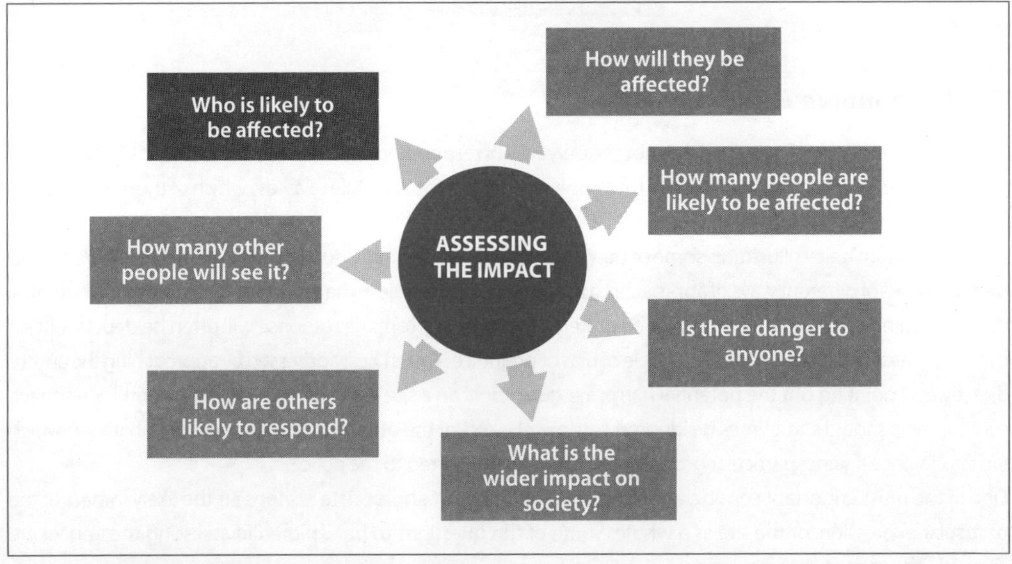

STAYING SAFE

Young people need to be aware of the potential dangers online, and they need to know about precautions they can take to avoid compromising their own privacy. There are also certain measures which can help to ensure that they are less likely to become targets of cyberbullying. Some of these are described in the section on Cyberbullying.

5.9 CYBERBULLYING

"... cyberbullying means any electronic communication including, but not limited to, one shown to be motivated by a student's actual or perceived race, colour, religion, national origin, ancestry or ethnicity, sexual orientation, physical, mental, emotional, or learning disability, gender, gender identity and expression, or other distinguishing personal characteristic, or based on association with any person identified above, when the written, verbal or physical act or electronic communication is intended to:

(i) Physically harm a student or damage the student's property; or
(ii) Substantially interfere with a student's educational opportunities; or
(iii) Be so severe, persistent, or pervasive that it creates an intimidating or threatening educational environment; or
(iv) Substantially disrupt the orderly operation of the school."

Responding to Cyberhate, Toolkit for Action (Anti-Defamation League)

Bullying takes place when one person or a group of people deliberately engage in hostile or abusive behaviour towards another individual. Normally, the abuse takes place over a period of time: the victim is persistently targeted.

In cyberbullying, the victimisation takes place online, or in electronic form. Cyberbullying makes use of emails, instant messaging, chat rooms, pagers, mobile phones, or other forms of information technology. The impact on the individual can be no less severe than in offline cases of bullying: cyberbullying is still a form of bullying.

Cyberbullying can be particularly difficult to address because the Internet allows for more anonymity than in offline communication. It can also be more intrusive, or more persistently intrusive, because it can take place even when the bully is not physically present. Once a bully knows how to contact his or her 'victim', the bullying can be constant and difficult to avoid. For this reason, it is important that young people are aware of the dangers of giving out personal details.

THE EXTENT OF CYBERBULLYING

Cyberbullying is a serious and persistent problem among young people. It can cause lasting damage and has led to suicide. A number of different studies have shown that large numbers of teenagers are affected by the problem. The figures below apply to the United States of America, but research and experience tell that the problem is equally serious in Europe:

- Over half of adolescents and teens have been bullied online, and about the same number have engaged in cyberbullying.

- More than 1 in 3 young people have experienced cyberthreats online.
- Over 25% of adolescents and teens have been bullied repeatedly through their cell phones or the Internet.
- Well over half of young people do not tell their parents when cyberbullying occurs.

Source: i-SAFE Inc., 'Cyber Bullying: Statistics and Tips'

CYBERBULLYING AND HUMAN RIGHTS

Both bullying and cyberbullying are forms of abuse and many instances fall under different human rights protections. In 'milder' cases, the right to private life is relevant, and very frequently engaged. In more extreme cases, the right to be free from inhuman and degrading treatment may also be engaged, or even the right to life. Inhuman and degrading treatment may include cases of sexual abuse, psychological violence and exploitation. For the right to life, this may be engaged both in cases where bullying offline results in physical risk to a victim's life, or if the suffering becomes so intense that the victim considers suicide. Failure to protect someone from such a risk is likely to constitute a violation of their right to life.

WHAT IS THE LINK OF CYBERBULLYING AND HATE SPEECH?

Cyberbullying is a power relation directed against an individual, while hate speech usually calls for hostility and violence against a whole group of people. However, for their victims, both are forms of violence and humiliation. Hate speech and cyberbullying use the same online channels. They are often happening against individuals who are considered different, either because of their background, disability, ethnicity, or other reasons. They both make use of insulting and harassing communication. In many instances, cyberbullying and hate speech are combined and this is very damaging to individuals and groups, for example, bullying that takes advantage of the victims' gender identity, sexual orientation or ethnic background.

At the same time, building the resilience of young people in combating hate speech can support their resilience in dealing with cyberbullying and vice versa. Internet literacy is a support in empowering young people to understand the issues at stake on the Internet and to protect themselves or react to abuse when it occurs.

KEEPING YOURSELF SAFE

Young people need to be made aware that the forms of behaviour listed in the next section are unacceptable – and probably illegal. Even a single case may be the start of a prolonged campaign or a precursor to stronger forms of abuse. Young people need to be able to recognise warning signs, to use their judgment about the best way to respond to individual instances, and to know the precautions they can take when a threat appears real. They should also be aware that there are organisations which may offer support or advice, or which will help if more 'official' steps need to be taken, including legal steps. Some of the national campaigns of the No Hate Speech Movement provide information about help lines reporting to police authorities. The InSafe network, for example, provides tips for reporting and numbers of helplines for young people to report or ask for help: www.saferinternet.org. InSafe is a project of Euroschoolnet, a European partner of the No Hate Speech Movement.

EXAMPLES OF ONLINE ABUSE

- Sending threats, provocative insults or racial or ethnic slurs
- Gay bashing, gender specific slurs or other forms of discrimination
- Attempting to infect the victim's computer with a virus
- Flooding an email inbox with abusive messages
- Posting or spreading false information about a person with the aim of harming the person or their reputation
- Singling someone out and inviting others to attack or make fun of them
- Pretending to be someone else to make it look like as if the other person said things they don't believe, or that aren't true about them.
- Sharing images of a person, particularly in an embarrassing situation, without their permission.
- Sharing emails without the writer's permission
- Pressurising others to exclude someone from a community (either online or offline)
- Repeatedly sending someone nasty, mean and insulting messages.

ONLINE SAFETY: A CHECKLIST FOR YOUNG PEOPLE

Limiting the possibilities for abuse

- Check your privacy settings on social networking sites regularly and update them.
- Do not give out personal details, for example, mobile phone number, email address, or home address, unless you know and trust the person.
- Do not share personal information with people whom you do not know (e.g. in online chatrooms where you are likely to meet strangers).
- Consider the 'space' you are using, the accepted rules of behaviour and the kind of people also using the space. Just as in the offline world certain locations present a greater safety risk, so in the online world we should react according to the particular context.
- Respect 'netiquette': treat others online as you would wish to be treated yourself.
- Be careful about protecting your profiles and email address: log out of public computers and change your passwords regularly.
- Report abuse that you come across online or that is addressed to you to the network hosting the content or comments, or to specialised police and justice services in your country (please see some tips at www.saferinternet.org).

If you receive threats or abuse

Consider the following actions. Every case is different and it is important that young people learn to use careful judgement when deciding on a course of action. It will always be helpful for them to discuss the case with people they trust.

- Do not respond! Very often a response is just what a potential abuser is wanting. Never retaliate as this will only escalate the problem.
- Share the problem with someone you can trust: ask their advice.
- Report the problem to an organisation working on youth safety online (see pages 204-205).
- Report the behaviour to the website owner / hosting provider.
- Block / report unwanted contacts and people who are behaving inappropriately.
- Change your email address or mobile phone number if either of these is being used to target you.
- If necessary, report the behaviour to the police or contact a lawyer. **Online abuse is illegal if it severely impacts on someone's health, safety or psychological well-being.**
- Always keep evidence of abusive messages received – including the email address or profile of the abuser. You may need this evidence if an official complaint becomes necessary.

ONLINE SAFETY: A CHECKLIST FOR EDUCATORS

Educators, parents and in general people working in regular contact with young people can take measures to protect them from the dangers of cyberbullying by:

- Taking a proactive approach, discussing this risk with young people and supporting them to avoid it, to the extent that it is possible. Be open to discussing this. Use examples in the class and do not shy away from raising these questions. Support a consistent policy against cyberbullying in your school.
- Becoming aware of the connection between offline and online hate speech: the two often go together!
- Empowering children through informing them and discussing the matter with them. If you feel you do not have the necessary skills to do this, you can get in touch with organisations and help centres for the victims. Make visible to young people the contacts where they can get help in case of need.
- Empowering parents, who need to become aware of the existence of cyberbullying and how they can counteract it.

5.10 THE COUNCIL OF EUROPE AND HATE SPEECH ONLINE

The Council of Europe is the continent's leading human rights organisation and it includes 47 member states. All Council of Europe member states have signed up to the European Convention on Human Rights, a treaty designed to protect human rights, democracy and the rule of law.

The work of the Council of Europe for democracy is strongly based on education: education in schools, and education as a lifelong learning process of practising democracy, such as in non-formal learning activities. Human rights education and education for democratic citizenship form an integral part of what we have to secure to make democracies sustainable.

The Youth Department of the Council of Europe runs the No Hate Speech Movement youth campaign with a specific focus on citizenship and human rights education as a means for young people to develop competences to recognise hate speech and to defend human rights online.

The Council of Europe's work on hate speech online has concentrated on four key areas:

1. Legal approaches to the problem, using the European Convention and the case law of the European Court of Human Rights
2. Policy instruments, through the Internet Governance work and through a series of recommendations and policy papers addressed to the Member States of the Council of Europe
3. Monitoring activities, through the work of the European Commission against Racism and Discrimination and the work of the Commissioner for Human Rights
4. Education, prevention and capacity building for various social actors, including journalists, NGO activists, teachers and young people.

Hate speech online has strong connections with a number of different issues, so the topic has also been a part of initiatives in various other areas. Some, but not all, of these include:

Children's rights	Protecting minorities	Training of judges
Fighting cybercrime	Fighting cyberbullying and protecting children	Media literacy
Freedom of expression	Promoting a pluralist society	Media education
Anti-racism policies	Promoting intercultural dialogue	Teacher training
Youth policies	Youth participation	Non-formal education and youth work

This long list is an illustration of the variety of concerns and issues which bear some relation to hate speech online. It is also an indication that the problem can be addressed from a multitude of different angles, using a huge variety of methods.
The following brief information covers only those areas of work which are most significant or bear a more direct relationship to combating hate speech online.

LEGAL INSTRUMENTS

- The European Convention of Human Rights has been ratified by every member state of the Council of Europe. It protects a range of civil and political rights, including rights to privacy, security and protection from inhuman and degrading treatment. Although the Convention also protects freedom of expression, this right allows for restrictions when forms of expression are likely to endanger others or harm society as a whole.
- The European Court of Human Rights is responsible for upholding the rights in the European Convention. The case law of this court has provided an interpretation of 'hate speech' which ensures that the worst abuses are not protected by the right to freedom of expression.
- The Convention on Cybercrime developed by the Council of Europe, and its Additional Protocol, is the only binding international treaty on the subject. It entered into force in July 2004 and lays down guidelines for all governments wishing to develop legislation against cybercrime.

STRATEGY AND POLICY INSTRUMENTS

- The Council of Europe's Internet Governance strategy (2001) outlines a number of key areas designed to ensure the future development of the Internet as safe space which protects freedom of expression and ensures free access to information.
- Policy recommendations relating to combating hate speech online have been drawn up by the Committee of Ministers and the Parliamentary Assembly of the Council of Europe. These include Recommendation CM/Rec(2009)5 which contains measures to protect children against harmful content and behaviour and for promoting active participation in the online world.
- The *Guide to Human Rights for Internet Users* is based on the European Convention on Human Rights and other Council of Europe conventions and instruments which deal with various aspects of human rights protection. The Guide is a tool for Internet users to learn about human rights online, their possible limitations, and available remedies for such limitations. The Guide provides information about what rights and freedoms mean in practice in the context of the Internet, how they can be relied and acted upon, as well as how to access remedies.

MONITORING INSTRUMENTS

- The European Commission against Racism and Intolerance (ECRI) is a Council of Europe human rights body. It is composed of independent experts and issues monitoring reports, including reports on the problem of hate speech. The ECRI has also addressed hate speech in its policy recommendation on combating the dissemination of racist, xenophobic and antisemitic material via the

Internet (Policy Recommendation 6). ECRI tracks this problem through country monitoring work and thematic reports.

- The Commissioner for Human Rights has drawn attention to hate speech as a human rights concern (for instance, in relation to Roma, refugees and asylum seekers). The Commissioner has also called for measures to be adopted against hate speech.

EDUCATION, PREVENTION AND CAPACITY BUILDING

- The Pestalozzi Programme of the Council of Europe is designed for educational professionals and includes modules on media education and intercultural learning.
- The online game 'Wild Web Woods' is a tool for children to learn basic methods of keeping safe online.
- The *Internet Literacy Handbook* is an online learning tool for parents, teachers and young people to develop their competences in using the Internet.
- The youth sector of the Council of Europe organises a human rights education programme for youth organisations and activists. Anti-racist work and intercultural dialogue occupy an important role. Training courses at local and international levels are organised for activists and human rights educators, and various educational materials have been produced, for example, *Compass*, *Compasito*, and *Gender Matters*.

OTHER ACTIVITIES ON COMBATING HATE SPEECH ONLINE BY THE YOUTH DEPARTMENT

- Research on hate speech online and the publication *Starting Points for Combating Hate Speech Online*: this addresses the realities of hate speech for young people and describes a number of projects and campaigns designed to address the problem.
- A survey on young people and hate speech, carried out in 2012, to analyse young people's perception of hate speech and the impact it has on them
- Grants from the European Youth Foundation have been awarded to youth organisations for projects tackling hate speech online.
- Training courses for online activists
- Workshops and seminars for campaign activists and organisers
- Study sessions with international youth organisations.

WHERE TO FIND MORE INFORMATION:

European Court of Human Rights cases tackling hate speech
www.echr.coe.int/ECHR/EN/Header/Press/Information+sheets/Factsheets/
http://echr.coe.int/Documents/FS_Hate_speech_ENG.pdf

List of Committee of Ministers Recommendations, Resolutions and Declarations adopted in the media field
www.coe.int/t/dghl/standardsetting/media/doc/cm_EN.asp

Pestalozzi Programme
www.coe.int/t/dg4/education/pestalozzi/Documentation_Centre/ML_resources_en.asp#TopOfPage

Wild Web Woods
www.wildwebwoods.org/popup_langSelection.php

Compass – A Manual on Human Rights Education with Young People
www.coe.int/compass

Internet Literacy Handbook
www.coe.int/t/dghl/standardsetting/internetliteracy/Source/Lit_handbook_3rd_en.swf

Manual on Hate Speech, by Anne Weber, Council of Europe Publishing, Strasbourg 2009

Guide to Human Rights for Internet Users
www.coe.int/en/web/internet-users-rights/guide

CHAPTER 6

APPENDICES

6.1 UNIVERSAL DECLARATION OF HUMAN RIGHTS (SUMMARY)

1. All human beings are born free and equal in dignity and rights.
2. Everyone has the right to be treated in the same way, irrespective of race, colour, sex, language, religion, political opinion, property, birth, or other status.
3. Everyone has the right to life and to live in freedom and safety.
4. No-one has the right to treat you as a slave nor should you make anyone your slave.
5. Everyone has the right to be free from torture and from inhuman and degrading treatment.
6. Everyone has the right to recognition by the law.
7. The law is the same for everyone; it should be applied in the same way to all.
8. Everyone has the right to an effective remedy when his/her rights have not been respected.
9. No-one has the right to detain or imprison you unjustly or expel you from your own country.
10. Everyone has the right to a fair and public trial.
11. Everyone should be considered innocent until found guilty.
12. Everyone has the right to have their privacy (including home and family life) respected.
13. Everyone has the right to live and travel freely within state borders.
14. Everyone has the right to go to another country and ask for protection if they are being persecuted or are in danger of being persecuted.
15. Everyone has the right to a nationality.
16. Everyone has the right to marry and have a family.
17. Everyone has the right to own property and possessions.
18. Everyone has the right to believe whatever they wish (including, but not confined to, religion).
19. Everyone has the right to say what they think and to give and receive information freely.
20. Everyone has the right to join associations and to meet others in a peaceful way.
21. Everyone has the right to take part in the government of their country, which should be chosen through free and fair elections.
22. Everyone has the right to social security.
23. Everyone has the right to work for a fair wage in a safe environment and to join a trade union.
24. Everyone has the right to rest and leisure.
25. Everyone has the right to a standard of living adequate for the health and well-being of themself and of their family, including food, clothing, housing, medical care and necessary social services.
26. Everyone has the right to education, including free primary education.
27. Everyone has the right to share in their community's cultural life.
28. Everyone is entitled to a social and international order in which the rights and freedoms set forth in this Declaration can be fully realised.
29. Everyone must respect the rights of others, the community and public property.
30. No-one has the right to take away any of the rights in this declaration.

6.2 THE EUROPEAN CONVENTION ON HUMAN RIGHTS AND ITS PROTOCOLS

SIMPLIFIED VERSION OF SELECTED ARTICLES

SUMMARY OF THE PREAMBLE

The member governments of the Council of Europe work towards peace and greater unity based on human rights and fundamental freedoms. With this Convention they decide to take the first steps to enforce many of the rights contained in the Universal Declaration of Human Rights.

ARTICLE 1 - OBLIGATION TO RESPECT HUMAN RIGHTS

States must ensure that everyone has the rights stated in this Convention.

ARTICLE 2 - RIGHT TO LIFE

You have the right to life.

ARTICLE 3 - PROHIBITION OF TORTURE

No-one ever has the right to hurt you or torture you. Even in detention your human dignity has to be respected.

ARTICLE 4 - PROHIBITION OF SLAVERY AND FORCED LABOUR

It is prohibited to treat you as a slave or to impose forced labour on you.

ARTICLE 5 - RIGHT TO LIBERTY AND SECURITY

You have the right to liberty. If you are arrested you have the right to know why. If you are arrested you have the right to stand trial soon, or to be released until the trial takes place.

ARTICLE 6 - RIGHT TO A FAIR TRIAL

You have the right to a fair trial before an unbiased and independent judge. If you are accused of having committed a crime, you are innocent until proved guilty. You have the right to be assisted by a lawyer who has to be paid by the state if you are poor.

ARTICLE 7 - NO PUNISHMENT WITHOUT LAW

You cannot be held guilty of a crime if there was no law against it when you did it.

ARTICLE 8 - RIGHT TO RESPECT FOR PRIVATE AND FAMILY LIFE

You have the right to respect for your private and family life, your home and correspondence.

ARTICLE 9 - FREEDOM OF THOUGHT, CONSCIENCE AND RELIGION

You have the right to freedom of thought, conscience and religion. You have the right to practise your religion at home and in public and to change your religion if you want.

ARTICLE 10 – FREEDOM OF EXPRESSION

You have the right to responsibly say and write what you think and to give and receive information from others. This includes freedom of the press.

ARTICLE 11 – FREEDOM OF ASSEMBLY AND ASSOCIATION

You have the right to take part in peaceful meetings and to set up or join associations including trade unions.

ARTICLE 12 – RIGHT TO MARRY

You have the right to marry and to have a family.

ARTICLE 13 – RIGHT TO AN EFFECTIVE REMEDY

If your rights are violated, you can complain about this officially to the courts or other public bodies.

ARTICLE 14 – PROHIBITION OF DISCRIMINATION

You have these rights regardless of your skin colour, sex, language, political or religious beliefs, or origins.

ARTICLE 15 – DEROGATION IN TIME OF EMERGENCY

In time of war or other public emergency, a government may do things which go against your rights, but only when strictly necessary. Even then, governments are not allowed, for example, to torture you or to kill you arbitrarily.

ARTICLE 16 – RESTRICTIONS ON POLITICAL ACTIVITY OF ALIENS

Governments may restrict the political activity of foreigners, even if this would be in conflict with Articles 10, 11 or 14.

ARTICLE 17 – PROHIBITION OF ABUSE OF RIGHTS

Nothing in this Convention can be used to damage the rights and freedoms in the Convention.

ARTICLE 18 – LIMITATION ON USE OF RESTRICTIONS OF RIGHTS

Most of the rights in this Convention can be restricted by a general law which is applied to everyone. Such restrictions are only allowed if they are strictly necessary.

ARTICLES 19 TO 51

These articles explain how the European Court of Human Rights works.

ARTICLE 34 – INDIVIDUAL APPLICATIONS

If your rights contained in the Convention have been violated in one of the member states, you should first appeal to all competent national authorities. If that does not resolve the problem for you, then you may appeal directly to the European Court of Human Rights in Strasbourg.

ARTICLE 52 – INQUIRIES BY THE SECRETARY GENERAL

If the Secretary General of the Council of Europe requests it, a government must explain how its national law protects the rights of this Convention.

PROTOCOLS TO THE CONVENTION

ARTICLE 1 OF PROTOCOL NO. 1 - PROTECTION OF PROPERTY

You have the right to own property and use your possessions.

ARTICLE 2 OF PROTOCOL NO. 1 - RIGHT TO EDUCATION

You have the right to go to school.

ARTICLE 3 OF PROTOCOL NO. 1 - RIGHT TO FREE ELECTIONS

You have the right to elect the government of your country by secret vote.

ARTICLE 2 OF PROTOCOL NO. 4 - FREEDOM OF MOVEMENT

If you are lawfully within a country, you have the right to go where you want and to live where you want within it.

ARTICLE 1 OF PROTOCOL NO. 6 - ABOLITION OF THE DEATH PENALTY

You cannot be condemned to death or executed by the state.

ARTICLE 2 OF PROTOCOL NO. 7 - RIGHT OF APPEAL IN CRIMINAL MATTERS

You may appeal to a higher court if you have been convicted of committing a crime.

ARTICLE 3 OF PROTOCOL NO. 7 - COMPENSATION FOR WRONGFUL CONVICTION

You have the right to compensation if you have been convicted of committing a crime and it turns out that you were innocent.

ARTICLE 1 OF PROTOCOL NO. 12 - GENERAL PROHIBITION OF DISCRIMINATION

You cannot be discriminated against by public authorities for reasons of, for example, your skin colour, sex, language, political or religious beliefs, or origins.

6.3 OTHER RESOURCES ON TACKLING HATE SPEECH ONLINE

In case you have time and are interested in learning more about hate speech online and what other educational activities you can use with your group, you can find here some starting points. This is not an exhaustive list, merely some suggestions to click further!

COUNCIL OF EUROPE

- **Compass** - A Manual for Human Rights Education with Young People; **Compasito** – Manual on Human Rights Education for Children and other educational resources for human rights education and anti-racist education with young people
  www.coe.int/compass
- **Internet Literacy Handbook** – an online learning tool for parents, teachers and young people to develop their skills in using the Internet
  www.coe.int/t/dghl/standardsetting/internetliteracy/Source/Lit_handbook_3rd_en.swf
- **Wild Web Woods** – an online game for children to learn basic Internet safety rules
  www.wildwebwoods.org/popup_langSelection.php
- **Manual on Hate Speech**, by Anne Weber, Council of Europe Publishing, Strasbourg 2009
- **Starting Points for Combating Hate Speech Online** – three studies about online hate speech and ways to address it, by Gavan Titley, Ellie Keen and László Földi; Council of Europe Publishing, Strasbourg 2012
- **The Council of Europe media and freedom of expression main page**
  www.coe.int/t/dghl/standardsetting/media/Themes/Education_en.asp
- **The Council of Europe Pestalozzi programme webpage on media literacy**
  www.coe.int/t/dg4/education/pestalozzi/Documentation_Centre/ML_resources_en.asp
- **The European Court of Human Rights factsheets on themes** (among which, also hate speech)
  www.echr.coe.int/ECHR/EN/Header/Press/Information+sheets/Factsheets
- **List of Committee of Ministers Recommendations, Resolutions and Declarations** adopted in the media field
  www.coe.int/t/dghl/standardsetting/media/doc/cm_EN.asp

OTHER RESOURCES AND LINKS

- **Insafe** is a European network of Awareness Centres promoting safe, responsible use of the Internet and mobile devices to young people.
  www.saferinternet.org/home

- **Insafe Good Practice Guide**, Survey of resources for teenagers, full report
www.saferinternet.org/c/document_library/get_file?uuid=eb60c451-5826-459e-a89f-d8aa6aa33440&groupId=10137
- **Teachtoday** is a portal with information and advice for schools about the positive, responsible and safe use of new technologies
www.teachtoday.eu
- The **MediaSmarts** website includes a wide variety of educational activities, background information and tools regarding the use of the Internet
www.mediasmarts.ca
- Childnet International's **Chatdanger** is an educational website for young people to learn about safety online in interactive services online, such as chat, instant messaging (IM), online games, email and mobiles
www.chatdanger.com
- The **Web We Want** is an educational handbook for use by 13-16 year olds, developed with and by young people on the topic of Internet literacy
http://webwewant.eu
- **European Schoolnet**, a network of 30 European Ministries of Education, offers teachers and pupils resources related to the knowledge society and the use of Internet
www.eun.org
- The **European Wergeland Centre** offers a wide variety of educational resources on human rights education
www.theewc.org
- The **Anti-Defamation League** toolkit includes suggestions for action against cyberhate
www.adl.org/assets/pdf/combating-hate/ADL-Responding-to-Cyberhate-Toolkit.pdf
- INACH – **International Network Against Cyber Hate** – unites and empowers organisations to promote respect, responsibility and citizenship on the Internet through countering cyberhate and raising awareness about online discrimination
www.inach.net
- **INHOPE Hotlines** offer the public a way of anonymously reporting Internet material including child sexual abuse material they suspect to be illegal
www.inhope.org/gns/home.aspx

6.4 GUIDE TO HUMAN RIGHTS FOR INTERNET USERS

(Adopted by the Committee of Ministers on 16 April 2014 at the 1197th meeting of the Ministers' Deputies)

SIMPLIFIED VERSION

YOUR RIGHTS ONLINE	AUTHORITIES' AND/OR INTERNET PROVIDERS' ROLE
Access to the Internet and non-discrimination • Your access to the Internet should be affordable • While communicating on the Internet, you must not be discriminated against by gender, race, colour, language, religion, age, sexual orientation or any other reason	• To provide you with access to the Internet if you live in rural and geographically remote areas, are on a low income or have disabilities • To react to discrimination online and provide protection and support
Freedom of expression and information • You have the freedom to express yourself online, except using expressions which contain discrimination, hatred or violence • You have the right to access information • You are free to create, re-use and share content respecting intellectual property, including copyright • You may use a pseudonym online but in some cases it can be revealed	• To instruct you on how to claim, or report violations • To react to your claims • To reveal someone's online identity in case of crimes or human rights violations
Assembly, association and participation • You have the right to associate with others using the Internet • You have the right to protest peacefully online • You may choose any online tools in order to join any social groups or to participate in public debates	• To provide you with tools for online participation • To consider your opinion

<table>
<tr><th>YOUR RIGHTS ONLINE</th><th>AUTHORITIES' AND/OR INTERNET PROVIDERS' ROLE</th></tr>
<tr><td>Privacy and data protection<ul><li>You have the right to private and family life on the Internet</li><li>You should be aware that in using the Internet your personal data is regularly processed</li><li>The confidentiality of your private online correspondence and communications must also be respected in the workplace</li></ul></td><td><ul><li>To respect specific rules and procedures when they process your personal data</li><li>To receive your consent regarding your personal data processing</li><li>To protect you from unlawful surveillance or interception</li><li>To provide you with assistance by data protection services</li></ul></td></tr>
<tr><td>Education and literacy<ul><li>You have the right to education, and access to knowledge</li><li>You should have the opportunity to develop skills to understand and use different Internet tools to check the accuracy and trustworthiness of content and services that you access</li></ul></td><td><ul><li>To provide you with access to education and cultural, scientific, and academic content</li><li>To provide you with the opportunity to develop media-literacy skills</li></ul></td></tr>
<tr><td>Children and young people<ul><li>You have the right to express your views freely and participate in public life</li><li>You should be aware that content you create on the Internet or content concerning you created by other Internet users may compromise your dignity, security and privacy</li></ul>This content can be accessible everywhere in the world, now or at a later stage in your life<ul><li>You have the right to education to protect yourself from interference and abuse on the Internet</li></ul></td><td><ul><li>To train you in safe use of the Internet</li><li>To give you clear information about online content and behaviour that is illegal (for example, online harassment) and the possibility to report illegal content</li><li>To provide you with advice and support with due respect for confidentiality and anonymity</li><li>To protect you from interference with physical, mental and moral welfare, in particular regarding sexual exploitation and abuse on the Internet and other forms of cybercrime</li></ul></td></tr>
<tr><td>Help and support<ul><li>You have the right to receive help and support when your rights are restricted or violated</li><li>You have the right to apply to a court</li></ul></td><td><ul><li>To inform you about your rights</li><li>To inform you about how to report on interferences</li><li>To inform you about available help and support if rights are violated</li><li>To protect your digital identity and your computer from illegal access and manipulations</li></ul></td></tr>
</table>

6.5 PROPOSALS OF WORKSHOPS BASED ON BOOKMARKS

1. INTRODUCTORY WORKSHOP ABOUT HATE SPEECH ONLINE (1-2 HOURS)

This workshop proposal is designed for a short introductory workshop using *Bookmarks* activities. During this workshop participants will:

- Learn about hate speech online, what it is and how it manifests itself
- Discover the online No Hate Speech Movement youth campaign

This workshop is designed for a group of up to 25 participants, with one facilitator.

INSTRUCTIONS STEP BY STEP:

1. Introduction to the workshop (5 minutes)

Explain to participants what the workshop is about.

2. Introduction to hate speech online (15 minutes)
   - Ask participants if they have encountered hate speech online and ask them to provide some examples; alternatively, you could provide participants with some examples yourself (for instance, by using some of the content of the Hate Speech Watch: www.nohatespeechmovement.org/hate-speech-watch).
   - Ask participants how those affected by hate speech online feel, and what the consequences of hate speech could be for those targeted, or for the others in society.
   - Introduce the concept of human dignity, which is at stake when people are confronted with hate speech; also introduce the definition of hate speech online. You can find the Council of Europe's definition of hate speech on page 11 of Bookmarks.
3. Proceed to the activity Saying it worse, from *Bookmarks*. (45-60 minutes)

This is an introductory activity to hate speech online. Participants rank different examples of anti-gay hate speech according to which they think are "worse". See more on page 112.

4. After this activity, you may want to: (20-30 minutes)
   - Show participants the video of the No Hate Speech Movement youth campaign (www.nohatespeechmovement.org) or the video of the No Hate Ninja project *A story about cats, unicorns and hate speech* (www.youtube.com/watch?v=kp7ww3KvccE) and tell them about the No Hate Speech Movement youth campaign. You can learn more about the Movement from Chapter 2 (Bookmarks): No Hate Speech Movement, on page 11.
   - Have a discussion about how young people could use the Internet in a way that does not promote

hate speech, and, from the discussion, draft a list of DOs and DON'Ts for a human rights-friendly use of the Internet by young people.
- Carry out a short evaluation of the workshop (for example, by having a round of keywords from each participant about what they learnt from the workshop). (5-10 minutes)

VARIATIONS

In case you want your introductory workshop to focus already on one of the more specific topics of the manual Bookmarks, you could run a different activity, for example:

- Changing the game, which looks at sexism in online games
- Confronting cyberbullying, which looks at ways of addressing cyberbullying
- Group X, which looks at racism affecting Roma people
- Web profiles, which looks into prejudice and stereotypes leading to hate speech online.

2. WORKSHOP ON HATE SPEECH ONLINE, HUMAN RIGHTS AND FREEDOM OF EXPRESSION (4 HOURS)

This workshop proposal is designed for a longer workshop using Bookmarks. During this workshop participants will:

- Learn about hate speech online, what it is and how it manifests itself
- Learn about the human rights framework and the limits to freedom of expression
- Discover the online No Hate Speech Movement youth campaign.

This workshop is designed for a group of up to 25 participants, with one facilitator.

INSTRUCTIONS STEP BY STEP:

1. Introduction to the workshop (5 minutes)

Explain to participants what the workshop is about.

2. Introduction to hate speech online (15 minutes)
   - Ask participants if they have encountered hate sppech online, and ask them to provide some examples; alternatively, you could provide participants with some examples yourself (for instance, by using some of the content of the Hate Speech Watch: www.nohatespeechmovement.org/hate-speech-watch).
   - Introduce the concept of human dignity, which is at stake when people are confronted with hate speech; also introduce the definition of hate speech online. You can find the Council of Europe's definition of hate speech on page 11 of *Bookmarks*.

3. Proceed to the activity Freedom unlimited? from *Bookmarks.* (60 minutes)

Participants explore the idea of freedom of expression using a number of case studies. They need to decide what to do with comments or communications which are controversial, abusive or potentially dangerous. See more on page 69.

4. After this first activity, you may want to look more deeply into the roots of hate speech online and its consequences. You can use, for this purpose, the activity Roots and branches from *Bookmarks* (60 minutes), on page 108. You could use any of the examples from the previous activity as a starting point for drawing the problem tree in this activity.
5. Have a short break. (20 minutes)
6. On the basis of the problem trees, you could ask participants to develop actions and campaigning activities to address some of the consequences of hate speech. You could divide participants into smaller working groups and ask them to choose one consequence of hate speech they would like to see changed, and find ways to address this. Give groups 20 minutes to discuss this, and another 20 minutes to present their findings. (40 minutes)
7. After this activity, you may want to: (30 minutes)
   - Show participants the video of the No Hate Speech Movement youth campaign (www.nohatespeechmovement.org) or the video of the No Hate Ninja project A story about cats, unicorns and hate speech (www.youtube.com/watch?v=kp7ww3KvccE) and tell them about the No Hate Speech Movement youth campaign. You can learn more about the Movement from Chapter 2 (Bookmarks): No Hate Speech Movement, on page 11.
   - Have a discussion about how young people could use the Internet in a way that does not promote hate speech and, from the discussion, draft a list of DOs and DON'Ts for a human rights-friendly use of the Internet by young people.
8. Carry out a short evaluation of the workshop (for example, by having a round of keywords from each participant about what they learnt from the workshop). (5-10 minutes)

3. WORKSHOP ON HATE SPEECH ONLINE, HUMAN RIGHTS AND FREEDOM OF EXPRESSION (4 HOURS) - ADVANCED

This workshop proposal is designed for a longer workshop using Bookmarks. During this workshop participants will:
- Learn about hate speech online, what it is and how it manifests itself
- Learn about the human rights framework and particularly about the relation between freedom of expression and hate speech
- Discover the online No Hate Speech Movement youth campaign.

This workshop is designed for a group of up to 25 participants, with one facilitator.

INSTRUCTIONS STEP BY STEP:

1. Introduction to the workshop (5 minutes)
   - Explain to participants what the workshop is about.
2. Introduction to hate speech online and human rights (20 minutes)
   - Ask participants if they have encountered hate speech online and ask them to provide some ex-

amples; alternatively, you could provide participants with some examples yourself (for instance, by using some of the content of the Hate Speech Watch: www.nohatespeechmovement.org/hate-speech-watch).

- Introduce the concept of human dignity, which is at stake when people are confronted with hate speech; also introduce the definition of hate speech online. You can find the Council of Europe's definition of hate speech on page 11 of *Bookmarks*.

3. Proceed to the activity A day in court, from Bookmarks. (120 minutes)

Participants act out a mini-trial, looking at a real case which came before the European Court of Human Rights. See more on page 25.

4. Have a short break. (20 minutes)

5. After this activity, divide participants into smaller groups and ask them to carry out a short search on their favourite interactive websites to check their policies related to racist abuse or other forms of hate speech. Give groups 20 minutes, and then bring participants back together to and discuss and compare the different policies they found. Discuss whether they feel any are inadequate for protecting users, and how they would like to adapt them. (40 minutes)

This is a variation of the activity Reading the Rules from *Bookmarks*. You can find more information about the activity on page 102.

6. After this activity, you may want to: (30 minutes)
   - Show participants the video of the No Hate Speech Movement youth campaign (www.nohatespeechmovement.org) or the video of the No Hate Ninja project *A story about cats, unicorns and hate speech* (www.youtube.com/watch?v=kp7ww3KvccE) and tell them about the No Hate Speech Movement youth campaign. You can learn more about the Movement from Chapter 2 *(Bookmarks)*: No Hate Speech Movement, on page 11.
   - Have a discussion about how young people could use the Internet in a way that does not promote hate speech and, from the discussion, draft a list of DOs and DON'Ts for a human rights-friendly use of the Internet by young people.

7. Carry out a short evaluation of the workshop (for example, by having a round of keywords from each participant about what they learnt from the workshop). (5 minutes)

Sales agents for publications of the Council of Europe
Agents de vente des publications du Conseil de l'Europe

BELGIUM/BELGIQUE
La Librairie Européenne -
The European Bookshop
Rue de l'Orme, 1
BE-1040 BRUXELLES
Tel.: +32 (0)2 231 04 35
Fax: +32 (0)2 735 08 60
E-mail: info@libeurop.eu
http://www.libeurop.be

Jean De Lannoy/DL Services
Avenue du Roi 202 Koningslaan
BE-1190 BRUXELLES
Tel.: +32 (0)2 538 43 08
Fax: +32 (0)2 538 08 41
E-mail: jean.de.lannoy@dl-servi.com
http://www.jean-de-lannoy.be

BOSNIA AND HERZEGOVINA/ BOSNIE-HERZÉGOVINE
Robert's Plus d.o.o.
Marka Maruliça 2/V
BA-71000 SARAJEVO
Tel.: + 387 33 640 818
Fax: + 387 33 640 818
E-mail: robertsplus@bih.net.ba

CANADA
Renouf Publishing Co. Ltd.
22-1010 Polytek Street
CDN-OTTAWA, ONT K1J 9J1
Tel.: +1 613 745 2665
Fax: +1 613 745 7660
Toll-Free Tel.: (866) 767-6766
E-mail: order.dept@renoufbooks.com
http://www.renoufbooks.com

CROATIA/CROATIE
Robert's Plus d.o.o.
Marasoviçeva 67
HR-21000 SPLIT
Tel.: + 385 21 315 800, 801, 802, 803
Fax: + 385 21 315 804
E-mail: robertsplus@robertsplus.hr

CZECH REPUBLIC/RÉPUBLIQUE TCHÈQUE
Suweco CZ, s.r.o.
Klecakova 347
CZ-180 21 PRAHA 9
Tel.: +420 2 424 59 204
Fax: +420 2 848 21 646
E-mail: import@suweco.cz
http://www.suweco.cz

DENMARK/DANEMARK
GAD
Vimmelskaftet 32
DK-1161 KØBENHAVN K
Tel.: +45 77 66 60 00
Fax: +45 77 66 60 01
E-mail: reception@gad.dk
http://www.gad.dk

FINLAND/FINLANDE
Akateeminen Kirjakauppa
PO Box 128
Keskuskatu 1
FI-00100 HELSINKI
Tel.: +358 (0)9 121 4430
Fax: +358 (0)9 121 4242
E-mail: akatilaus@akateeminen.com
http://www.akateeminen.com

FRANCE
Please contact directly /
Merci de contacter directement
Council of Europe Publishing
Editions du Conseil de l'Europe
FR-67075 STRASBOURG cedex
Tel.: +33 (0)3 88 41 25 81
Fax: +33 (0)3 88 41 39 10
E-mail: publishing@coe.int
http://book.coe.int

Librairie Kléber
1 rue des Francs-Bourgeois
FR-67000 STRASBOURG
Tel.: +33 (0)3 88 15 78 88
Fax: +33 (0)3 88 15 78 80
E-mail: librairie-kleber@coe.int
http://www.librairie-kleber.com

GREECE/GRÈCE
Librairie Kauffmann s.a.
Stadiou 28
GR-105 64 ATHINAI
Tel.: +30 210 32 55 321
Fax.: +30 210 32 30 320
E-mail: ord@otenet.gr
http://www.kauffmann.gr

HUNGARY/HONGRIE
Euro Info Service
Pannónia u. 58.
PF. 1039
HU-1136 BUDAPEST
Tel.: +36 1 329 2170
Fax: +36 1 349 2053
E-mail: euroinfo@euroinfo.hu
http://www.euroinfo.hu

ITALY/ITALIE
Licosa SpA
Via Duca di Calabria, 1/1
IT-50125 FIRENZE
Tel.: +39 0556 483215
Fax: +39 0556 41257
E-mail: licosa@licosa.com
http://www.licosa.com

NORWAY/NORVÈGE
Akademika
Postboks 84 Blindern
NO-0314 OSLO
Tel.: +47 2 218 8100
Fax: +47 2 218 8103
E-mail: support@akademika.no
http://www.akademika.no

POLAND/POLOGNE
Ars Polona JSC
25 Obroncow Street
PL-03-933 WARSZAWA
Tel.: +48 (0)22 509 86 00
Fax: +48 (0)22 509 86 10
E-mail: arspolona@arspolona.com.pl
http://www.arspolona.com.pl

PORTUGAL
Marka Lda
Rua dos Correeiros 61-3
PT-1100-162 LISBOA
Tel: 351 21 3224040
Fax: 351 21 3224044
Web: www.marka.pt
E mail: apoio.clientes@marka.pt

RUSSIAN FEDERATION/ FÉDÉRATION DE RUSSIE
Ves Mir
17b, Butlerova.ul. - Office 338
RU-117342 MOSCOW
Tel.: +7 495 739 0971
Fax: +7 495 739 0971
E-mail: orders@vesmirbooks.ru
http://www.vesmirbooks.ru

SWITZERLAND/SUISSE
Planetis Sàrl
16 chemin des Pins
CH-1273 ARZIER
Tel.: +41 22 366 51 77
Fax: +41 22 366 51 78
E-mail: info@planetis.ch

TAIWAN
Tycoon Information Inc.
5th Floor, No. 500, Chang-Chun Road
Taipei, Taiwan
Tel.: 886-2-8712 8886
Fax: 886-2-8712 4747, 8712 4777
E-mail: info@tycoon-info.com.tw
orders@tycoon-info.com.tw

UNITED KINGDOM/ROYAUME-UNI
The Stationery Office Ltd
PO Box 29
GB-NORWICH NR3 1GN
Tel.: +44 (0)870 600 5522
Fax: +44 (0)870 600 5533
E-mail: book.enquiries@tso.co.uk
http://www.tsoshop.co.uk

UNITED STATES and CANADA/ ÉTATS-UNIS et CANADA
Manhattan Publishing Co
670 White Plains Road
USA-10583 SCARSDALE, NY
Tel: + 1 914 472 4650
Fax: +1 914 472 4316
E-mail: coe@manhattanpublishing.com
http://www.manhattanpublishing.com

Council of Europe Publishing/Editions du Conseil de l'Europe
FR-67075 STRASBOURG Cedex
Tel.: +33 (0)3 88 41 25 81 – Fax: +33 (0)3 88 41 39 10 – E-mail: publishing@coe.int – Website: http://book.coe.int